DAUGHTERS OF TIME

Women and
Culture Series

The Women and Culture Series is dedicated to books that illuminate the lives, roles, achievements, and status of women, past or present.

Fran Leeper Buss
Dignity: Lower Income Women Tell of Their Lives and Struggles
La Partera: Story of a Midwife

Valerie Kossew Pichanick
Harriet Martineau: The Woman and Her Work, 1802–76

Sandra Baxter and Marjorie Lansing
Women and Politics: The Visible Majority

Estelle B. Freedman
Their Sisters' Keepers: Women's Prison Reform in America, 1830–1930

Susan C. Bourque and Kay Barbara Warren
*Women of the Andes: Patriarchy and Social Change in
Two Peruvian Towns*

Marion S. Goldman
*Gold Diggers and Silver Miners: Prostitution and Social Life on the
Comstock Lode*

Page duBois
*Centaurs and Amazons: Women and the Pre-History of the Great Chain
of Being*

Mary Kinnear
Daughters of Time: Women in the Western Tradition

Lynda K. Bundtzen
Plath's Incarnations: Woman and the Creative Process

Violet B. Haas and Carolyn C. Perrucci, editors
Women in Scientific and Engineering Professions

Sally Price
Co-wives and Calabashes

Patricia R. Hill
*The World Their Household: The American Woman's Foreign Mission
Movement and Cultural Transformation, 1870–1920*

Diane Wood Middlebrook and Marilyn Yalom, editors
Coming to Light: American Women Poets in the Twentieth Century

Leslie W. Rabine
Reading the Romantic Heroine: Text, History, Ideology

Joanne S. Frye
*Living Stories, Telling Lives: Women and the Novel in Contemporary
Experience*

E. Frances White
*Sierra Leone's Settler Women Traders: Women on the
Afro-European Frontier*

Catherine Parsons Smith and Cynthia S. Richardson
Mary Carr Moore, American Composer

DAUGHTERS OF TIME

Women in the Western Tradition

MARY KINNEAR

The University of Michigan Press

Ann Arbor

1990   1989   1988   1987   9   8   7   6

Library of Congress Cataloging in Publication Data

Kinnear, Mary, 1942-
  Daughters of time.

  (Women and culture series)
  Bibliography: p.
  Includes index.
    1. Women—History. 2. Women—Social conditions.
I. Title. II. Series.
HQ1121.K5   1982   305.4'2'09   82-11152
ISBN 0-472-08029-6 (pbk.)

For David, Andrew, Sara, and Lucy;
and, especially, for Michael.

Acknowledgments

I would like to acknowledge the support and vitality of colleagues and students in St. John's College, and in the history department and the Women's Studies program at the University of Manitoba. I thank Marilyn Baker, Associate Professor in the School of Art, University of Manitoba, for her advice on the illustrations; the University of Manitoba Photography Service for reproducing photographs; Arthur Millward, librarian of St. John's College, for his efficiency in acquiring books; and Anthony Waterman, St. John's College, for his help with the index. I am grateful to the publisher's readers who improved the draft typescript with their constructive comments: Louise Tilly, Professor of History at the University of Michigan; E. William Monter, Professor of History at Northwestern University; Robert Weeks, professor in the humanities department of the Engineering School at the University of Michigan; and Jens C. Zorn, Professor of Physics and Associate Dean for Curriculum in the College of Literature, Science, and the Arts at the University of Michigan.

I acknowledge the following holders of copyright for illustrations: Mr. James Mellaart, for the picture from Catal Huyuk; Mr. Leonard von Matt, for the pictures of women in Crete; Mr. Abner Scram, for the pictures of women in Crete, Greece, and Rome and women in the Middle Ages; Phaidon Press, for the picture from the Bayeux Tapestry; the dean and chapter of Westminster, London, for the picture of Saint Wilgefortis; the Austrian Nationalbibliothek, Vienna, for the portrait of Maria Theresa; the Tate Gallery, London, for the portrait of Mary Wollstonecraft; the New York Public Library for David's sketch of Marie Antoinette; Barbara Evans Clements, for the photograph of Aleksandra Kollontai; Leila J. Rupp, for the illustration of the ideal Nazi woman; the Curtis Publishing Company for Norman Rockwell's painting of Rosie the Riveter reprinted from *The Saturday Evening Post* (© 1943 The Curtis Publishing Co.); and Dr. Richard Pankhurst for Sylvia Pankhurst's pictures.

Above all, I want to thank my husband Michael for his help, comfort, and encouragement over the years.

Contents

CHAPTER 1

Introduction

Women compose more than half the population of Western society. Symbols of success announce a radical change in their status over the last hundred years. In the media, a multitude of images mirror the variety of livelihoods women have. On television, the universal medium, women report the news, direct programs, write drama, and act in plays and commercials. Schools and institutions of higher education are accessible to girls as well as boys. Politically, women have the same rights as men to vote for democratically elected governments and to run for office. Legally, women sue and are sued in the courts. In the Western industrialized economies, women work in factories, offices, schools, farms, retail outlets. In families, women provide companionship and material and emotional support to husbands and children. The signs of emancipation are all recent.

Beneath the surface there is dissonance. There are women journalists and writers but few women producers, directors, or technicians; still, not many women *make* the news. Female students remain concentrated in traditionally female areas of study. Women are political officeholders in only miniscule numbers. There is only a small proportion of women lawyers and judges. Women earn less than men in work of comparable skill and responsibility. The married women who work in the labor force experience a double burden by their simultaneous management of the household. In the United States, the most potent opposition to enactment of an equal rights amendment to the Constitution came from women themselves.

How are we to make sense of these discordant messages? One message implies that women are presently on a one-way road to the inevitable goal of equality with men. Another tells us that severe barriers impede such progress. Another questions the value of the enterprise altogether. It is difficult to assess the size and strength of the constituencies behind each viewpoint, but their existence cannot be denied.

To help us understand and explain the present, we can explore the past, to see where we have come from. This book is a contribution to the charting of what is still largely unfamiliar territory. It examines the development of Western society to discover the social, economic, cultural, and political foundations for the status of women in modern times. It describes, analyzes, and assesses the roles of women at various times in Western history, in those European and North American societies which inherit traditions forged in Greece, Rome, and Palestine. Its format is essentially chronological, but also thematic: each chapter treats the subject matter within a particular time period and geographic area. The more nearly we approach the twentieth century, the more specific is the topic under discussion and the more precise are the illustrations. This results in a certain emphasis on more recent developments, in that the book chronicles more about women in nineteenth-century Britain, for example, than in fifth-century Greece. Imbalance is unavoidable if we are to write at this time a history with some attempt at an overall view. Clearly there is a tension between the desire to incorporate as much information as possible about women in the past and the need to produce a coherent account with an orderly argument providing some clues to women's position in the West today. In this work, I have set aside the encyclopedic approach in favor of a brief and selective study of women in the history of Western society.

In the works of major Western philosophers whose thought underlies both past and present society, we see women excluded from the discussions of the nature of the good life, the characteristics of the good person, the political features of an ideal society.[1] Insofar as they are mentioned at all, with few notable exceptions, it is in the context of reproduction and family life. This thought process, whereby "man" in the language of philosophers is to be interpreted literally as the male of the species, has pervaded Western attitudes toward women and has inhibited the conceptualization of ideas which apply indiscriminately to both men and women. It has also tended to relegate women primarily and often exclusively to reproductive activity only, and simultaneously assigned secondary social importance to reproduction while according the highest esteem to productive, and public, activities. Lorenne Clark and Lynda Lange, in a recent work on Western philosophical ideas, identify two essential assumptions for the creation of a new set of egalitarian social and institutional practices. "The first is that an adequate political theory must allow the same rights, duties, privileges and liabilities to all persons regardless of gender. The second is that reproductive labor is as socially necessary and humanly important as productive labor."[2] While such assumptions could inspire radical change in future society, they can also illuminate our attitudes and questions about the past. Much recent feminist historical scholarship has benefited from an application of those principles to orthodox historical interpretation, with disturbing consequences. It has led to suggestions that the Renaissance, for example, was a period of humanism and delight in individual accomplishment for men only, and that women did not even *have* a renaissance in early modern Italy. Similarly, one can question whether the French Revolution marked any lasting change in the status of women: the Rights of Man did not, even briefly, become rights for women as far as governments were concerned.

A new wave of feminist scholarship, flourishing most recently in the last fifteen years, has been able to draw on the women's history produced by previous historians who still held, to a greater or lesser degree, the basic assumptions of a sexist society. The nineteenth-century women's suffrage movements generated considerable research on women in history, mainly to prove that women in the past had indeed been capable of exercising public, and productive, skills and responsibilities. Historical evidence was then used to buttress their immediate argument that women should have access to higher education and training for professional work, and that women should have political rights on a par with men. Those historians and activists were able to detach themselves from the albatross of sexism at least to the extent that they believed that women were not destined by nature for a role dictated solely by reproductive determinants: a woman had a mind, and a moral sense, as well as reproductive organs. Some women in the nineteenth-century movement went so far as to insist that women not only possessed an ethical understanding, but that this was naturally superior to men's. This was grist to their argument that they had a special and distinct contribution to make to political life once enfranchisement came, but we cannot avoid the observation that their attitude reflected the sexist framework of Victorian society.

Most of the early historical research concentrated on women with a claim to fame in public life: a great warrior, or ruler, or artist. Amazons, queens, female writers, and painters were rediscovered and accorded belated recognition, and the process is by no means completed. One recent book, Germaine Greer's *The Obstacle Race,* shows how much can be learned and appreciated from such discoveries of unknown artists, for example.[3] In a similar vein is Mary Beard's *Woman As Force in History,* in which she argues that women did in fact exercise public and legal powers from medieval times to the nineteenth century.[4] Their absence from the history books was not a function of their powerlessness, but of male historians' myopia and bland assumption that women in the past, like their own middle-class wives, were concerned only with household matters and child rearing.[5] The discovery and reevaluation of women in the past who were involved in public, and productive, livelihoods, continue to be topics which conscientious historians must tackle.

Exceptional women are rightly appropriate subjects for study. But so are ordinary women, particularly in the light of contemporary social history. The English historian Trevelyan as late as 1942 defined social history as "the history of a people with the politics left out."[6] Now, influenced especially by French historians, social history can be defined more positively as the total history of a society: history with not only the politics, but also the people's attitudes (or mentality) and everything else, left in.[7] Social history now uses interdisciplinary perspectives, and is an expression of the shift in focus among historians from public events to private experience; from a study of separate events to the examination of long-term patterns. It also reflects a shift away from the exclusive concerns with influential elites toward the inclusion of broad and sometimes inarticulate social groups. Women's history in this context is basically a study of the relations between the sexes: economic, political, and social as well as sexual. Women's history is concerned not only with the activities but also with the status of women at any point in time, with the term *status* defined as broadly as possible.[8]

Social history can achieve a great deal in helping us to understand Western civilization. At the least, it enriches the old-style history—that is, accounts of how wars were conducted, how wealth was accumulated and distributed, how laws were made and carried out, how knowledge was transferred and disseminated, how governments communicated with each other. Questions about how people lived, what their attitudes were, and how they related to each other add a vital dimension to our understanding of the past. Also, of course, it renders women visible in history.

We can attempt to find out what was important to a woman in a particular time and reconstruct life-styles and livelihoods for women in certain parts of society. Women, like men, never comprised a single monolithic and homogeneous group. The useful divisions, from the point of view of a contemporary social historian, are age, economic class, region, and occupation: often other categories are useful too, for example religion, and, in multiracial societies, ethnic origin.[9] In any investigation of these questions, women must be compared not only with men but also with other women.

If we ask what it was like to live in Athens in 400 B.C., or in London in 1910, we must organize the information in a way which illustrates what we in the present think useful and important to know. Work matters; so does politics; personal interactions—at work, at home, in clubs—are important; religion may matter. In order to respond to that simple question, we must delve deeply into areas which until recently the historian has left alone, sometimes because of the complexity of what is found, sometimes because of the paucity of evidence available.

The family must play an important part in this history. Most people live in a family for many years from birth; there, social training takes place as attitudes begin and become ingrained—attitudes toward politics and toward practically everything else in society too. The family mediates messages of all sorts—political, economic, psychological, social—from institutions and groups. There, children learn social skills which later are practiced and develop in larger groups. It is a channel of communication from a wider world to an individual, and at the same time the first of many channels through which that individual moves en route for adult life. A family has always been more than a group of people related to each other by blood: it has been a primary social unit, and within that unit women have been indispensable.[10]

What kinds of evidence do historians of the family, and of the role of women in past families, use? They are interested in anything that can throw light on the structure of the family and on its functions—size and composition of families, birth and death rates, methods of controlling family size, attitudes and feelings which people had about their family life. Reliable and comparable statistics, however, are a product of powerful and centralized institutions, especially the Christian church and the modern state. Our study of Western civilization therefore is heavily weighted toward the relatively recent time periods for which adequate written evidence exists.

The historian attempts to find a quantitative base, and seeks registers of births, marriages, and deaths. These were never totally complete. Bastards were born whose births were not recorded, abortions happened, and some children died, either naturally or by infanticide, whose deaths were not always brought to the attention of the local recorder, usually the village priest. Rudimentary records exist, but it is not easy to flesh out the vital statistics by clothing them with attitudes. The difficulty is of a different sort. Diaries, autobiographies, family correspondence give insights into people's attitudes— what can be called *descriptive* evidence. In addition, there is the *prescriptive* evidence, of what contemporary moralists, or philosophers, or sometimes ordinary people, felt *ought* to be the attitudes and roles of various people within a society. Both kinds of evidence, descriptive and prescriptive, present problems for the historian. When a homily in the Anglican church, for example, chides women for nagging, do we take this as an indication that women hearing the homily will obediently go home and mend their manners? Or do we deduce from the frequency of such comments that the women were ignoring the passive subordinate role enjoined on them by church doctrine?

Either type of evidence has its limitations, particularly with reference to the restricted social groups which are affected. Until the nineteenth century most people, and most women, were not literate. Few people could record their feelings even if they had seen the point of doing so. To some extent the history of the family which has so far been published tends to be a history of upper-class elite families, and similarly with women generally: we know more about women from the higher ranks in society.[11]

Study of the family can remind us that what happened for women was important. This can encourage us in turn to examine traditional concepts or periods in history from the point of view of women who lived then. This may lead to provocative questions concerning orthodox periodization. We talk about the Golden Age of Greece during the fifth and fourth centuries B.C. For Athenian women, this meant segregation from men, internal confinement to a gyneceum, little opportunity to do anything save direct a household. For other women, there was the life of a concubine or *hetaera*, an entertainer and high-class prostitute who was expected to interact intellectually as well as sexually with men. The *hetaera* however did not attract social approbation, and for both groups of women the historian must ask whether this was really a golden age. Paradoxically, this was the time too of great Greek tragedies in which women characters are accorded strong and directing roles. Yet it is hard to know whether to interpret this drama as descriptive literature, prescriptive literature, or as imaginative work of good entertainment.

The study of women in Western civilization is fraught with ambiguity. Through history we can gain an insight into the roots of this condition and thereby a greater understanding of our present and continuing contradictions. Perhaps we can start to explain the irony, expressed in 1928 by Virginia Woolf, of the "very queer composite being":

> Imaginatively she is of the highest importance; practically she is completely insignificant. She pervades poetry from cover to cover; she is all but absent from history. She dominates the lives of kings and conquerors in fiction; in fact she was the slave of any boy whose parents forced a ring upon her finger.[12]

The objective of this book, two generations after Woolf, is to demonstrate that women have not been "all but absent" from history. In Western civilization they have played a crucial role, producing, processing, and reproducing the cultural and economic resources of each generation. We are only now beginning to interpret that role with a realistic appreciation of the benefits and costs it has generated for Western society and for Western women.

Suggestions for Further Reading

Davis, Natalie Zemon. "Women's History in Transition: The European Case." *Feminist Studies* 3 (1976):83–103.

Lerner, Gerda. *The Majority Finds Its Past: Placing Women in History.* New York, 1981.

Okin, Susan Moller. *Women in Western Political Thought.* London, 1980.

Richards, Janet Radcliffe. *The Sceptical Feminist: A Philosophical Enquiry.* London, 1980.

Woolf, Virginia. *A Room of One's Own.* London, 1975.

CHAPTER 2

Early Civilizations

Prehistory was the time before people deliberately left records of their activities. In the absence of written records, myth and fiction have attempted to explain the origins of creation and social habits. In the last few centuries a scientific dimension has been introduced to the study of prehistory. Ethnologists and anthropologists can observe the few contemporary communities of peoples still living in isolated pockets almost untouched by more modern civilization, and can use their experience to throw light on societies existing thousands of years ago. Archaeologists can learn much of ancient social and political organization from the ruined buildings and buried artifacts of past cultures. Twentieth-century technology makes the identification and dating of pottery, bones, weapons, and other materials more accurate. New discoveries of remains and of deciphering techniques continue to expand our knowledge of human existence in the millennia before people saw any point in writing down records. Still, it is hard to describe prehistoric time with any degree of assurance. This difficulty, however, has not inhibited scholars and theorists from evolving a chronology of human existence and formulating portrayals of the earliest human communities.

Development of the Species

Fossil remains of apelike species have been found in east Africa, north India, and Europe, and from these animals were descended hominids who at some point regularly walked on two legs. Arms and hands could then be used for holding infants and for other purposes: for movement, for gathering food for later consumption, for fashioning shelter, and for making tools. Communication could be developed, and it seems that the brain became larger while the jaws and snout became smaller, since tools and hands could help make food more accessible and digestible. Biped remains found in Africa are estimated to be five million years old. Remains found in Asia and Europe of *Homo sapiens* with the skeletal construction, including braincase, of people today, are thought to be about two hundred fifty thousand years old.

During most prehistoric time, people lived in communities sustained by a hunting and gathering economy. Wild game was hunted, and fruit, seeds, other vegetation, and honey were gathered. The prime source of energy was human muscles, and the main materials used for tools and shelter were stone, wood, and bone. For literally thousands of years communities survived in many different climatic areas pursuing basically the same hunting and gathering way of life. Evidence for this comes from fossilized human bones, from the dismembered bones of animals, from the surviving weapons and tools used for killing game and processing it for consumption, from indications that as long as four hundred thousand years ago fire was used, and from the primitive painting, sculpture, and engraving dating from about thirty thousand years ago depicting both animals and humans. Most of the early human representations are of the female body.

Approximately ten thousand years ago the glaciers of the Ice Age receded northward and the temperature elsewhere became warmer. Trees grew in areas previously covered by ice. The hunting tools of bow and arrow became more common, fishing became more important, and farming, the cultivation of crops with its concomitant social changes, began. During the Ice Age, lasting for roughly two and a half million years, *Homo sapiens* had been largely confined to areas south of the zone where the temperature was below freezing point. There were some exceptions: as early as thirty-five thousand years ago it seems as though some communities had developed effective animal skin clothing and heated dwellings, according to remains found in Siberia. Earlier still, seventy-five thousand years ago, the cave dwellers of the Dordogne in present-day France possessed bone needles, tools for scraping furs, and cooking hearths.

Early Social Groups: Cooperation before Competition

The study of surviving artifacts from this preagrarian culture has been supplemented by the ethnography of the few hunting and gathering peoples surviving into the nineteenth and twentieth centuries. Pygmies in central Africa, bushmen in South America, Eskimos in the Arctic, and Australian aborigines presently total only a few hundred thousand people, and their hunting life seems unlikely to continue in its still primitive form. We can observe several features of their lives which may well have been characteristic of the lives of all human beings during those thousands of years of prehistory.

Their material culture is simple. They do not accumulate individual wealth. They are mobile, living in small groups of kinfolk and friends who work together. Subsistence requirements necessitate a modest effort of a couple of days work a week by each adult, and they do not compete over food resources. They are flexible in their living arrangements and in the number of people they support. They have a considerable number of old people, and the number of young child dependents is controlled through long intervals between births. Self-sufficiency is a highly valued virtue, and the group is able to cope with the occasional hazards of illness, accident, or even the migration of normal food supplies. They experience an intimate and necessary relationship with their natural environment, and clearly have evolved a satisfactory way of survival.[1]

Hunter-gatherer communities existed for millennia, but gradually from about 7000 B.C. more people turned to other ways of living made possible by a complex of developments connected with agriculture. Agriculture is producing rather than just collecting food—the deliberate interference with nature in order to effect an abundance of certain species, animal, or plant. One outcome was that crops could be cultivated to feed more people than the producers. More complex social and political organization developed. Larger populations could be supported. The food supply had to be protected from both natural disaster—too much or too little rainfall, for example—and from people it was not designed to serve. Whereas the earliest agricultural settlements still retained many of the self-sufficient features of the hunter-gatherer societies, and specialization seems to have been small, they also exhibit some of the organizational features of the first civilizations which later grew up in the fertile crescent of the Tigris and Euphrates valleys.

Problems of Evidence: The Eye of the Beholder

Where prehistory stops and civilization begins is a moot point. A convenient signpost is the development of writing, which occurred around 3000 B.C., probably independently, in several agricultural societies developing in Egypt, in Mesopotamia, in northern India, and in China. A cluster of other developments occurred at about the same time, in particular the technological inventions allowing smelting and working of bronze. Different parts of the world, indeed different parts even of the Western world, did not experience the changeover to civilization at the same time, nor in the same way. Nor was it a question of once civilized, always civilized: demographic catastrophe, geological disaster, or political disturbances sometimes shattered the fragile balance constructed between and among human settlements and their environment. The haphazard and fortuitous survival of evidence of how people lived during those several thousand years makes generalizations difficult, and further discoveries might seriously alter our knowledge. It is possible to make some substantiated observations concerning the role of women in these prehistoric and early civilized societies.

When archaeology and anthropology were in their infancy, practitioners naturally enough asked questions of early societies which were important in their own, nineteenth-century, North American or European, culture. Bachofen, Lewis Henry Morgan, and others used accounts by travelers, missionaries, and administrators in still-primitive societies to develop and illustrate theories of the role of women in primitive societies at any time, in any place. The prejudices of the firsthand reporters were frequently duplicated in the scholars: they were all men, middle-class, and often came from an evangelical background.[2] They were all influenced too by the evolutionary theory of Darwin, and by the prevailing belief of Victorian times in the inevitability and desirability of progress.

In the twentieth century, anthropological interpretation has been influenced in addition by the theories of Freud and biological determinism. It is extraordinarily difficult, perhaps impossible, for a scholar to discount the contemporary cultural climate when investigating other cultures. So we observe prehistoric women through the prism of modern sensibilities, and we have to evaluate the few remaining pieces of hundreds of jigsaw puzzles as well as we can. Much of our understanding of prehistory, as well as of early civilization, is necessarily derived from inductive reasoning: scholars reason what the most likely way of life was, on the basis of the evidence (fossils, bones, artifacts, knowledge of nonhuman primates, and knowledge of living humans) available to us. In three significant stages of development, we can make tentative reconstructions of women's everyday life: in a hunter-gatherer society, in an early agricultural community, and in an early civilization. An example of a modified hunger-gatherer society is the culture of the Twana Indian band, an example of an early agricultural community is that revealed by excavations at Catal Huyuk, and an illustration of one of the first civilizations is Minoan culture on the island of Crete.

The Twana: Ambiguity in the Interpretation of Women's Roles

The important notion of sharing food for consumption by people besides the person who acquired it probably originated with mothers sharing food with weaned infants who were still unable to gather sufficient food for themselves. Humans have a lengthy gestation period, and also take a long time to grow to maturity. During that time, other people have to help them. Earliest social groupings were likely collections of females and their children. The father of each child may or may not have been the same man. The fact that women cared for their own dependent children enabled adult males to apply their skills of coordination, endurance, sharp vision, planning, and cooperation to hunting activity, and men could make their particular contribution to the sharing of food by providing large game which could not be trapped by women invariably accompanied by children. The blood relationship of mother and children, and a child with its siblings, underlies the universal taboo concerning incest, especially between mother and son, but also between brother and sister.

The division of labor in early social groups primarily addressed subsistence needs and care of the next generation. The group's requirement for protection also put a premium on cooperative skills, rather than on competition and aggressiveness.[3] Our knowledge about the social and political structure of hunter-gatherer groups comes to a large extent from those who have survived into modern times, and we cannot be sure that identical arrangements existed in the past, in most places. Still, it is interesting to see how the several contemporary cultures distribute tasks.

Populations of hunter-gatherer groups are between twenty and two hundred people, with most living in groups of under fifty. Within the band, the group is subdivided in families of an adult couple and kin who share a common dwelling. The band forages and hunts in a large area and moves camp frequently. The division of labor is based on sex and age: men hunt, fish, and protect the community. Women gather plants, nuts, fruits, and process the food for consumption. They also care for the children and do most to process animal hide and woodbark into household objects. In groups with knowledge of pottery making, women make pots. Some tasks are shared: building dwellings, making ornaments and tools, and training the children for adult roles. Whereas most family groups are nuclear—a couple with their children—half of the 175 twentieth-century hunter-gatherer cultures examined by Murdock in 1967 had different kinds of families: either stem families, where a nuclear family also has the addition of the parents of one partner, or laterally extended families, where several married brothers or sisters with spouses and children live together. The place of residence varies: the majority of families are virilocal, with the man of the family determining family location, but in an appreciable number, about a sixth, a man locates with his wife's family, and in another sixth, the location of an adult family can be either virilocal or matrilocal.[4]

Studies of the Twana Indians illustrate many of these general features. They also serve to remind us of the ambiguities regarding women's roles even at this very simple stage of social development. The Twana were seminomads located in the present-day state of Washington in the United States. They fished, hunted, and gathered food and were largely self-sufficient within their own small (one thousand total) group. They engaged with neighboring tribes in a limited barter exchange of food and other goods but these potlatch exchanges were more for prestige than for subsistence purposes. They exhibited several indications of sexual inequality: men provided the bulk of the food; men built and owned the houses; the community leaders were men; the few specialists, like canoe makers, were men. General male domination of women was suggested too by a double sexual standard, which closely controlled unmarried daughters and punished adulterous women more severely than men. At the same time, however, women enjoyed some rough equality, in domestic authority, in the value placed on women's lives, in much joint participation with men, in ritualized female solidarity, in religious life, and in their ability to acquire and control property independently of their husbands. Martin King Whyte has utilized the example of the Twana to illustrate his contention that women's status in preindustrial communities must be seen not as a single composite phenomenon, but as a list of several discrete scores.[5] Modern research into a community widely removed in place and time from the Twana, but nevertheless sharing several economic and cultural features, gives some other indications of positive status for women.

Neolithic Urban Life: Catal Huyuk and the Fertile Goddess

Catal Huyuk was a Neolithic city in Anatolia in present-day Turkey, located on a river bank in a fertile alluvial plain three thousand feet above sea level. Its remains are contained in two mounds. One mound, covering thirty-two acres, was partly excavated by James Mellaart in the early 1960s. Observations about the settlement derive from evidence discovered then, and from knowledge of other settlements in the same geographical area.

Between 6000 and 7000 B.C., the millennium before the date of settlement excavated, game animals were hunted in the plain and nearby hills which today are deforested. Then, there was more vegetation and also probably a greater rainfall. The wild botanical precursors of wheat and barley grew in the surrounding hills, and furnished the seeds for horticulture in the flood pools of the river by Catal Huyuk. By 6000 B.C. the inhabitants had developed hybrid strains of barley and wheat, produced peas and lentils, and domesticated sheep, goats, and possibly cattle. They varied their diet by foraging for acorns, apples, and almonds, and by collecting hackberries which were used for wine production. Hunting and fishing augmented this abundant food supply. Catal Huyuk probably contained between eight and ten thousand people. They made pottery; they could extract copper and lead ores; and they traded their own surplus products for tools whose raw material was absent, for flint from Syria, for example. They were adept at wall painting and sculpture and produced luxury goods out of local material, like polished obsidian mirrors. Woven textiles, probably made out of cultivated flax as well as animal wool, were in use. Radiocarbon dating fixes the time of the excavated material between 6500 and 5600 B.C.—three thousand years or so before the urban and imperial civilizations of Mesopotamia, but two thousand years after the date of the first known urban civilization of Jericho, uncovered by archaeologist Kathleen Kenyon.[6]

There are some indications of the social and religious position of women in this community straddling the hunter-gatherer and early agricultural economies. Houses were arranged in long lines, and each house, containing a room and a storage room, was contiguous with the next. Entry was through a hole in

Catal Huyuk: goddess giving birth

the roof. Alongside the east and north walls were set two raised platforms, for sitting, working, and sleeping, and underneath were buried the bones of the dead. In each house the larger platform, against the east wall, was the woman's, and was constructed more elaborately. Mellaart has inferred that there existed considerable specialization of occupations and skills from the wide variety of artifacts found, and also from the fact that its large population was sustained by well-organized food production and conservation. It is assumed that here, as with other societies at a similar stage of development, women performed and probably controlled food production, made the household objects, and were also responsible for their preservation.

It is not clear who was responsible for the general administration of the settlement, but the primacy of a goddess-dominated religion is clear. The goddess, depicted most frequently either pregnant or giving birth to a human or to a bull, is represented in sculpture, painting, and plaster reliefs. Pairs of heavy breasts also decorate shrines, in multidimensional wall reliefs. Male figures do not appear in the relief work, but the bull and the ram, both symbols for male fertility, are present. Male humans are depicted in wall paintings of hunts, and in representations of large birds picking the flesh of dead bodies, a ritual which apparently preceded the burial of the bones inside the houses. Thirty-three representations of the goddess have been found in the excavation, as compared to eight of a god. He was sometimes represented as an adolescent son of the goddess as well as a more mature consort. Mellaart has drawn attention to the absence of explicit sexual representation in the art: reproductive organs are not shown, and the offspring of the goddess giving birth appears nestling between her knees. He hypothesizes that this absence is due to the absence of male perceptions and desire on the part of the art's creators. He believes that women created the religion and its symbolism in which creativity was connected with the breast and pregnancy, and horns or horned animal heads symbolized male principles. The higher proportion of women than men found in the buried remains, the association of women with the processes of agriculture, the taming and nourishing of domesticated animals, and the ideology of increase, abundance, and fertility, all suggest female centrality, he argues. "Hence a religion which aimed at exactly the same conservation of life and death, birth, and resurrection . . . (was) evidently part of her sphere rather than that of man." Moreover, it seems "extremely likely that the cult of the goddess was administered mainly by women."[7]

Early Civilization: Minoan Crete and the Feminine Spirit

It was people from Anatolia who at some time, possibly even at the time Catal Huyuk was flourishing, sailed across the Aegean and settled on the island of Crete.[8] Not until around 2000 B.C. was there a crystallization of economic and cultural factors which gave rise to the impressive civilization known as Minoan, and not until the end of the nineteenth century were the remains of this first European civilization found. Schliemann's spectacular discoveries of Troy and the citadel at Mycenae were the forerunners of Evans's digging at Knossos and his naming the Cretan palace civilization Minoan after Homer's legendary King Minos, a Cretan ruler who had exacted tribute of Athenian youth to be sacrificed to the minotaur on the island. The Cretan civilization was found to be a precursor of the Mycenean culture on mainland Greece, but we do not know when or how the Minoan ascendancy ended, whether it was in the fifteenth century B.C., or about 1300 B.C.; nor whether the Cretans were overcome by invading Greeks from the mainland or deluged by volcanic eruptions known to have occurred at intervals between about 1700 and 1400 B.C. What is clear from the remains is that by about 1350 B.C. the palace at Knossos was destroyed by fire, never to be rebuilt. This date is generally considered the end of high Minoan civilization.

There are other unknown factors. In his early excavations, Evans found tablets covered in writing, but was unable to decipher it. This script was described as Linear A, and was found on the island but not on mainland Greece. A later form of Linear A, known as Linear B, was found both on Crete and on mainland Greece and was deciphered by an architect cryptologist named Michael Ventris, who pronounced it an early form of Greek. Linear A remains undeciphered.

What is certain is that an island civilization, familiar with writing, flourished on Crete for many centuries. Its relationship with the mainland in its declining years is unclear, but what is especially interesting about Crete is that many political features typical of Mesopotamian and Egyptian civilizations are absent. Unlike them, Crete was not a martial society. There were no warriors, and defense structures were not a part of the architecture. The state was not highly centralized, and did not exact heavy taxation to finance war, defense, and large scale funerary and irrigation projects. Crete contained some grand palaces, but also small village settlements in the hills, and the sea offered an adequate alternative for fortified frontiers. The climate too was more temperate than in Egypt or Mesopotamia. Public works did not show grandiose figures of male rulers confronting masculine deities, nor the triumphs of war nor even of hunting. Cretan civilization was imbued with what more than one archaeologist has termed "the feminine spirit."[9]

Whereas in Catal Huyuk the settlement's economic strength appears to have rested primarily on its agricultural surplus, in Crete, prosperity was built on a carrying trade. The island's geographical position, good harbors, and plentiful timber provided favorable circumstances for ships trading the length of the Mediterranean. Cretans imported raw materials, like gold, tin, lead, copper, ivory, and possibly Egyptian linen, for their own use, and exported their manufactured goods, for example pottery and finished fabric, as well as their agricultural surplus. Above all, they furnished carriers for transshipment among other countries. Cretan silver and gold cups were found in Egypt in the tomb of a pharaoh who reigned in 1900 B.C., and Cretan pottery found its way to palaces of Mesopotamia.

In Cretan towns, the focal point was the palace. Four palaces have been discovered, of which the greatest is Knossos. All palaces were built on harbors. Their architecture was similar: each had a large central rectangular court running north and south, overlooked by windows and balconies approached by columned staircases. Knossos covered twenty-four thousand square yards, and

Crete: the small snake goddess   *Crete: the large snake goddess*

had three, possibly in places five, stories. The palace housed the royal family and attendants, incorporated the settings for religious ritual, and also included storerooms for tax and tribute goods, administrative offices, and artisans' workshops. Some storerooms may also have been used as warehouses for local and export trade. Defense needs were satisfied only by strong outer walls and narrow entrance ways, sometimes overlooked by towers.

The towns around the palaces had paved and drained streets, with private houses of two or three stories. Altogether, Knossos had a population of possibly a hundred thousand, yet there were no city walls. In other Cretan settlements, a large mansion was situated in a rural setting not far from a harbor, serving as the center of a cluster of artisans' dwellings. A paved highway joined towns on the southern shore of the island with Knossos and other roads linked the main towns. Wagons supplemented litters and donkey transportation.

Frescoes, pottery decoration, sculpture, and other artifacts testify both to the highly developed skill and creativity of the artists and artisans and to the ubiquity of women. Women are portrayed everywhere—in solitude, with other women, with children, with men. They appear in a crowd of excited people talking to each other, apparently forming the audience for a spectacle; young girls appear with young boys, bull-leaping and in other acrobatic positions; they appear with their hair elaborately dressed on the top of their heads and again with curls around their faces and falling down the back; a pottery

15

Crete: priestess sacrificing bull

Crete: the poppy goddess

Crete: group of dancing women

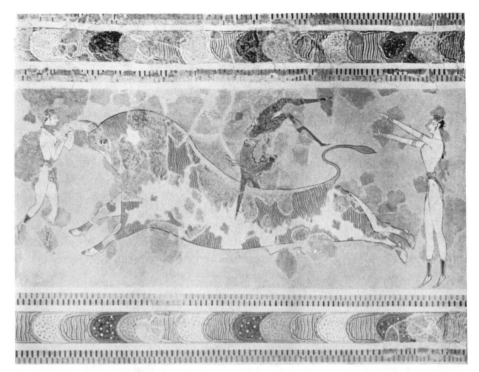

Crete: girl acrobats in the bull dance

Crete: gold seal ring depicting a ritual dance

portrayal of dancing women shows three joining hands around a fourth; goddess figures from the palace of Knossos show the goddess's dress fitted tightly around her waist opening to reveal full breasts, and snakes coil under her bosom and down her arms. The goddess's most frequent symbol was a double-headed axe, the labyris, depicted in gold, in miniature, and in all other materials and fashions. She is seen dancing sedately, and also in ecstasy. She is seen with a child, and with a consort. She is seen with female priestess attendants and with male bearers. The supreme divinity on Crete was feminine, and took many forms. Priestesses shared most functions with priests, but in artistic representation women were set above men.

We do not have sufficient evidence to deduce the sex of Minoan rulers and administrators. Women clearly took part in public life, but the later patriarchal rulers of Crete, coming from mainland Greece with warrior traditions, seem to have destroyed older evidence concerning women's legal and customary status. Besides the preponderance of the goddess, Jacquetta Hawkes points to other manifestations of the psychological and social ascendancy of women which may have resulted in actual political rule. She cites the celebration of sexuality, and the love of nature and gardens shown in the art: one of the few representations of a male god shows a young man dressed in a peacock feather headdress walking in a garden with flowers and butterflies. All point to a society where women felt secure and self-confident. It seems odd that the art shows no representations of a masculine ruler, if there were one in actuality. Many of the pictures of the goddess show her seated on a throne. In other cultures, even less surviving evidence suggesting the notion of masculine rule has nevertheless been used to show that the ruler was a king. It seems as though generations of classical scholars, and the classical tradition which has inspired modern archaeologists, prefer to accept the familiar notion of a masculine king even when the prolific art of Crete does not portray such a person. However, future archaeological finds may well decide the issue in a more satisfactory way.[10]

Matriarchy: The Iroquois and the Influence of the Matrons

Matriarchy, meaning rule by women, has been considered to mean a reversal of patriarchy. Some nineteenth-century scholars surmised that matriarchy did in fact exist at some undefined period of prehistoric time. Of these the most outstanding was Bachofen, whose *Mutterrecht*, or *Mother Right: An Investigation of the Religious and Juridical Character of Matriarchy in the Ancient World*, was published in 1861. Bachofen of course wrote before the discoveries either of Troy, or, more poignantly, of Crete, but it is questionable whether he would have recognized his own females in the confident sexuality of the uninhibited Cretan women as portrayed in art. It was Bachofen's view that "mother right" had once been a historical fact, stemming from the natural association of mother and child. The dominion of the mother over family and state—political rule—developed after women banded together and militarily defeated lustful males. Individual monogamous marriage, and matrilineal transmission of property and names accompanied the gynocracy, or rule by women, and the domination of society by women was reflected in goddess-worshiping religions. Bachofen's prototype matriarch incongruously resembled the Victorian middle-class man's ideal woman romanticized in Ruskin's *Sesame and Lilies,* a work published at the same time as Bachofen's *Mutterrecht:* she was modest, sexually chaste, conscientious of her domestic responsibilities, and beautiful.[11] Her rule was not to last. The males manfully overthrew matriarchy and successfully established patriarchy. The only surviving memories of the earliest political situation remained in the religious customs, and in the enduring stories—myth.

In the fashion of archaeologists and anthropologists, this story was hotly debated. Morgan supported Bachofen, and the two influenced Engels in his consideration of the earliest forms of social organization. Engels concluded that matriarchy was overthrown when property became private rather than com-munal. After the changeover to patriarchy, inheritance was traced in the male line. Men wished to ensure the paternity of their children and consequently controlled the sexuality of their wives through legal and customary sanctions. Class society emerged along with the institution of private property. These developments produced Engels's "world historical defeat of the female sex."[12] Other writers denied that matriarchy had ever existed, and even Bachofen had argued that matriarchy occurred only as a brief overture to patriarchy. Whereas Bachofen had drawn his evidence from Greek and Roman mythology, Henry Maine used the Old Testament, Roman law, and Hindu law to argue that patriarchy had always governed the human race.[13] He was supported by Ed-ward Westermarck, who demonstrated that matrilineal societies need not have matriarchal political systems: property inheritance customs were distinct from political power.

Contemporary anthropologists have concluded that there is no evidence for the past existence of matriarchy.[14] The furthest one will go is to describe as a "quasi-matriarchy" the Iroquois of North America, studied by the nineteenth-century anthropologist Lewis Morgan. Strictly speaking, even when they had been first observed in the sixteenth century, they could not be described as primitive.[15] By then they practiced settled agriculture and had organized large-scale offensive and defensive alliances. The Iroquois had long used firearms and were heavily involved in fur trade entrepreneurship by the time Morgan did his field work. Nevertheless they preserved memories of their history when their longhouse culture was simpler. A longhouse was the single dwelling shared by up to twenty-five families. Agriculture, performed by the women, was an inte-gral feature of the economy. In historical time, and in the memories of prehis-toric time, Iroquois women did not receive deferential treatment. On the other hand, they did exercise power over basic resources and concerning important decisions, economic, military, and political. Iroquois matrons nominated the chiefs, who were male; matrons determined whether prisoners of war lived or died; they participated, through male speakers, in political council meetings discussing diplomatic alliances; they could veto a declaration of war; they could intervene in bringing about a peace. Nineteenth-century anthropologists famil-iar with other Indian tribes noted that the Iroquois were singular in vesting this political power in the matrons, who enjoyed social and institutional recognition as éminences grises. In addition, women both helped select and were themselves selected for the important positions of religious leaders.[16] A recent observer confirms a previous student who in 1934 considered that the Iroquois "approach most closely to that hypothetical form of society known as the matriarchate," and concluded that this position of shared political power with men was "the result of their control of the economic organization of their tribe."[17] However, the assumption that women's economic authority is the key to their standing within their society is presently being called into question.

Status of Women in Preindustrial Societies: Simple and Complex Structures

Martin King Whyte has examined the position of women relative to men in ninety-three preindustrial cultures around the world. His sample includes many from outside the geographical boundaries of the Western tradition, but the breadth of his work provides valuable comparative data. Approximately one-third of his sample were nomadic hunter-gatherer cultures, one-third were peasant communities within complex agrarian civilizations, and one-third were cultures intermediate in scale and technological development. Although this comprehensive sample includes preliterate hunting bands along with communities in settled agrarian empires, all are social forms existing prior to industrialized nation-states. Whyte found no single pattern of universal male dominance. Rather, "there is substantial variation from societies with very general male dominance to other societies in which broad equality and even some specific types of female dominance over men exist."[18]

Whyte questions prevailing orthodoxy in two major conclusions. First, he cogently argues that there is no such "coherent phenomenon" as the status of women. Rather, different components measuring status vary from culture to culture, and there is only a weak interrelationship between these measures. "We can compare the domestic authority of women relative to men . . . or their subsistence contribution or property rights, but the total picture is a series of pluses and minuses that are different in each culture and that cannot be summed up easily to form an overall measure of women's status."[19] His second major conclusion, drawing extensively on the work of anthropologist Jack Goody, significantly modifies the existing materialist view in an explanation of the one pattern he discerns amidst his data.

The pattern is the following:

> In the more complex cultures, women tend to have less domestic authority, less independent solidarity with other women, more unequal sexual restrictions, and perhaps receive more ritualized fear from men and have fewer property rights, than is the case in the simpler cultures.[20]

A simple society is described as small, without a hierarchy of specialized organizations. There are few recognized social differences beyond those of age and sex, and it is personal qualities and skills which determine ranking, rather than birth or inherited wealth. A simple society relies mainly on hunting and gathering, and there are no large amounts of inheritable property. Living is frequently nomadic, and there are few tools. Such a society experiences little or no pressure from its population on the available land: when more land is needed, for herding, or hoe-type agriculture, it is readily accessible. There is consequently little direct competition for the basic means of production. Prevalent in simple societies is the custom of the bride price, whereby the groom gives money or goods to the bride's family at the time of marriage. There tends to be a large age gap between bride and groom, and polygyny is common: an older man with economic resources can acquire extra wives who will not be a financial burden since the land resources are elastic. More wives and more children are an asset, in that they perform labor. There is little economic imperative to limit the reproductive capacity of the women. Simpler societies therefore exercise little control over women's sexual and marital lives.

A complex society, on the other hand, tends to rely on intensive plow cultivation of limited land where there is more competition from a denser population for access to this strategic resource. There is social stratification based on land ownership, and parents are concerned to preserve the status of their children by bequeathing to their sons assets in the form of land, and to their daughters assets in the form of moveable wealth at marriage: dowries. In order to attract a desirable husband for a daughter, a family accumulates as large a dowry as possible. A daughter however could undermine carefully laid marriage plans if she were to fall in love with an undesirable man or if she became pregnant. In order to limit her opportunity for independent female action, parents and the community attempt to control a woman's sexual activity and marriage choice. A sexual double standard exists. A family is more inclined to limit the number of its offspring in order not to disperse its precious property in either divided bequests or numerous dowries. Because of the need for her family to amass a dowry, a daughter may be quite old when she marries, possibly even older than her husband, and there is a distinct tendency in the society to monogamy, since there is insufficient land to support multiple spouses with their children.[21]

Whyte shares with Engels a stress on the underlying importance of the ownership and control of economic resources in determining both the structure of a society and the status of its women. Whyte convincingly suggests, though, that the overriding significance of private property ownership and control is not as crucial as Engels argued. Whyte points out that even in simple societies, private ownership already exists. Also, his researches have indicated that there are other aspects which help determine women's status besides the existence of private property. "Private property does not seem to be the crucial variable in producing most of the changes in the role of women."[22] Rather, it is the cluster of components within a complex society which in combination disadvantage women. These he identifies as the differentiation of extrafamilial social roles, which give men greater opportunity for male domination; the increased political hierarchy which is reflected in social and domestic life; and the increased importance of intensive agriculture, which, as described above, involves the need to control the family's property and labor force and translates into the control of women and their sexuality.[23]

Looking again at Jacquetta Hawkes's sympathetic presentation of women in Crete, which appears to have been a complex society while retaining many of the advantages for women associated with more simple societies, we can perhaps learn from the terminology she employs. Hawkes does not invoke matriarchy as a mirror image of patriarchy, with its features of domination, subordination, and exploitation, but talks instead about "queenship." In a society where art and creative skill were so highly valued, and where the state was not tightly centralized nor in need of perpetual protection from external marauders, the sex of the ruler might not have been so significant. And in the absence of a strong central temporal authority, important events could enjoy more of a domestic character. Prehistoric hunter-gatherer societies, Neolithic towns, and Cretan civilization did not experience strong centralized state structures and there seems to have been no need to compete for the abundant food resources. Perhaps that was the reason why they were so well able to celebrate, at least on the level of art and religion, the contribution of women.

Suggestions for Further Reading

Hawkes, Jacquetta. *Dawn of the Gods.* New York, 1968.

Mellaart, James. *Catal Huyuk: A Neolithic Town in Anatolia.* New York, 1967.

Reiter, Rayna R., ed. *Toward an Anthropology of Women.* New York, 1975.

Rosaldo, Michelle Zimbalist, and Lamphere, Louise, eds. *Woman, Culture and Society.* Stanford, 1974.

Whyte, Martin King. *The Status of Women in Preindustrial Societies.* Princeton, 1978.

CHAPTER 3

Greece

Aristotle in the *Politics* approvingly quoted Sophocles' dictum: "Silence is a woman's glory." The sentiment also found expression in Pericles' funeral oration in 430 B.C. to those warriors fallen in the Peloponnesian War:

> If I now mention the women who have become widows, and speak of womanly virtue, I can say all that is needed with a brief exhortation. Fulfill diligently the tasks that nature has assigned you and you will be praised; and the highest praise you can win is to be spoken of by men as little as possible, whether for good or ill.[1]

Respectable women in classical Greece were supposed to keep their peace, and not give rise to others' talk. Yet women were not inaudible, nor invisible. Drama accorded to women protagonist roles, painting portrayed women at work and at play, philosophy gave attention to women. With few exceptions, the images of women in Greek society are man-made. They are fraught with paradox and contradiction.

The Golden Age of classical Greece was the fifth and fourth centuries B.C., centered in Athens. This was the time of the tragedy of Sophocles, Euripides, and Thucydides, of the sculptor Phidias. In pottery the "red figure" vases were produced, and in architecture the Parthenon was constructed. Socrates trained his pupils in philosophical inquiry, to be followed by Plato and Aristotle. The attention of scholars has been drawn ever since to this cultural splendor, particularly when western Europe rediscovered classical Greece during the Renaissance. Between the sixteenth and twentieth centuries, the standard education for literate men was study of the classical writers of Greece and Rome. The classical Greeks not only created a spectacular culture; they also profoundly influenced the ways of thought of hundreds of successive generations as well. What they wrote, or drew, or believed about women has had a similarly long life.

What we know about ancient Greece is not confined to Athens in the Golden Age. We have already noted the conjuncture of material remains and poetry in the archaeological discovery of Troy, Crete, and Mycenae: their days of glory preceded the Athenian ascendancy by over six hundred years. The lands bordering on the Aegean Sea shared a common language and culture, with important variations, and evidence in law codes and political theory as well as literature and art extend our knowledge beyond the city-state of Athens. After the Macedonian Alexander defeated and unified the Greek cities and other areas of the Middle East before his death in 323 B.C., the geographical area under Greek influence expanded even further. The periodization of ancient Greek history starts with the Bronze Age to the fall of Troy (1184 B.C.); the Dark Age followed, when Homer, Hesiod, and Semonides created their poetry and the Phoenician alphabet was adopted; then came the Archaic Age, during which Sappho wrote in the sixth century and Solon was archon of Athens; the classical period of cultural supremacy, ending in Alexander's reign, ensued; finally came the Hellenistic period up to the death of Cleopatra, Alexander's Egyptian descendant, in 30 B.C. In a period of over a thousand years, the images of women drawn from a variety of geographical locations are varied and changing.

The Bronze and Dark Ages: Epic Protagonists

The Amazons were a group of women said to have resided in northern Anatolia. Homer's *Iliad* alludes to their warrior activities and relates how several heroes proved their manhood by successfully defeating Amazons in battle. Plato in his *Laws* repudiated the notion that contemporary girls should be raised in military skills like Amazons.[2] Whether or not such a group existed outside mythology is doubtful. Their multifarious depiction in art is no necessary evidence for historical fact. Similar doubts exist as to whether any kind of matriarchal society existed in the Bronze Age, roughly 1400–1200 B.C. There are stories of goddesses and heroines set at some supposed time in the Bronze Age which so impressed Bachofen that he considered they must have some basis in fact. The Trojan War was caused when, according to the myth, the Spartan queen Helen abandoned her husband for the pleasures of the Trojan prince Paris: her father-in-law Agamemnon led the Greeks against the Trojans in a ten-year war in order to recapture her.

The power and influence of a woman was a recurrent feature of epic poetry derived from Bronze Age exploits. The royal characters of Clytemnestra, who outwitted and murdered her husband in Aeschylus's *Agamemnon*, and of Antigone in Sophocles' play, who flouted conventions of passive and deferential feminine behavior, are complex and profound personifications of tragic forces.[3] Not only do the female characters in Greek tragedy and comedy act out parts which are consciously heroic, but they also comment directly on the inhibiting customs by which they were expected to deny their autonomy. Medea, in Euripides' play, mourns the limitations a woman was subjected to and deplores the total lack of an alternative way of life:

> Surely, of all creatures that have life and will, we women Are the most wretched. When for an extravagant sum We have bought a husband, we must then accept him as Possessor of our body. . . . Then the great question: will the man We get be bad or good? For women, divorce is not Respectable; to repel the man, not possible.[4]

Epic characters in Dark Age poetry and Golden Age drama were modeled on memories of people who, according to myth, had lived in some prehistoric time. This literature can enhance our understanding of ambition, hatred, jealousy, grief, and other ever-present emotions, but cannot provide evidence that matriarchal power was wielded systematically by women. As one recent historian concludes, "there is little evidence available to a classical scholar indicating the historical existence of matriarchy in the Bronze Age," and another points out that "Greece weathered and emerged from the Dark Age as a patriarchal culture."[5] Matriarchy, however, need not be the acid test of women's status, and there is considerable evidence culled from the centuries before the Golden Age to suggest that women's status and sphere of action were greater then than during the heyday of Pericles and Aristotle.

This conclusion reflects the location of the surviving evidence. Law codes of Sparta and of Gortyn in Crete were established and written down in the seventh century B.C., and furnish evidence for those particular areas of regulations governing women's behavior and status. For other parts of the Greek world, more fragmentary indications are provided by archaeological finds in graves, by pottery, and also by contemporary literature. On the whole, it appears as though the women of Sparta and Gortyn enjoyed a less circumscribed life than those in Athens or those of the later classical period. Their life could still by no means be described in terms of freedom. All women in Greece, from the Dark Age through the classical, came under a man's tutelage. They had no choice other than to marry, but at times this imperative could be used as an advantageous lever.

During the Dark Age the city-state, or polis, became the standard unit of government in Greece. The polis was most often a commercial city, located near a harbor, supported by the agricultural products of its rural hinterland and by trade with other centers of population. The polis was ruled by one man, a "tyrant," or a group of aristocratic families. The prosperity of such ruling groups depended largely on their dynastic alliances and loyalties, and women were clearly significant pawns in the game of internal security and external relations. Women were not only the reproductive tool for the continuation of one family's influence, but were often visible representatives of that family's political and economic power. Alliances and allegiances were forged and maintained through marriage, which was not a means to personal fulfillment, but a manifestation of a family's bargaining power. The law codes which survive testify to the state's concern in protecting a family's interest in its daughters, before, during, and after marriage—not for the benefit of the women concerned, but for the preservation and extension of the family's property and good name.

Sparta: Willful Women

A second principle operated uniquely in the Spartan code, attributed to Lycurgus. This was the separate interest of the state itself, distinguished from the dynastic interests of its powerful families. From early times, Sparta was a society organized on a war footing. This put a premium on women's ability to bear many male children—the next generation of warriors. Moreover, since warriors must be physically fit, the Spartans recognized the desirability of their mothers' physical well-being. From childhood, Spartan girls were fed as well as the boys, and like the boys, underwent gymnastic training. Upper-class Spartan wives and mothers of Spartan citizens continued their athletic activity and enjoyed musical pursuits as well as child rearing and organizing their households. Unlike women elsewhere in Greece they did not themselves do housework, nor did they spend time spinning and sewing. In Sparta these were the jobs of slave women and the wives of noncitizens. Spartan women's dress was distinctive: they wore the peplos, with slit skirts allowing freedom of movement, and some art portrays Spartan women in the nude, giving rise to the notion that they possibly did their exercises without clothes on.

Spartan marriage was singular: women were married when full grown to young men of comparable age, that is, at about eighteen. The bride at the wedding was dressed as a boy and had her hair cut short by her attendant bridesmaid. If the bride did not become pregnant, both parties could claim no marriage had taken place. Only after a baby was born did a wife take up residence with her husband's family. Until the groom was thirty years old, he continued to reside in the warrior barracks, and met his wife only occasionally. Plutarch observed that children of both sexes were "not the individual possession of fathers, but the common possession of the state." Since the state wished to promote the number of its warriors, extramarital affairs were encouraged as a means to more children. Large increases in the population might have been expected, but in fact the perpetual state of war led to an imbalance in the sex ratio. Adult women competed for husbands among the men who were not killed in battle, and in order to enhance their daughters' prospects, fathers bestowed on them large dowries of both land and movable property. Even for rich families, this could cause hardship if there were many dowries to fund, and this tradition, of the rich endowment of the daughters of citizens, encouraged citizens to limit the size of their families. A daughter with some economic support of her own, however small, could act in a more independent manner. With men continually absent on military campaigns, married women in Sparta had an opportunity to manage property and to act outside the close supervision of their husbands. By Aristotle's time, Spartan women had a reputation for willfulness, and the population had already begun to fall.[6]

Gortyn: Legacy from Crete

Elsewhere, the Gortyn law code of the seventh century B.C. also assigned an appreciable area of activity to women. Gortyn was located in the Mycenean sphere of influence and it is tempting to see a continuity between Minoan culture on Crete and the Gortyn experience. However it must be remembered that the Minoans were probably overcome by conquering Greeks from the mainland, and the Gortyn code shows the Greek heritage as well as Hawkes's "feminine principle." The code is a series of inscriptions produced in the fifth century B.C., referring to an earlier time, and the surviving tablets are not a comprehensive code, but laws dealing with exceptional circumstances, including disputes over slaves and loans. However, they include regulations concerning sexual assault, divorce, the division of property, children of mixed marriages, and the marriage and property of a patroikos, or girl heiress. Hence, considerable information about women can be gleaned from the code.

At Gortyn as in Sparta, the sexes were separated and young men lived together in barracks where they trained as warriors. Unlike Sparta, however, Gortyn does not appear to have experienced incessant warfare. Men first married at the age of about sixteen, before they entered the andreion, or barracks, but girls were obliged to marry immediately after puberty at about twelve years old. The Gortyn code allowed some free women to possess and even control their own property: this may have been a device whereby the family of a patroikos, a girl who inherited a family's property in default of a male heir, kept control of that property out of the hands of the girl's husband's family. Such a woman retained some personal stake in that property, for in the event of divorce, she kept her own property and in addition half the produce of the household. Not all married couples lived together. Possibly the custom was similar to Sparta's, where a bride resided apart from her husband, although in his family's home, until he was released from his barracks duty. One authority pointed out that a bride resided with her husband only after she was old enough to manage a household herself.

Detailed regulations concerning the patroiki testify to the Gortynian concern to protect unmarried girls who might inherit considerable wealth by default of a male heir. A patroikos should first select a husband from the ranks of her father's brothers, if they were willing and able. If not, their sons, that is, her cousins, were eligible. Third in succession to her hand was any other member of her father's tribe. However, if the girl did not care for a man in the third category then she could divest herself of that obligation by paying him a fine and marrying a man of her choice. This man could even be unfree, since there were regulations governing the children, and adultery, of free and unfree persons. For example, if a free woman married an unfree man and lived in his house, the children were unfree, but if her husband lived in her house, the children were free. Normally children were at the disposal of the father: if a child were born after a divorce, the natural father could either accept it as his own, or reject it, in which case the mother chose whether to rear it or "throw it away." The nominal ownership of property enjoyed by some women at Gortyn in certain circumstances could well have been translated into relative independence for adult women, but whereas Spartan women developed a reputation for selfishness with later Greek observers, Gortyn women did not. Possibly the lack of wars to divert the men from their own control of domestic property reduced opportunities available to women.[7]

Until the sixth century B.C. women elsewhere in Greece are elusive, but two sources of information survive from archaeology and literature. Graves particularly provide some fascinating insights. The sex of the deceased can be inferred from the bone structure of the skeleton, from the grave marker, if used, and also from the gifts furnishing the grave. When cremation occurred, male remains were put in neck-handled amphorae, whereas female ashes were interred in either belly-handled or shoulder-handled amphorae. Often the decoration on these amphorae, and on others accompanying them, indicated the sex of the deceased. Offerings placed in the grave tended to reflect masculine roles, like warrior paraphernalia, or feminine roles, like cooking pots, weaving and spinning tools, and certain jewels. Two studies have examined the age at death, as indicated by skeletal remains, and the sex ratio of male to female deceased in a seventh-century B.C. burial plot near Athens. Archaeologist Lawrence Angel discovered that adult women died young, and that there were more graves of men than of women. This might suggest that there were fewer women accorded elaborate funerals than men. It could also be that there were fewer adult women than men among the living, possibly because more female babies than male babies suffered infanticide. Generalizations are impossible, but literary sources also indicate greater numbers of living sons, and men, than of females.[8]

Dark Age Greek literature abounds in misogynist statements about women, to be repeated many times in later centuries, but it also contains the few fragments of observations on love and life from a woman's voice. Sappho lived in sixth-century Lesbos where, according to her account, other women poets also wrote lyrics and songs which were performed at public festivals as well as in private houses. Her surviving work exhibits delight in sensual pleasures, in love for girls and other women, and also describes the sorrow brought by parting, or death. Sappho's poetry probably reflected the feelings young women could have for each other before their marriage to men often a generation older than themselves. It parallels the public approbation bestowed on the glorification of boys' beauty. Sappho's poetry is singular both in its subject matter, speaking of the confidence and delight and emotional sovereignty of women, and in its authorship, for few other poets of the entire ancient and medieval Western world were known to be women.[9]

Athens in the Golden Age: Democracy for Men Only

The classical image of women evolved during the heyday of Athens in the fifth and fourth centuries B.C. Despite comprehensive treatment in the hands of philosophers, playwrights, and artists, this picture can never be complete, since we lack the testimony of the women themselves. We do not know to what extent our evidence is prescriptive rather than descriptive; whether contemporary women actually behaved as Aristotle, for instance, said they should, or whether his comments were those of an unheeded scold. It is hard to differentiate between prescription and description even when he considered political matters, and our confusion extends to an assessment of both the roles and the status of women.[10] This is exacerbated by the dichotomy between the heroines of Greek drama on the one hand, and what we know about the seclusion of respectable Athenian women on the other. Even when the female population is differentiated according to the status and wealth of men, the picture is not at all clear.

Basic vital statistics are blurred. Average adult longevity has been computed at forty-five years for males and thirty-six for females. Since women predeceased men by five to ten years, there were few elderly women in the population, and a natural majority of men. The interval between births has been estimated at four years, so with menarche at approximately fourteen, when a girl first married, one might expect a woman to bear about six children. An average of 1.6 died as infants. Skeletal investigation suggests that the actual number of births per woman was about four.[11] There are indications that through concern for the limited amount of material resources available to Athens, there were both generalized and individual mechanisms used to limit the population.

Generalized sanctions included the prevailing misogyny. There was a lack of respect for women, accompanied by abstinence from heterosexual activity. Male homosexuality was accepted by wealthy Athenians in early adulthood.[12] The sexual activity of citizen wives was reduced also by their husbands' preferred intercourse with prostitutes or slave women, through widowhood, and by subsequent failure to remarry. The citizenship law enacted by Pericles in 451 B.C. offered a formal check to population growth. It stipulated that a man's parents must both normally be of citizen stock in order to qualify him in turn as a citizen. However, when there was an insufficient supply of free female Athenians, a citizen was allowed to marry a foreign woman. When on the other hand there were too many eligible free Athenian women, the law could be tightened up, and marriage with a foreigner prohibited, lest, according to Pericles, the daughters of the citizens could not have marriages procured for them.[13] Exogamy was thereby controlled. Individual limitations on births included abortion, sanctioned by Aristotle before the fetus "quickened."[14] At birth, a newborn infant was at risk even in normal circumstances, but deliberate infanticide, especially of females, probably was practiced also.

A male citizen's education normally continued well into his twenties, and contained the Aristotelian subjects of reading, writing, gymnastics, music, and drawing. This was to fit a citizen for the duties of citizenship, and also for the enhancement of his adult life. An adult Athenian woman, in contrast, could not participate in government, nor in war. Moreover, after the age of fourteen she was to spend her life married to a man at least fifteen years older, rearing children and helping organize a household, tasks for which different skills were important. It was sufficient for a girl to learn domestic skills from her mother. A teenage bride could well live in her husband's house, tending an infant, while his teenage brother, her brother-in-law, could be living in the same residence, attending a school, learning the arts of rhetoric and developing intellectual skills. Age and educational discrepancy alone ensured supremacy of the husband: there was no notion of companionate marriage in ancient Greece. When Aristotle in the *Politics* emphasized the importance of the household, and at the beginning of the book set out his definition, we can interpret it literally in the context of his own fifth-century B.C. Athens. "The state . . . consists of villages which consist of households. The household is founded upon the two relations of male and female, or master and slave; it exists to satisfy man's daily needs." The state, however, had a superior purpose to either the village or the household, which was sufficient for a woman, for the state's raison d'être was to provide "the good life" for its male citizens.[15] Women, in this schema, helped to support the men that the men might participate in the good life. A woman's task therefore was confined to bearing a man's children and to providing him with everyday needs.

Before marriage, the daughter of a citizen was under her father's care, or that of his male next of kin. At marriage the bride exchanged his guardianship for that of her husband, for in law she was perpetually a minor. Her father and her own family retained some interest in her despite her marriage. If she became a widow, her guardianship reverted to her father's family if she had no sons of majority. This extended to her dowry, as well as to her person, and it was encumbent on her father to provide a daughter with a dowry appropriate to his own economic status. If he personally was unable to provide a large enough dowry, his own wealthier relatives might contribute. A bride would also take to the marriage a small trousseau. The dowry was inalienable, and interest derived from it was used for the woman's maintenance during the marriage. In the event of divorce, or widowhood, a woman's dowry remained intact and rendered her attractive for remarriage. Divorce could be initiated on behalf of either spouse, and by the woman's father or other male citizen in the few examples known of a wife attempting divorce.

Superficially, procreation within marriage was its justification. Biologically, the woman was thought to be an incubator for the embryo provided exclusively by the man: at the fulfillment of term, she could then expel the baby. "She who is called the mother is not her offspring's parent, but nurse to the newly sown embryo." This idea was tempered, in Aristotle, by his observation that a pregnant woman ought to take care, since "the offspring derive their natures from their mothers as plants do from the earth." He thought that by furnishing part of the environment for a fetus, if not, perhaps, its essence, a mother clearly had a significant part to play, but the classical Greeks went to considerable length to downplay a woman's role even in producing a child.[16]

The loyal wife had certain prescribed pastimes. Athenian living was ur-

Greece: mother and child

ban, and the citizen woman was secluded even within her house. Women who resided in smaller urban centers, or in rural settlements, may not have experienced the almost total withdrawal from public sight of the respectable Athenian woman.[17] The glorious Greek architecture dating from this period provided the context for their husbands' lives; their own was circumscribed by houses with separate women's quarters, the gyneceum. In a two-story house, free women and slave women lived upstairs, males downstairs. This domestic apartheid furnished the background for much domestic drama, as the case of Euphiletus, a man accused of murder about 400 B.C., makes clear. In his defense he argued that the victim was his wife's seducer, and he described some of the evidence which led him to believe his wife was being unfaithful.

In the beginning, she was the best of women. She was a clever house-wife, economical and exact in her management of everything. But then, my mother died, and her death was proved to be the source of all my troubles, because it was when my wife went to the funeral that this man Eratosthenes saw her; and as time went on, he was able to seduce her. He kept a look out for our maid who goes to market; and approaching her with his suggestions, he succeeded in corrupting her mistress.

Now first of all, gentlemen, I must explain that I have a small house which is divided into two—the men's quarters and the women's—each having the same space, the women upstairs and the men downstairs.

After the birth of my child, his mother nursed him; but I did not want her to run the risk of going downstairs every time she had to give him a bath, so I myself took over the upper story, and let the women have the ground floor. And so it came about that by this time it was quite customary for my wife often to go downstairs and sleep with the child, so that she could give him the breast and stop him from crying.

This went on for a long while, and I had not the slightest suspicion. On the contrary, I was in such a fool's paradise that I believed my wife to be the chastest woman in all the city.

Time passed, gentlemen. One day, when I had come home unexpectedly from the country, after dinner, the child began crying and complaining. Actually it was the maid who was pinching him on purpose to make him behave so, because—as I found out later—this man was in the house.

Well, I told my wife to go and feed the child, to stop his crying. But at first she refused, pretending that she was glad to see me back after my long absence. At last I began to get annoyed, and I insisted on her going.

"Oh, yes!" she said. "To leave *you* alone with the maid up here! You mauled her about before, when you were drunk!"

I laughed. She got up, went out, closed the door—pretending that it was a joke—and locked it. As for me, I thought no harm of all this, and I had not the slightest suspicion. I went to sleep, glad to do so after my journey from the country.

Towards morning, she returned and unlocked the door.

I asked her why the doors had been creaking during the night. She explained that the lamp beside the baby had gone out, and that she had then gone to get a light from the neighbors.

I said no more. I thought it really was so. But it did seem to me, members of the jury, that she had done up her face with cosmetics, in spite of the fact that her brother had died only a month before.

. . . An interval elapsed. . . . Then, one day, I was approached by an old hag. She had been sent by a woman—Eratosthenes' previous mistress, as I found out later. This woman, furious because he no longer came to see her as before, had been on the look out until she had discovered the reason. The old crone, therefore, had come and was lying in wait for me near my house.

"Euphiletus," she said, "please don't think that my approaching you is in any way due to a wish to interfere. The fact is, the man who is wronging you and your wife is an enemy of ours. . . . Your wife is not the only one he has seduced—there are plenty of others. It's his profession."[18]

The trial verdict is unknown.

Few opportunities presented themselves for women to meet other men: besides a funeral, which was where Euphiletus's wife saw her chance, outside the home there were religious festivals and probably dramatic performances, although women's parts in the plays were performed by male actors. Most women stayed home most of the time, spinning and weaving, caring for their children, and preparing food. Slaves were sent to the market to buy food and to the well for water. Some women became knowledgeable about the management of family property and Socrates implied approval of a woman's acquaintance with such family business matters. Poor women, even citizen women, worked, particularly as shopkeepers in retail trade.[19] However, most economically comfortable women were confined both to the home and within it. The heightened intimacy which most likely ensued among the children, the slaves, and the adult women inspired sociologist Philip Slater to formulate an interesting theory on the relationships among men and women and among the gods and goddesses. A young boy growing up in the cramped, hothouse atmosphere became the object of his mother's repressed hostility toward her absent husband. The boy in turn became narcissistic, a woman-hating homosexual whereby he compensated for the lack of adult male models in his formative childhood years. Subsequently the boy's feelings for women alternated between desire for the close protection of infancy and hatred for an adult woman's parasitism on his own life.[20] Such a theory may help explain some of the classical drama of Euripides and Sophocles, but it is unclear whether it can help explain the denigration of women by contemporary philosophers. Aristotle used study and observation of animal life to conclude that in all species, the female was inferior to the male and that male domination was the will of nature: in the body politic, passivity was the virtue of woman, who was to obey while man commanded.[21]

There was another option available for women, beside domestic seclusion. As well as the few girls and women who became priestesses in the

service of generally female cults, there were prostitutes, not all of whom were slaves.[22] Their existence has been glamorized by writers and historians who testified to the political and emotional influence on great men such as Pericles, whose friend Aspasia was his close companion as well as bedmate. Greek art sympathetically portrayed the slender and beautiful female figures entertaining men during symposia with food, drink, music, and sex. The prostitutes or hetaerae could also probably converse in a manner unlikely in a child-wife. Certainly the courtesan-whore had access to the Greek culture, access shared by no other woman. But if it were available only to hetaerae, the very meaning of "Golden Age" should be revised.

Hellenistic Period: Widening Options

The historian Sarah Pomeroy has characterized the three centuries after the Golden Age as a period of broadening opportunity for women. The political background was the erosion of democratic forms of government in the city-states, and a reversion to monarchical forms.

Under the domination of Hellenistic monarchs the implications of citizenship and its privileges were less far-reaching for men that they had been in the independent city-states of the Classical world. . . . On the one hand the gap in privileges between men and women was much nar-

33

rowed, and on the other the men . . . became more ready to share with women the less-valued privileges they had.[23]

The subjugation of Athenian democracy by Alexander the Great and his Macedonian successors may have been deplored by liberal historians, but it held more promise for women in the lands of the eastern Mediterranean. Two documents illustrate the change, and the underlying continuity. One is a marriage contract of a Greek couple living in Egypt in 311 B.C., which illustrates their expectations of marriage. The other is a Neopythagorean letter of advice to young girls.

Two standards of marital behavior were explicit when Heraclides married Demetria of Cos.

He is free; she is free. She brings with her to the marriage clothing and ornaments valued at 1000 drachmas. Heraclides shall supply to Demetria all that is suitable for a freeborn wife. We shall live together in whatever place seems best to Leptines (Demetria's father) and Heraclides, deciding together.

If Demetria is caught in fraudulent machinations to the disgrace of her husband Heraclides, she shall forfeit all that she has brought with her. But Heraclides shall prove whatever he charges against Demetria before three men whom they both approve. It shall not be lawful for Heraclides to bring home another woman for himself in such a way as to inflict contumely on Demetria, nor to have children by another woman, nor to indulge in fraudulent machinations against Demetria on any pretext. If Heraclides is caught doing any of these things, and Demetria proves it before three men whom they both approve, Heraclides shall return to Demetria the dowry of 1000 drachmas which she brought, and also forfeit 1000 drachmas of the silver coinage of Alexander. Demetria and those helping Demetria shall have the right to exact payment from Heraclides and from his property on both land and sea, as if by a legal judgment.[24]

Demetria was protected against her husband's "fraudulent machinations" and against extravagant behavior from Heraclides in the event of her own machinations. Her contract gave her more secure protection than that enjoyed by Athenian women. Neopythagoreans, by way of contrast, still envisioned a totally dependent and deferential wife whose main qualities were moderation and chastity, as seen in the text giving advice to young ladies:

We must deem the harmonious woman to be one who is well endowed with wisdom and self-restraint . . . for from these qualities fair deeds accrue to a woman for herself as well as for her husband, children, and home; and perchance even to a city, if in fact such a woman were to govern cities or peoples, as we see in the case of a legitimate monarchy. . . . To be consumers of goods from far-off lands or of items that cost a great amount of money or are highly esteemed is manifestly no small vice. And to wear dresses that are excessively styled and elaborately dyed with purple or with some other color is a foolish indulgence in extravagance. For the body desires merely not to be cold, or for the sake of appearances, naked; but it needs nothing else.

. . . So that a woman will neither cover herself with gold or the stone of India or of any other place, nor will she braid her hair with artful device; nor will she anoint herself with Arabian perfume; nor will she put white makeup on her face or rouge her cheeks or darken her brows and lashes or artfully dye her greying hair; nor will she bathe a lot. For by pursuing these things a woman seeks to make a spectacle of female incontinence.

. . . A woman must live for her husband according to law and in actuality, thinking no private thoughts of her own, but taking care of her marriage and guarding it. For everything depends on this. A woman must bear all that her husband bears, whether he be unlucky or sin out of ignorance, whether he be sick or drunk or sleep with other women. For this latter sin is peculiar to men, but never to women. Rather it brings vengeance upon her. Therefore, a woman must preserve the law and not emulate men. And she must endure her husband's temper, stinginess, complaining, jealousy, abuse, and anything else peculiar to his nature. And she will deal with all of his characteristics in such a way as is congenial to him by being discreet. For a woman who is affectionate to her husband and treats him in an agreeable way is a harmonious

woman and one who loves her whole household and makes everyone in it well disposed. But when a woman has no love in her, she has no desire to look upon her home or children or slaves or their security whatsoever, but yearns for them to go to perdition just as an enemy would; and she prays for her husband to die as she would a foe, hating everybody who pleases him, just so she can sleep with other men. Thus, I think a woman is harmonious if she is full of sagacity and temperance.[25]

The Neopythagorean dispenser of advice clearly envisioned much opportunity for a wife to utilize her wisdom and self-restraint.

Women in wealthy and aristocratic families had opportunities for public service, limited and segregated to be true, but nevertheless more than classical Athens could offer. The girls who produced clothing for the image of Athena every fourth year during the festival honoring the patron goddess of Athens were themselves commemorated by political decree. Some royal queens in various regions of Greece exercised considerable power behind the throne during the reigns either of their husbands or, more often, of their sons. At least one woman, Cleopatra, came to rule Egypt in her own right and was a shrewd and able monarch. In some areas women came to act in a legal capacity on their own behalf, without the intercession of male guardians, and their economic status improved by direct ownership of property, including slaves. Women's increased visibility was manifest in art: after the fourth century B.C. the heavily draped female figure gave way to nudity in sculpture.

The fleeting and incomplete glimpses we have of women in the Greek world in the thousand years or so before the birth of Christ leave us with contradictory impressions. In the democratic city-states, considered as exemplars of economic, political, and cultural organization by so many generations of cultivated European men, respectable women were secluded and hidden; in the same period, however, they were powerful forces in the drama. Earlier, in some areas like Sparta and Crete at least, women were less dependent on male guardians, and later in the Hellenistic period, male domination was not so intense. Certainly throughout the millennium, the expectation suvived that mortal women should be protected, by their male kin and by law. Yet the mythology of Zeus's partners and female progeny gives rise to role models of women well able to take care of themselves. And what could be more at odds with the prevalent image of the invisible woman than the idea of the triumphant, ecstatic maenad, the woodland nymph, whose presence pervaded every stream and grove, and who experienced total freedom from ordinary restraints?[26]

Suggestions for Further Reading

Lacey, W. K. *The Family in Classical Greece.* Ithaca, N.Y., 1968.
Pomeroy, Sarah B. *Goddesses, Whores, Wives, and Slaves: Women in Classical Antiquity.* New York, 1975.
Slater, Philip E. *The Glory of Hera: Greek Mythology and the Greek Family.* Boston, 1968.

CHAPTER 4

Rome

Spectacular sights in three continents remind twentieth-century tourists of Roman splendor. The public buildings in Rome, the mosaics of Pompeii, villas along the highways of Roman communications, baths and fortifications along Hadrian's Wall in Britain, still testify to the scope, the immensity, and the skill of the Roman builders. Viaducts and aqueducts across gorges and chasms are still awesome in their design, and the bureaucratic, legal, military, and political organization devised to maintain the imperial structure was remarkably successful. The Roman heritage includes a legend of the emancipated Roman matron, a notion that Roman women did not tolerate the repressive treatment meted out to the women of classical Greece. The contemporary reality was more complex. Although women in the Roman Empire possibly had more options, that does not negate the very real limitations they experienced. As one classicist expresses it, "even the most emancipated and self-assertive Roman woman lived in a state of bondage if we compare her to the most retiring Roman male."[1] One very necessary reminder of similarity with Greek culture is that women were excluded from public life. Women were not politicians, rulers, lawyers, engineers, architects, soldiers, or public officials. On the other hand, one very important difference was that women were not confined to the same domestic seclusion as fourth-century Athenian women. Roman women were more visible, and more active.

Although we miss statements by women themselves, there is evidence describing the lives of women comprehensively, particularly for the early empire. Debates on proposed legal changes in women's status, the sumptuary laws regarding dress, marriage and divorce customs, letters and poetry, and grave descriptions combine with representational art to produce several images of Roman women from approximately two hundred years before the birth of Christ to two hundred years after. During those four centuries the position of the city of Rome grew from the political leader of a single Italian confederacy to ruler of most of the northern shore of the western Mediterranean by 146 B.C. During the first century A.D. her rule extended to Gaul in the west and Syria in the east, and further afield both on the southern shore of the Mediterranean and, beyond Gaul, to Britain. The empire was a free trade unit with a single currency. Commerce was aided by a network of straight, paved roads and protected harbors. Grain was regularly transported from one end of the empire to another, as were metals, papyrus, luxury cloth, and olive oil. Armies occupied imperial territory, staffed the local bureaucracy, and provided mobile fighting forces to protect the boundaries of the empire. Merely keeping the army supplied oiled the commercial routes. Nevertheless people engaged in either manufacturing or commerce did not enjoy the prestige of landowning notables or the Roman aristocracy. When historians describe the emancipated Roman woman, it is the women of this latter elite who furnish most of the evidence. Within the context of a large and variegated empire, with several millions of population, that elite numbered only thousands.

Guardianship

The basic feature of a Greek woman's life—the legal protection of a male guardian—was true also for a Roman woman, but with significant differences. With the exception of vestal virgins, all Roman women were under the control of the oldest male member of their family, the paterfamilias, who also had jurisdiction over all male offspring until his death. There were only six vestal virgins at a time, and they came from a select group of noblest families. Since a virgin left the cult at the age of forty and reverted to normal custodial arrangements, this exception affected few women. The paterfamilial authority was invoked when a woman accepted an inheritance, made a will, assumed any contractual obligation, or performed any transaction of importance. However, by late republican times, guardianship had become more onerous for the guardian than for his ward, who could apply to a magistrate for a different guardian if her present one was not sufficiently compliant. This de facto situation was recognized de jure by the first emperor, Augustus. As an incentive to increase the birthrate, Augustus offered total exemption from guardianship to women who bore a certain number of children: three in the case of free women, and four in the case of freedwomen—women born slaves but manumitted into freedom. Mature women could benefit from this change, but on the major transaction of a woman's life, her first marriage, the paterfamilias still exercised authority.[2]

Marriage: Legal Subordination

There was also significant development in the type of marriage. The paterfamilias had the power to determine whether or not the girl would be transferred from his authority to that of her new husband. Either way, she would technically be subjected to a male guardian. When the marriage went with manus, or authority, to the husband, the bride then became a member of her husband's family, and worshiped her husband's family's household gods. If her own paterfamilias retained manus over her at marriage, she was excluded from her husband's family's religious worship, and retained her celebration of her paterfamilial cult. Since the supervision of the household hearth and the worship of its gods was one of the main responsibilities of the mistress of the household, the question of whose gods she cultivated was a matter of significance. The nature of the husband's supervision, however, is not clear. It appears by late republican times that in this matter also women did not experience too close a control by a husband, and this was a matter of regretful comment by male legislators for some time.[3] The historian Livy, writing during Augustus's reign, put the following words into the mouth of Cato the Censor in his attempts to keep the sumptuary Oppian Law in effect in 195 B.C.

> If each of us citizens had determined to assert his rights and dignity as a husband with respect to his own spouse, we should have less trouble with the sex as a whole; as it is, our liberty, destroyed at home by female violence, even here in the Forum is crushed and trodden underfoot, and because we have not kept them individually under control, we dread them collectively. . . . Our ancestors permitted no woman to conduct even personal business without a guardian to intervene in her behalf. . . . Give loose reign to their uncontrollable nature and to this untainted creature and you cannot expect that they will themselves set bounds to their license. . . . It is complete liberty, or rather, complete license they desire. . . . The moment they begin to be your equals, they will be your superiors.[4]

The marriage without manus (*sine manu*) had become the common form by Augustus's day, but this did not necessarily mean that the woman, through lack of subjection to her husband, was necessarily better off. Marriage *sine manu* freed the husband from an obligation to maintain the wife after divorce. Moreover, the paterfamilias could still decide his daughter's partner in remarriage, and since military and political alliances could be furthered by marriage, a woman could be much married as a means for her paterfamilias's ambition.[5] The women concerned were not invariably passive pawns. Balsdon remarks on the novel "self-assertion" of certain of the women once they were married. Sallust described Sempronia, wife of the consul in 77 B.C.:

> Well-bred, handsome, and with children of her own, she had little of which to complain. She was well-read in Greek literature as well as in Latin; her singing and dancing were rather too professional for a lady, and she had many other accomplishments which made for dissipation. Self-restraint and chastity ranked lowest in her scale of values; and it was hard to say which she thought less of squandering, her money or her reputation. . . . Yet she had a good brain; she wrote verses; she was amusing; and, whether in the language of the drawing-room or the brothel, she was a good talker, full of wit, even of charm.[6]

Marriage *sine manu* did not guarantee either economic prosperity or happiness for the woman concerned, but it did free her from the intimate supervision of guardian or husband, and if she had no access to her husband's property, neither could he encroach on hers, if she had any. There is also evidence that some women initiated marriage alliances not only to benefit their families, but also on their own behalf. Few women, it seems, initiated divorce proceedings, leaving that to their technical guardian. Divorce was not difficult, and no reason was legally required although one was frequently given, especially when the husband was charging his wife with adultery. When Julius Caesar, then serving as high priest, divorced his barren wife Pompeia in 62 B.C. since an intruder had attended one of her parties with the intention of debauching her, he remarked, "The High Priest's wife must be above suspicion." Adultery was a legal offense for women, but not for men, by Augustus's declaration: he wished to restore respect for marriage, chaste wives, and the prolific family in Rome. Similarly, fornication was by law totally forbidden for women but allowed for men with prostitutes. Many women went unpunished, however, if the gossip recorded by Ovid, Juvenal, and other writers is to be believed, and a "perfect wife," thought Juvenal, was "rare as a black swan." Well-born women, however, had a much narrower choice of extramarital partners than their husbands did. Not only were the penalties for male infidelity less severe, but the double standard recognized the inevitability of men sleeping with prostitutes, slave women, freedwomen, and concubines. If a woman, married *sine manu*, was found to be an adulteress, her paterfamilias was legally permitted to kill her. Vice versa, however, an adulterous husband was not subject to criminal prosecution and his wife was not obliged to divorce him, even though she could. The discrepancy was recognized by contemporaries. The jurist Ulpian observed that it was "very unjust for a husband to require from a wife a level of morality that he does not himself achieve."[7]

Marriage was supposed to produce an advantageous family connection, and also legitimate heirs for the family's future protection. It was concern for the birthrate which led Augustus to pass laws encouraging procreation; besides rewarding fertile women, he also introduced punitive measures against the unmarried and childless. He, and many other rulers before him, felt that the birthrate was too low. Exactly what the birthrate was of Romans as compared with other residents of the empire is not known, but there was perpetual concern particularly for citizens to man the armies, and the history of the late republic and early empire abounded with examples of marriages which produced one child or none.[8] Studies of tombstones show many more males than females were commemorated. This could mean that the society considered that males were more deserving of a tombstone, but, as in classical Greece, it could also reflect a population surviving childhood which contained fewer women than men. Contraception and other means of curtailing the population were practiced. Magic remedies were common. One writer advocated the placing of a cat's liver in a tube and wearing it on the left foot. Another said the woman should hold her breath at ejaculation, and afterward sneeze and drink something cold. More effective techniques were suppositories of soft wool and oils to block the entrance to the womb. Some ointments were thought to be spermicides, and probably coitus interruptus was practiced.[9] Abortions were not subject to legislation until the third century A.D., and the exposure of newborn infants was not forbidden by law until late in the fourth century.[10] Together with the normal risks attendant on pregnancy and childbirth, these devices probably curbed population growth, even without recourse to witchcraft.

Daily Life: Options for the Rich

When women were commemorated on tombstones, they were described traditionally in variations on the same theme: personal attributes, the achievements of children, and household management. "You bore me children completely like myself; you cared for your bridegroom and your children; you guided straight the rudder of life in our home and raised high our common fame in healing—though you were a woman you were not behind me in skill," declared Panthia's widower in the second century A.D.[11] Yet even the clichés announce occupations unknown to classical Greek women. A Roman woman's life had not ended its usefulness when she produced a male heir: her day was more varied than that of the admired paragons of Aristotle's day. Young girls received vigorous academic and musical education either from tutors at home or possibly by attending school, and then as married women used their intellectual agility and artistic skill at social gatherings which provided entertainment for both men and women. A Roman elite woman's household contained slaves to do the housework. Although there was a convention for some wistful writers to claim a preference for the early rustic simplicity of Rome, when Cincinnatus plowed his own land and the women spun their own yarn, wove their own clothes, and tended personally their own households, the elite Roman matron paid them no heed.[12] After 21 A.D. she was able to accompany her husband on tours of duty in the Roman provinces, which could involve opportunities for closer involvement with his career. On that ground, the new law was opposed, but its supporters argued that the alternative was even worse:

> Women are naturally weak; and Caecina is proposing that they should be deserted by their husbands and left victims to the temptations of their own flesh and the lusts of other men. When you consider that, with husbands present to keep watch on their wives, marriages are only just saved from running on to the rocks, you can easily imagine what will happen if for a number of years on end they are annulled by what to all intents and purposes amounts to a divorce. In our zeal for effecting reforms in outlying parts of the Empire, it would be a mistake to shut our eyes to the scandals which occur here in Rome.[13]

Besides an active role in her husband's public life, a wealthy Roman woman could spend her day out of her house shopping, going to the baths, paying social calls, worshiping at temples, or attending public spectacles and entertainments. In the city she traveled in a litter or chair, accompanied by attendants. For such excursions her preparations, in dress, makeup, coiffure, and jewelry, were extensive. The styles of clothes changed little, but interest was maintained by variations in fabrics. Her clothing formed a backdrop to hair and jewels. Hair arranging varied according to the fashion of the moment but could be very elaborate and intricate, as the sculpture and paintings of women demonstrate.[14] Men were excluded from the dressing ritual, and Lucian subjected it to sarcastic criticism.

If you saw women getting out of bed in the morning, you would find them more repulsive than monkeys. That is why they shut themselves up and refuse to be seen by a man; old hags and a troupe of servant maids as ugly as their mistress surround her, plastering her unhappy face with a variety of medicaments. For a woman does not just wash away her sleepiness with cold water, and proceed to a serious day's work. No, innumerable concoctions in the way of salves are used to brighten her unpleasing complexion. As in a public procession, each of the servants has some different object in her hand; a silver basin, a jug, a mirror, a multitude of boxes, enough to stock a chemist's shop, jars full of mischief, tooth powders or stuff for blackening the eyelids.[15]

Jewels were an obvious declaration of the family's wealth and were worn by men as well as women. One of Petronius's characters, Trimalchio, relates an after dinner sequence in his home when his wife shows off her jewelry to friends. "By god," says Trimalchio, "she must be wearing six and a half pounds of solid gold. Still, I must admit I've got a bracelet that weighs a good ten pounds on its own."[16]

Working Women: Options for the Poor

The vast majority of women did not have access to sufficient wealth to lead the kind of life described, and often deplored, by Roman writers and poets. Certainly in all the many urban centers of the empire the Roman matron was seen in either crude or sophisticated imitation. In the rural areas, or in the cities too, most women had to work for their living, many in service occupations for the upper-class Roman women. Much of this service industry was populated by slaves—women enslaved as adults from a conquered part of the empire, or daughters of slaves. Slaves' previous training was probably the traditional female one of learning by example to do household tasks, and this was what a slave in a large household in Rome would have to do. Slaves did the work which the Roman matron supervised, but this was not entirely a mirror image of what Greek women had done for themselves. Romans did not normally have to fetch water from a public place, as it was transported in pipes to the larger houses. Not all clothing was made in the home. Because there were more public events in which wealthy women participated, more women, both slave and free, worked in occupations connected with them, as companions on outings, bath attendants, entertainers, actresses, beauticians, and so on. Slave women too offered sex to the men of the household and were also employed in brothels.[17]

A slave could not legally be married, but frequently slaves within the same household experienced a long and faithful relationship. Their children legally belonged to the master of the household. A slave could acquire money through tips, and keep savings: this could be used to buy other slaves, or to purchase his or her manumission. Slaves could be awarded their freedom at the pleasure of the owner, or by payment of their own purchase price, or by providing their owner with a certain number of children, probably four. A

Rome: lady at her toilette

Rome: imperial family in procession

Rome: young woman with writing materials

Rome: girl athletes

Rome: priestesses in Isis cult procession

female slave could marry her free master and become free but men of senatorial rank were forbidden to marry either slaves or freedwomen.[18] Most freedwomen either continued to work in personal service, or became shopkeepers or artisans, working predominantly in textiles. Their grave inscriptions also testify to a variety of occupations: a female physician, commercial entrepreneur, brickmaker, tavern keeper, waitress.[19]

Rich Roman women do not appear notably repressed. We do not know how they felt about their exclusion from earning direct political kudos or bureaucratic salaries, but they did have the compensations of wealth, personal comfort, and considerable personal freedom. Poor women in Rome and throughout the empire were not at all emancipated. As slaves, they could experience wrenching emotional heartbreak when captured, and were also perpetually subject to the caprice of their owner. We know what Roman men thought about women, for much of the literature is given to formulas of praise for virtuous wealthy women who performed their family duties adequately. An additional dimension is noted by classicist Judith Hallett, which might be interpreted as evidence that some women at least were self-possessed beyond the expectations of a satisfied lady of leisure. Hallett contrasts the platitudinous praise for women's submissiveness, support, and stability with a development newly discerned in the Augustan love elegists. These poets cast their beloved in an active role normally assumed by a man. The woman, in the elegies, is a female master commanding a male slave. Her romantic liaisons are absorbing, praiseworthy pursuits for her lover—parallel even to his orthodox occupations of business or public service. Within the liaison, the woman is portrayed as an intellectual and emotional equal, with the undisputed power to enthrall her partner. Hallett argues that this poetry was a departure from conventions which essentially patronized women, and offered instead a model for human interaction which did not require the woman to be basically dependent and deferential.[20]

If the model was realized, only a very few exceptional women in Roman times were in a position to benefit. The possibility could remain, however, to inspire the image of a different kind of woman who would have to live in a different kind of society. The beginnings of Christianity were contemporary with the Augustan poets. Christianity provided the image not only of a different kind of social organization, but of a different kind of man, and woman as well.

Suggestions for Further Reading

Balsdon, J. P. Dacre. *Roman Women.* London, 1962.

Lefkowitz, Mary F., and Fant, Maureen, eds., *Women in Greece and Rome.* Toronto, 1977.

Pomeroy, Sarah B. *Goddesses, Whores, Wives, and Slaves: Women in Classical Antiquity.* New York, 1975.

Late Roman Empire: Empress Theodora and retinue

CHAPTER 5

The Early Christians

Christianity echoes many other spiritual developments found around the Mediterranean at the time of Christ. Literate men, and some women, were familiar with the socially conservative ideas of the Stoics, and with the more questioning ideas of the Epicureans and Cynics. Christians inherited belief in only one God from the Jews, but a search for monotheism was widespread throughout the Roman Empire, and a multiplicity of local cults gradually gave way to acceptance of a handful of almost universal religions, including the worship of the Egyptian goddess Isis. Mysticism and asceticism and a strong feel for the dualism of, for example, life and death, mind and matter, were prevalent in much Gnostic thought contemporary with the early Christians. The new religion always exhibited the tension between prevailing spiritual and social mores on the one hand, and a vision of what life should be on the other. Like the Jews, the Christians believed that their religion included an interpretation of the whole of life. Their life was permeated with their faith.

Information on the early church depends initially on the accounts of Jesus' ministry written by his immediate followers and by his early interpreters. These accounts were refined, purged, and filtered through the understanding of the early church fathers and senior church officials in the critical first few centuries, and emerged as Christian orthodoxy. In the process, much that was important to the early Christian congregations was censored out of later Christian experience.

The Christian church was able to consolidate its organizational structure to the extent of becoming a permitted religion of the Roman Empire after 312, when the emperor Constantine won a victory at the Milvian Bridge against his military rival with the help, he concluded, of the God of the Christians. After the political disintegration of the western part of the empire during the fourth and fifth centuries, the Christian church did not find evangelical expansion easy, but was nevertheless able to attract men, and women too, of remarkable ability and energy. Entrenched in the eastern, hellenized part of the empire, the church managed to spread in the more rural and unsettled west slowly but surely. By 1100 not only had the sect survived, but it had proselytized to the extent of monopolizing the spiritual allegiance of practically all political rulers and enjoying the protection of the established legal authorities. This favored position was developed still further in the following two centuries. The internal organization of the church extended horizontally through personal contact of priests with almost every inhabitant of Europe, and vertically, the hierarchy centered on Rome was able, most of the time, to insist on conformity with official church doctrine. Culturally the Christian church became an integrated and dominant part of the fabric of people's lives. The most imposing building in a rural as well as an urban settlement was the church; some of the most colorful art was sacred; much of the decorative arts utilized holy themes; music and ritual were similarly used to reinforce ordinary people's loyalty to the church. Clearly the success of Christianity as the monopoly religion was due to many factors. One of the major reasons for its early appeal was its message, and the universality of that message. One group particularly susceptible to the ideology of Christianity was women.

Religious Experience: Service and Ecstasy

Religious experience of one sort or another had always been accessible to women. Participation in public religious festivals, either mixed, or all female, was one of the few chances a Greek woman had to get out of her house. In the Hellenistic period, a Greek family in Egypt ordered some music and food for a festival:

> Send us at your earliest opportunity the flutist Petoun with the Phrygian flutes, plus the other flutes. If it's necessary to pay him, do so, and we will reimburse you. Also send us Zenobius with the soft drum, cymbals, and castanets. The women need them for their festival. Be sure he is wearing his most elegant clothing. Get the special goat from Aristion and send it to us. . . . Send us also as many cheeses as you can, a new jug, and vegetables of all kinds, and meat if you have it.[1]

As well as joining in the music, dancing, and worship, in some cults women were the interpreters. At Eleusis, for example, Demeter and her daughter Persephone were commemorated every year in Lesser and Greater Mysteries connected in the remote past with the death and rebirth of grain. Although the chief priest and some of his officials were men, there were also priestesses of whom the most prestigious was the chief priestess of Demeter. The festival's importance was symbolized by the fact that at Eleusis, events were dated by the name of the priestess and her tenure of office. Worship in the cult was demonstrated by participation in the rites, which included a bath of purification, fasting, sacrifices, and drinking. The sacred vessels were carried only by female initiates, who could watch sacred dances performed by other women.[2]

The Romans had a wide variety of cults in which women could participate, both as officials and priestesses, and as worshipers. The most regular daily ritual a Roman wife undertook was officiating in the cult of her husband's family: she served the guardians of the hearth.[3] Outside the home, ceremonies and festivals centered around one cult or another gave occasion for much female visiting about town. A young girl would dedicate to Fortuna Virginalis the small toga worn in childhood, and after the ceremony could wear a stola. Many other cults and rites provided opportunities for an aunt to dedicate her niece, for a mother to celebrate her maternity, for a respectable woman to honor domestic harmony, or for a courtesan to honor love. The emperor Augustus used these customs to promote his ideals of childbearing and sexual fidelity and restored even more temples and cults celebrating women's fecundity. Many of these cults were for women only, and the sense of mystery and exclusivity attached to them led some satirists, Juvenal in particular, to deride their pretended solemnity and charge instead that the cults covered gross immorality and lewd promiscuous behavior on the part of women.

One popular cult which Augustus attempted to restrict was that of Isis, which was open to both men and women. Originally Egyptian, Isis loosely represented everything: "light and dark, day and night, fire and water, life and death, beginning and end," according to Plutarch. She was a single supreme goddess whose guidance could be seen behind everything. She was loving and merciful. She was a wife and mother but also had been a prostitute. A hymn to Isis dating from the second century A.D. praised Isis in that "she made the power of women equal to that of men." Isis condoned eroticism, for she was supposed to have been a whore herself, but also asceticism, for some of the rites sanctioned abstinence from food and sex. Women as well as men served as her functionaries. The Romans also provided the image of a highly influential woman priestess in the persons of the vestal virgins, revered as the guardians of the city's continuity. Their virginity was maintained by the severe deterrent of burying alive any unchaste vestal. Paradoxically, obedient and orthodox vestals, of whom there were six at a time, were allowed total legal independence, the privilege of driving through Rome in a two-wheeled wagon, and prominent seats among the imperial family at spectator events.[4]

Religious experience, apart from spiritual challenge or comfort, could offer women relief from monotony and possible fun and games. Men could get this too, but their daily life offered more opportunities for variety anyway. Some cults hinted at redemption or salvation, concepts which were frequently debated in the Mediterranean world around the time of Christ. Upper-class women in Rome and other sophisticated centers were often well educated in the ideas of the Stoics and other philosophical schools. Although Juvenal railed against bluestockings, other writers, like the Stoic Musonius Rufus, recommended that women receive the same education as men, for philosophy was a good foundation for the attributes of a good wife.[5] Apart from advocating rigorous intellectual training, the Stoics had a conservative attitude toward women despite the ideas of their founder Zeno who, like Plato in *The Republic*, imagined a utopian society where wives were held in common. Stoics did believe in equality, but only among men. Women were to be wives and mothers, and, despite Zeno, to belong to their male protectors. Spiritually, Stoicism taught that happiness was found internally. "Before the external disorder of the world and bodily illness, retreat into yourself and find God there," wrote the emperor Marcus Aurelius in the second century. Meditation, introspection, rejection of sensual pleasure, and a disdain for worldly business were features present in other philosophies or in cults. They were also expressed in the Gnostic spirituality which took inspiration from eastern religions of Hinduism and Buddhism as well as from Greek philosophers (Plato, for instance) and Judaism.[6] *Gnosis* is the Greek word for reflective knowledge: Gnostics claimed to possess a special knowledge of the nature and destiny of man derived from appreciation of a myth which explained the origin of the universe and mankind. Gnosticism pervaded first- and second-century Christianity until many of its ideas were declared unorthodox by the fourth-century church. In its mythology and its beliefs and practices some women could find a favorable reception.

Gnosticism: The Dyad God

There were many Gnostic communities, many Gnostic Christian congregations, and several versions of Gnostic myth and ideology, but all believed that the material world was controlled by evil forces and moreover had been created not by the supreme good God, but by the evil Demiurge. Only the elect few could be redeemed, at the time of death. They possessed the gift of a divine spark from the true God, and their souls must be aroused during life to an awareness of a high destiny. The material world was irrelevant. An elect individual need acknowledge no obligation toward society, or the state, or other people, although it might be prudent and respectful to do so. At death the freed soul would journey through the planets to find its heavenly home. En route, special passwords determined admission to the correct pathways, so during life these had to be learned. Rival Gnostic communities, both those professing the Christian faith and those denying any special status to Jesus, set up rival lexicons of passwords, causing considerable confusion about the most appropriate way to live while awaiting death and spiritual liberation. Most Gnostics advocated ascetic behavior, with a prohibition on marriage or at least on procreation, so that even on earth the soul might not be diverted from contemplation of its eventual destiny. Some Gnostic Christians, however, preached that since material constraints were of no moral value, and since only spiritual matters ultimately counted, sensual license might be indulged. Plato had taught that love was a mystical communion with God: if one could experience that, all other experiences were subordinate and might therefore be either enjoyed or rejected.[7]

Gnostic Christians interpreted their faith in a way threatening to the maintenance of the Christian church, or so its early guardians complained. Gnostic differentiation of the true God from God the creator allowed them to regard the true God as indescribable. The true God was all things, and was in all things, and moreover was female as well as male.[8] For most Gnostic Christians, Jesus was the redeemer, but some sects regarded Jesus as secondary and instead considered other persons as the major redeemers. Even those Gnostics who acknowledged the central place of Jesus in Christianity held a view which was distinctly unorthodox. The divine Christ could not simultaneously be human, they preached. Therefore, Jesus was divine, not human. The resurrection was spiritual, not of the flesh. Jesus had not literally been born of a woman, for he existed only in a spiritual sense, so there was no need to believe in a Virgin

Birth. Gnostics questioned the supremacy of scriptural and official authority. They believed their own inner light could lead to the truth about God. Neither the Old Testament nor contemporary interpreters could usurp this special relationship or erode its legitimacy. Consequently, traditional documents and contemporary priests were not infallible. Priests might be helpful, depending on their intimate relationship with the true God, who did not discriminate according to ingrained social customs of the material world as to who might appropriately be a priest. In other words, a priest might be a woman, displaying in human form the feminine side of the true God's nature, and mirroring the influence of Mary Magdalene as a disciple of Jesus. Residual fragments of Gnostic thought still abound in much orthodox Christianity, but the so-called Gnostic Gospels, writings paralleling the orthodox Gospels but pronounced heretical in the early fourth century, were ordered destroyed. Twelve books of Gnostic writings which were buried in Upper Egypt at Nag Hammadi were dicovered in 1945 and allow us a glimpse of a church in which the traditional Greek, Roman, and Judaic woman could be transformed.[9]

The Hebrew Tradition

Hebrew women at the time of Christ in many ways shared the subordination of their Hellenistic and Roman counterparts, but their tradition contained unique elements too. Part of this tradition gave undoubted emphasis to the importance of Jewish women as trustees of the uniqueness of the Hebrew race and culture. Legally and commercially Jews were bound by the laws of the Roman Empire, whether they lived in Palestine or in the Jewish quarters of cities elsewhere in the empire. Their religious and family life was governed by tradition as displayed in the Old Testament, and in the later corpus of commentary and interpretation known as the Talmud. The Old Testament tradition, like Greek and Roman culture, offered no monolithic image of woman, but rather several, many of them antithetical, testifying simultaneously to the power and the powerlessness of Jewish women. Since Christianity started out as a Jewish sect, since its first practitioners were Jews, and since the first congregations were in Palestine or other Jewish settlements, Jewish customs regarding women were crucial in forging Christian customs regarding women.

The laws of the Old Testament were collected over a long period of time, from before 1000 B.C. until around 400 B.C., and represent widespread Middle Eastern practice at the time of Minoan culture in Crete, and Mycenean culture in Greece until the beginning of Aristotelian Athens. They shared some features not only with those cultures, but also with the more immediate neighbors in Mesopotamia: all had mainly patrilineal descent, patrilocal residence, concubinage, slavery, and a double standard for sexual behavior. In two ways the Hebrew laws differed from those of their neighbors. Sexual transgression was punished more severely, and the exclusive and undefiled worship of Yahweh, the one God, was preserved carefully. Both were aspects of the same concern, to preserve the purity and strength of the Hebrew tribes. Most of the laws were addressed to the adult male head of household, who was regarded as responsible for all his dependents both economically and religiously. His main concern was to transmit the property and values of his forebears to the next generation. To do this, he had to have the security of knowing his wife's reproductive power was harnessed exclusively to him. Adultery therefore demanded the death penalty, but for the man as well as for the woman; fornication required that the woman, who had thereby violated her virginity and the honor of her male guardian (usually her father), either be married by her seducer or be put to death. Monogamy was the norm, but a man could have more than one wife, could keep a concubine, and was not punished for consorting with harlots. A wife experienced economic protection, but a single woman without means—such as a widow—did not enjoy the use of property by right, and was dependent on the goodwill of close kin. Religious practice was in the exclusive care of men, and even as worshipers women were regularly restricted by the wide interpretation of "uncleanness," for during periods of impurity no person could participate in religious observance. Since uncleanness included menstruation and sexual intercourse and childbirth, with the birth of a son rendering a woman unclean for seven days, and of a daughter for fourteen days, a woman's opportunity to demonstrate purity was clearly limited.[10]

Simultaneous with these derogatory tenets were strictures on young people of both sexes to honor and respect both their parents, and in some parts of the Old Testament woman, as mother, wife, and emotionally autonomous adult, was recognized as possessing qualities desirable for men as well as women. Prudence, wisdom, industriousness, foresightedness, efficiency in the management of resources and servants, kindness in teaching, generosity toward the poor—all were features of the good wife of quality in Proverbs 31. A man was admonished to beware the seductions of a harlot or adventuress whose sexual attractions could only result in his unhappiness and ruin: sexual pleasure should only be enjoyed in marriage. This advice, seemingly grudgingly given, nevertheless introduced into marriage an element which was absent from classical Greek culture and only fortuitously present in Roman: the notion of a companionate relationship, where sex was enjoyed, and a married couple loved one another. Most Old Testament references to women were associated with nonsexual attributes of character. Many historical anecdotes took woman as protagonist, usually in epic stories defending the interests of the Hebrews. The Old Testament also contained powerful erotic poetry, where the writer rejoiced in the sensual pleasure of a beautiful body and returned affection.[11] Despite the general lack of a legal or public personality, a woman's power, both to absorb a man's attention and to contribute to his worldly success, was clearly acknowledged in the society into which Jesus was born.

Christianity: the Promise of Equality

The founder of Christianity was born in Bethlehem in Judea and at the age of thirty began to preach that the Kingdom of God was at hand. Many Jews were predisposed to believe this message, for in many particulars Jesus' preaching was in accordance with Old Testament prophecies, and the particular political circumstances of Palestine, annexed as a Roman province in 6 A.D., encouraged the development of an indigenous, nationalist savior. His ministry at first attracted crowds, but the religious hierarchy disapproved of him. After three years he was handed over to Roman authorities who with the support of the crowds crucified him as a revolutionary. His disciples' faith in him lapsed, until their experience at Jesus' Resurrection renewed their belief and galvanized them into declaring the news of the Messiah not only to fellow Jews, but to Gentiles also. Christianity became accessible to all people. Jesus in his preaching and teaching had many remarkable points to make regarding women, and in the early generations of gospel spreading women took a prominent role, as they did later. Only in recent years has research into the early church recovered the significance of women quashed by the later orthodox patristic tradition developed after the Council of Nicaea in 325.

The Gospel according to Luke was distinctive among the other canonical Gospels in that it recorded more instances of Jesus' teaching in which he demonstrated an awareness of women in his audience. The "pairing parables" were stories where Jesus was emphasizing a particular moral point which he illustrated by a pair of parables, illuminating the point in one for men and in the other for women. An example is the pair illustrating the notion that the Kingdom of God was open to the most obscure and forgotten soul, provided he or she repented. The message was brought home in a direct way to his mixed audience by two stories, one of a man rejoicing after a successful search for a lost sheep, and the other of a woman, happy when she found a coin which had been lost. In another telling example, Jesus showed that the Kingdom of God would have inauspicious beginnings, but a magnificent achievement. Luke reported Jesus comparing the Kingdom first to a grain of mustard seed, which a man sowed, and could then observe growing into a very large plant, and second to leaven, which a woman used as the raising agent for bread.[12] These stories indicate that women formed a large part of Jesus' hearers, and other stories showed that Jesus could approve of nontraditional roles which women might take.

Outstanding was the story of Mary and Martha. Martha was making domestic preparations for Jesus, and was resentful that her sister Mary, instead of helping her, was listening at Jesus' feet, not an expected activity for a Jewish woman. Martha asked Jesus to reprimand Mary and send her about her proper business. Jesus however affirmed that Mary had chosen the right thing to do. A young woman should be allowed to learn about the Scriptures. Luke's Gospel especially, but the others too, carried the message that in the new faith it was as important to educate the women as the men. Luke included accounts of Jesus' teaching which showed, sometimes dramatically, how Jesus regarded women as souls deserving of the same salvation and as persons deserving of the same respect as men. He repudiated the double standard when discussing the woman taken in adultery, and was in favor of a secure matrimonial system whereby capricious divorce on the part of the husband would not be countenanced. In one of Jesus' most vivid metaphors describing the rewards of Christianity, he likened the joy of knowing God to the joy of a woman who underwent the travail of childbirth and then was delivered of a child: her joy knew no bounds.[13] Jesus also had women helpers in his ministry. Mary Magdalene "spoke as a woman who knew the All," according to a Gnostic text called *Dialogue of the Saviour*, and was the favored companion of Jesus. "Christ loved her more than all the disciples."[14]

Paul: Mitigated Misogyny

Paul and other Christian missionaries preached in Asia Minor, the Aegean islands, Greece, Italy, and possibly even in Spain. Their first targets were the Jewish congregations in the main urban settlements, and their Gentile associates. Very soon, most converts came not from the Jews but from Gentiles. The Acts of the Apostles alluded to the many women, both Jewish and Gentile, frequently literate and wealthy, who became Christians.[15] Paul's Epistles made continual reference to the women on his journeys who gave him hospitality and often organized his visits. Early assemblies of Christian communities were all in the houses of women.[16] One woman, Tabitha, also known as Dorcas, was described in the orthodox literature as a "disciple" and of sufficient importance to be raised from the dead by Peter.[17] There were women serving as prophets, clarifying and explaining the faith in accordance with the prophecy of Joel: "And your sons and your daughters shall prophesy."[18] In Christian tradition, however, all the evidence of women's early participation paled beside the fulminations of Paul in his first letter to the Corinthians, where he inveighed against women for praying with their heads unveiled, and witheringly told them to keep silence. "For they are not permitted to speak, but should be subordinate, as even the law says" (I Corinthians 14:34–35). Recent studies, building on increased knowledge of Gnostic practice, are instructive in softening the severe misogynist strain in these particular Pauline remarks.

Constance Parvey claims that Paul's insistence that women cover their heads when in church was consistent with the traditional Jewish habit whereby a woman's covered head was a sign of her respectability and a symbol of protection against fallen angels who might otherwise be able to attack her weak spirit. However, Parvey then draws attention to Paul's subsequent remark, which suggested that he did not necessarily believe in the natural weakness of woman. "Nevertheless," wrote Paul, "in the Lord woman is not independent of man nor man of woman; for as woman was made from man, so man is now born of woman. And all things are from God" (I Corinthians 11:11–12). This, argues Parvey, is to be interpreted as heralding an age of interdependence in a community living in God's faith, where each person's gifts, not necessarily distributed according to sex, could be maximized for the collective good of the community and God.[19] Parvey is similarly able to wrest a more favorable meaning from Paul's insistence on silence. The Corinthian congregation was heavily influenced by its Gnostics, preoccupied with their individual ecstasies, and considering themselves immune from the rebukes of church officials.[20] Possibly women were among the more eloquent of those talking and asking questions. The particular context is unknown, but Paul questioned the arrogance of those who thought themselves unaffected by the teaching of others. Then, Parvey notes, he advised the Corinthians to continue to prophesy and even to speak in tongues, so long as it was done "decently and in order." Decency and order could include women, whereas had he said "according to the law," they would have been excluded. So far from reinforcing the repressive Judaic tradition, and acting as precursor to later undeniably misogynist church fathers, a case can be made for Paul as a liberal.[21] This interpretation is strengthened when his revolutionary statement about equality is considered.

Galatians 3:28 states: "There is neither Jew nor Greek, there is neither slave nor free, there is neither male nor female; for ye are all one in Christ Jesus." The traditional categories of race, economics, and sex were to be no longer relevant in the new, immanent, Christian society. This was definitely true for the life in the world to come, but by way of preparation, people could start to live immediately according to new Christian ethics. Paul did not always counsel total abandonment of existing customs. After all, he thought women's headcoverings were important enough to maintain, and he thought the runaway slave Onesimus should be returned to his owners, though Paul did hope that in Christian charity, the owners would give Onesimus freedom.[22] But Paul acknowledged that spiritually women were not to be differentiated from men, and that a woman's gender did not disqualify her from teaching, preaching, and other important work in disseminating God's word. Compared with other Epistle writers, Paul was generous. Timothy, for example, considered that only motherhood could "save" women, whereas men, on the other hand, could be saved by coming to Christ (I Timothy 2:15). In this matter also Paul broke new ground. His observation that it was better to marry than to burn, in order to avoid fornication, was a profoundly negative attitude toward marriage (I Corinthians 7:1–12). Also, since in the context of existing society, an adult woman had no economic alternative to marriage, the remark unavoidably branded every woman as an influence for ill. Yet in context, he was not so much decrying marriage as he was venerating celibacy for the unmarried and widowed. In this, he was advocating a respectable alternative to marriage for those called by God, and these could be women as well as men. The chaste unmarried woman need not be regarded as an interim object, but as a person whose commitment to God absorbed all her energy. She was to be venerated, not eradicated.[23]

Women Believers

During Jesus' life, women were among his audiences and among the early congregations of believers, and Paul's Epistles gave much evidence of women active in first-generation Christian communities. There is further evidence of women acting as overseers, as well as teachers, healers, helpers, administrators, and protectors (I Corinthians 12:28). The word *episcopa* has been translated as *overseer* whereas *episcopus*, the masculine version, is rendered as *bishop*. It is not clear what specific functions the episcopae performed, but mosaics and inscriptions which include the designation *episcopa* show women officiating in churches. They might have been deaconesses, helping instruct women catachumens in the faith before baptism. They might have owned the house in which church services took place. They might have been members of a community of women, among the first converts. Or possibly a fresco in the catacomb of Saint Priscilla in Rome, dating from the first century A.D., was true to life in its depiction of seven women celebrating mass as priests.[24] Certainly Gnostic Christian communities were attacked by the orthodox for, among other things, their ordination of women. Irenaeus, bishop of Lyons in the second century, attacked the Gnostic Marcus for having in his circle women prophets and women priests who together with men celebrated the Eucharist. Irenaeus also denounced Marcus's theology. His followers gave prayers to the "Mother" as the feminine component of God.[25] By the beginning of the third century Tertullian inveighed against "heretical women" in the church: "They have no modesty: they are bold enough to teach, to engage in argument, to enact exorcisms, to undertake cures, and, it may be, even to baptise!" Marcion, who was excommunicated by the church in 144, was a Gnostic Christian leader in Asia Minor where he appointed women as priests and bishops.[26] By the time of Tertullian few Orthodox churches retained officiating women, but the proscribed Gnostic congregations continued for over a hundred years, and their ideas, which contained markedly heterodox views on women, were to resurface in various heresies during the Middle Ages. These were not always indisputably attractive. The Gnostic Gospel of Thomas related a story where Peter, jealous of the influence of Mary Magdalene on Jesus, suggested to the disciples that she be excluded from their group, "for she is a woman, and not worthy of Life." Jesus responded enigmatically. "Behold I will take Mary, and make her a male, so that she may become a living spirit, resembling you males. For I tell you truly, that every female who makes herself male will enter the Kingdom of heaven."[27] It is not clear whether the Gnostic strain of androgyny signified that sexual differences were irrelevant, or meant that their apparent androgyny was really total assimilation into male values.

Gnostic thought, censored from official Christian doctrine, bequeathed many legacies to orthodoxy. One of particular interest to women was the ascetic ideal whereby a person wishing to attain gnosis retreated from the world in contemplation of inner insight and God's will. Early Christians acknowledged that women might be the vehicles for God's grace and that the single celibate life was an honorable calling, indeed, to be regarded as superior to the married state. In the early fifth century Palladius, bishop of Helenopolis, wrote a history of Egyptian monasticism in which he asserted that twice as many women as men were by that time living in desert communities of nuns or anchoresses: twenty thousand as compared with ten thousand hermits.[28] Even after monastic life became more regulated, each community retained considerable autonomy and was able to provide not only a haven for disaffected women, and a respectable setting for religious persons, but also administrative opportunities for those women capable of managing the property and work which made the convents economically self-sufficient. Communities of religious women became famous for their social and educational services to local settlements, as well as continuing to serve as an alternative life-style for women who for a variety of reasons preferred not to conform to the prevalent pattern of marriage, motherhood, and subordination.

The Church Fathers: Woman as Carnal Temptress

Individualism and rejection of a strong institutional hierarchy were important tenets of the Christian Gnostics. These characteristics help account for the vehement and eventually successful opposition of Christians more mindful of the need for a strong, preferably united, church to protect its members and faith against persecution and hostility. Gnostics had always attracted critics, but their ideas were effectively exorcised from authoritative Christian thought by the fourth century "fathers." Their suppression of Gnostic attitudes about the creation of the world, about the Old Testament, about the humanity/divinity of Christ, about the trinity, and about religious authority led to the supression of Gnostic congregations in which women had officiated. Also, the particular ideas of the Gnostics regarding the dyad God, and the status of Mary Magdalene, were set aside. While consolidating their interpretation of Christianity, the fathers also imposed on the church their particular view of women, which was basically negative. Images of women in the Old Testament were much more favorable, as were those reaching us from Rome and the Hellenistic Mediterranean.

Paradoxically the fathers drew on Gnostic attitudes in many ways to buttress their misogynist approach. The Gnostics had stressed the importance of the spiritual world as distinct from the material: the fathers identified woman as the representative of the material world. As such she was not only a distraction to Christian men who wanted to lead the good life, but a definite incentive to carnal indulgence.[29] Yet the fathers could not ignore teachings which allowed women to be spiritual beings too. It was difficult for them to argue that by nature a woman was of the flesh, which should be subject to the spirit, and at the same time to appreciate that a woman possessed a spirit too, despite her nature. Tertullian addressed woman in fulsome language.

> You are the Devil's gateway. You are the unsealer of that forbidden tree. You are the first deserter of the divine law. You are she who persuaded him whom the Devil was not valiant enough to attack. You destroyed so easily God's image, man. On account of your desert, that is death, even the Son of God had to die.

The fathers' solution to this intellectual dilemma echoed the Gnostic Gospel of Thomas. In virginity a woman could be "forgetful of her natural feminine weakness" and could live "in manly vigor." She could transcend her female nature and become transformed into a male. So virginity became an entirely real option for the religious woman just as for religious men. On their scale of values, the virgin state produced a hundredfold return as compared with sixtyfold for widowhood and merely thirtyfold for marriage.[30]

The fathers were preoccupied with sexual continence and used it as the touchstone of all morality. Possibly their obsessions mirrored personal experiences: Tertullian, Jerome, and Augustine all left records of dissolute sinful lives prior to conversion which signified a shift from a fascination with the worldly to the spiritual.[31] Their clear preference for a life free of sexuality led them into difficulties regarding marriage. They stressed the problems of marriage often, and its joys rarely. Marriage was a nuisance, producing physical pain in child-bearing for women and irritating distractions for men. Its only advantage was that it provided a useful vehicle for procreation and reduced opportunities for lust in those weak souls unable to bear the discipline of celibacy. The fathers displayed an almost unrelieved antagonism to marriage and the family, in distinct contrast to the Judaic tradition and even the customs of Greece and Rome, where the family was considered as the basic natural unit of society and the state. Only Clement of Alexandria offered a modified view. Acknowledging that celibacy was to be preferred, he nevertheless considered that a Christian family offered opportunities for happiness and also gave a devout man more chances for exercising self-discipline, since more temptations were offered to him. Clement followed up his comparatively less jaundiced view of marriage with a few good words on women. Woman was man's equal, having exactly the same human nature, different in sex and therefore in function and vocation, but capable of attaining the same degree of perfection. Men, nevertheless, were always better at everything than women. The fathers' misogyny led them to deplore the notion of married clergy, and in the fourth century regulations were formulated requiring abstinence from coitus on the part of bishops, priests, and deacons. Synods of the church repeatedly declared the rule, so, quite likely, clergy did not willingly conform. Pope Leo in the mid-fifth century said the married clergy should be permitted to retain their wives "as though they had them not."[32]

For lay Christians, marriage was seen as the most likely state. Although Christians were enjoined to marry with the consent of a bishop, so that the marriage would be "according to the Lord, and not for the sake of lust," no marriage service was included in the rites of the church for several centuries: in 866 a pope first described an appropriate ceremony. Divorce between Christians was permitted for adultery in either party, but remarriage was normally condemned as a form of adultery. Augustine developed the idea of marriage as a sacrament between husband and wife which was permanent and indissoluble. It symbolized "the unity of us all made subject to God, which shall be hereafter in one heavenly City."[33] Marriage was a concession to human frailty, not regarded as highly as celibacy, but nevertheless preferable to sexual license which would inevitably predominate in its absence. Marriage therefore was to be strengthened by ecclesiastical injunctions to permanence.

The patristic tradition, while rejecting most Gnostic mysticism, still drew deep on the Gnostic juxtaposition of matter (bad) and spirit (good). The symmetry of the sexes allowed the fathers to identify woman as by nature opposite to man, who alone had the capacity for spiritual growth. This identification gave rise to much tortuous argument, for Jesus and Paul, their intellectual and spiritual masters, had allowed spiritual equality to women. Many unresolved dilemmas on the subject of women and sex can be found in the writings of Augustine, John Chrysostom, and other early church authorities. Moreover, the vituperative style of some fathers was an exhortation to hatred, disdain, or, at best, condescension toward women. Their basic attitude was the same as the fifth-century Martin of Tours when he described three fields: the ungrazed field of virginity, the field of marriage cropped by cattle, and the field of fornication uprooted by swine.[34] A Christian woman was worthy of the highest respect only when she denied her sexuality and remained chaste. In this respect, an alternative life-style was opened up to women, but at the price of demeaning all other women who chose not to remain virgin, or who had that choice made for them. In the very long term all women could benefit from the Christian insistence on equality. In the meantime, the Christian faith which emerged from its early doctrinal battles could not be described as the same open religious opportunity for women of its first two centuries.

Suggestions for Further Reading

Bailey, Derrick Sherwin. *The Man-Woman Relation in Christian Thought.* London, 1959.
Chadwick, Henry. *The Early Church.* London, 1977.
Pagels, Elaine H. *The Gnostic Gospels.* New York, 1979.
————. "What Became of God the Mother? Conflicting Images of God in Early Christianity." *Signs* 2 (1976):293–303.
Reuther, Rosemary, ed. *Religion and Sexism.* New York, 1974.

CHAPTER 6

The Middle Ages

"Eva/Ave" was the medieval palindrome which crystallized the two predominant pictures of woman in the literary imagination.[1] This Janus-like imagery was not confined to the tiny numbers of literate and educated people, for it reverberated also through the law codes, especially canon law. When politically strong units emerged from the period of unsettling tribal invasions and colonizing of the early Middle Ages—the Italian states from Ostrogothic settlements, Spain from the Visigoths, Britain from the Angles, Saxons, Danes, and Normans, France from the Franks and Burgundians—secular law enforcement was allied with the power of the church in a reciprocally advantageous connection. Church and state together permeated medieval mentalities with the representation of woman which was both wicked ("Eva" from Eve, the first woman) and holy (the "Ave" from the angel Gabriel's greeting to Mary at the annunciation of her conception of Jesus). In the idea of courtly love, the noble lady was depicted in a perpetually elevated position, and there were similarities between chivalry as seen by troubadours and the worship of the Virgin Mary. Fundamentally the knight's lady, Mary the mother of God, and Eve were integrated into a single notion of females which was inferior, weak, and subordinate to males. Still there were women in literature and even more in real life who did not fit completely any of these paradigms. Peasant women in the countryside and women earning wages in the towns could rarely be characterized wholly as an Eve, or a Mary, still less a noble lady carrying the colors for her paramour. In the course of this millennium, evidence suggests that for ordinary women, conditions in their daily life changed quite considerably just as there were changes in the lives of elite women.

Evidence as always is ambiguous. For the status and roles of medieval women we possess a wide variety of sources: place-names, graves, scattered demographic records, and secular and devotional literature. Historians have examined the remains of animal bones for a clue to the food consumed, and have even taken cross sections of a peat bog to discover the accumulation of vegetable matter as an indication of cereal crop production.[2] Laws and regulations, both secular codes and canon law, offer by far the most important material, and can additionally provide pointers to problems of everyday life. The

Salic Law (ca. 511) severely punished the stealing of fruit from trees. A normal diet was always on the verge of insufficiency, not only because of poor means of distribution but also because of a low yield of the cereal crops producing flour for the major daily nourishment of bread and its accompaniments. Similarly, trespassing on growing crops carried heavy punishment.[3] This same Salic code prohibited women from inheriting property in the areas of northern Europe subject to its jurisdiction. The law codes indicate the social and economic value men placed on women, for, as in the past, men controlled the society and made the laws.

Women Troubadours and Courtly Love

One valuable variation on this general theme is the remarkable corpus of women troubadours' poems dating from twelfth-century Occitania in the south of France. A legacy of Roman and Visigothic law and practice allowed women from noble families a comparatively privileged status, so that it was not uncommon for fiefs to be held by heiresses. The Crusades decimated the ranks of male nobility and at the same time encouraged younger noble sons to seek their fortune at the courts of patrons endowed with more resources than their own families. Some Occitanian courts were controlled by women who were not only the patrons of male troubadours but sometimes troubadours themselves; Meg Bogin has identified twenty women poets of the period 1150–1250.[4] Their work expands our understanding of the courtly love phenomenon and also reflects the women's own consciousness of chivalric society.

Veneration of a lady was the theme of the male troubadours. The female troubadours extended and modified the theme to include a more comprehen-

Women's experience of war in the Bayeux Tapestry

sive celebration of love in many forms. The standard model for *midons*—the hermaphroditic code name used by the first troubadour Guilhelm de Poitou to describe "my lord" who was the lady, and the ruler, of his affections—was the wife of the male troubadour's employer. She was, in their poems, passive: the knightly worshiper, by way of contrast, became more worthy, more happy, more spiritually ennobled through his worship of her. She was a "conduit of status" in that she had the power to intercede with her husband on behalf of the suitor and, if she were herself in control of the fief, had the potential to share her own inherited property with a new husband. The women troubadours did not utilize the formulas to the same extent. They sang of love affairs with reciprocated affection, hurt feelings, melancholy, pride, and sensuality. With sensitivity and intimacy they expressed passion and affection and saw a court society devoid of the worshipful knight stereotype who manned the stanzas of the male troubadours' poetry. "The women seek two things in their relationships: to be acknowledged for who they are, as women and as individuals, and a determining voice in how the relationship is conducted."[5] The very least we can conclude from this ray of evidence illuminating the high Middle Ages from the perspective of women is that for some noble women in Occitania, life held joy as well as sorrow, and the means of shaping the outcome of a love affair. The women troubadours provide a welcome leaven for the rather heavy dough of medieval evidence primarily fashioned by men.

Aquinas and Medieval Christianity: Marriage as Positive Good

Easily the greatest number of record creators, writers, and keepers in medieval times were men of the church, and it is church documents which provide the richest collection of information on medieval women, real and imaginary. Clerical attitudes informed the opinion makers of the society, and were themselves profoundly influenced not only by the patristic tradition but also by the Dominican friar theologian Thomas Aquinas who died in 1274. The historian R. W. Southern wrote of him that no writer was "better equipped to convey to an alien world the intellectual qualities of his own age," and in some significant respects Aquinas was able to soften slightly the dour ascetic insistence of the church fathers.[6] They had considered that a Christian man was a soul imprisoned in material flesh, a body which would only hinder communion with God. Aquinas too was suspicious of corporeal temptations, but he saw man as a composite of body and soul. Unlike the church fathers, Aquinas was readier to recall the Pauline statement of equality of male and female, but traditionally translated this as an equality in salvation rather than during a person's lifetime. He was, however, able to imagine a situation in which a living woman could aspire to holiness—by the renunciation of her sexuality.

On this the medieval church was clear. Sexuality for either sex was not recommended. It both distracted from attention to God and reduced intellectual consciousness in that it involved a lack of rational control. A man who wished to devote himself to God had to vow chastity, and the same requirement was made for a woman. The appearance of an equality in sacrifice was superficial. Following Aristotle's announcements of woman's inferior, subordinate, and irrational nature, Aquinas believed that man was a rational creature, woman was not, and indeed that woman could only be defined in relation to her reproductive capacity. For a novice monk to renounce sexuality was to give up something secondary to his nature. For a novice nun to surrender sexuality was to deny her womanhood, for a woman's sex drive was considered stronger than a man's and she had not the benefit of a man's naturally stronger will to help in its suppression. If successful, she then assumed, to a limited degree, the nature of a male, and had a certain access to religious insights and to a good life.

Aquinas added the patina of Aristotelian thought to commonplace views on the nature of woman, and of sexuality. With respect to marriage he introduced a tentative note which had been lacking in the reluctant toleration given by the church fathers. Marriage, they had recognized, was for the majority, who could not be expected to maintain celibacy throughout their lives. It could be justified not only by expediency, but also on the grounds that it was a remedy for lust, channeling carnal desire toward one person, and, additionally, because it produced children who might thereby have a stable environment for their growth. Aquinas added to these two reasons a third, the idea that marriage was a sacrament, going further than Augustine in this regard. Later theologians and poets developed the idea further still, but Aquinas contributed a positive theory of reciprocity and indissolubility to the idea of medieval Christian marriage.

Reciprocity included the recognition that sexuality was an inevitable and not necessarily bad part of marriage: each partner had a right to the body of the other. This was not a simple statement of equal rights. In his *Summa Theologica*, Aquinas illustrated some of the implications. For example, a woman was not allowed to seek sexual relations during menstruation, lest the child then conceived be malformed. (Correct knowledge of reproductive mechanics was centuries away.) However, a wife was not allowed to refuse her husband's advances during menstruation, for she would then expose her husband to the danger of the sin of lusting after another woman. The remedy for his sin took precedence over the good of a child. The idea that marriage was a sacrament carried with it permanence. For a few centuries, canonists had been advocating the indissolubility of marriage, and Aquinas's advocacy of this carried with it overtones of the potential for spiritual growth and communion with God inside marriage. It was left for later writers to develop the notion of marital growth and communion between the partners, but he allowed marriage to appear a positive emotional good and at least introduced the suggestion that in marriage it was reasonable for a woman to have some sexual expectations which the man should meet. Aquinas also accorded some dignity to a woman in the sense that he thought a marriage was invalid without the prior consent of the bride.[7]

Pagans and Christians: Triumph of Monogamy

The Christian championship of indissolubility was generally accepted in Aquinas's time, but it had emerged as orthodoxy only after coexisting with previous very different tribal customs. In most barbaric law codes, concubinage, for example, was not forbidden, nor was polygamy. Divorce was regulated, but not forbidden. The Burgundian code, for instance, compiled in the early sixth century, required a husband to prove his wife guilty of one of three crimes before he could legitimately repudiate her: adultery, witchcraft, or the violation of graves. Without proof of her guilt, however, he could leave her, so long as he left household property behind for the use of her and her children. If he had no cause to repudiate her, he could repay her the bride price of money paid to her or her guardians at marriage. For women, repudiation of a husband carried with it the punishment of being smothered in mire.[8] In a code five hundred years later, issued by the Danish king Cnut who conquered Britain in the early eleventh century, women of high rank at least were assumed to have some dignity and independence. "No woman or maiden shall ever be forced to marry a man whom she dislikes, nor shall she ever be given for money, unless the suitor wishes to give something of his own free will." Within marriage, she was not under the total tutelage of her husband, for she was deemed responsible for her storeroom, her chest, and her cupboard. If any stolen goods were put in these receptacles, she was considered guilty in the event her husband was a proven thief; otherwise, she was not automatically associated with him. This was a change from the law code issued two hundred years earlier by Ine of Wessex, wherein a man's wife was given no separate duty at all apart from obedience to her lord.[9]

Still, marriage for the barbarians, like marriage for the Greeks and Romans, centered around the desire to protect a family's interest in its property. It was an economic transaction safeguarding property in both present and future generations. The Christians could not expect to eradicate such longstanding and sensible undertakings, but they made their mark in ways which could be considered beneficial to women. First, they insisted on a woman's consent. How far this could be freely given when a woman was married at puberty, and with little or no economic self-sufficiency, is doubtful. Roman law tradition also insisted on a dowry, which could be interpreted as an attempt to provide some residual economic security for the woman within marriage and in the event she was left without a husband.[10] Third, they considered marriage to be indissoluble, and by the end of the ninth century, the Carolingian bishops, led by Hincmar of Reims, were carrying this principle to the extent that if a married couple separated and either one remarried, that would be considered fornication. Ironically, legitimate grounds for separation could be found in the elaborate lists of consanguinity constructed by the eighth- and ninth-century papal councils. Incest taboos existed in the pagan tribes, but the Christians introduced many more forbidden degrees of relationship. Consequently, if either spouse wished to separate or divorce, they could apply for an annulment on the grounds of incest if a forbidden relationship was belatedly discovered. Also, sexual relations with anyone were thought to create a blood tie, so the incest net was cast wide.[11] Since it was a wife who stood to suffer most by divorce or repudiation, an insistence on indissolubility was to her benefit.

Women in the Church: The Vita Apostolica

Even before Aquinas painted a more appealing view of woman for Christianity, women had responded in a variety of ways to the church. Communities of women pursuing religious perfection during their lifetime had been established since the very early days of the church. Convents never had the clarity of monasteries, for a religious woman, no matter how strong her vocation and how respected she was by the church hierarchy, was not to be ordained. Convents therefore usually contained a colony of monks nearby to perform the religious services, but they were administered and supervised by the female abbess. At the outskirts of Christianity, in seventh-century Britain, many communities of women or women and men together were established, all under the rule of an abbess. Novices or children educated there later became priests, scholars, or missionaries: for instance, a British monk named Wynfrith, later known as Boniface, before his death in 754 converted many of the German tribes to Christianity with the help of women from monasteries in Wessex trained by two outstanding abbesses, Tette of Wimborne in Dorset, and Eadburg of Thanet.[12] Another famous abbess was Hild of Whitby, who hosted a convention to decide how the date of Easter would henceforth be calculated.

Nuns in most of Europe came from the elite. Their motives for taking vows were not always religious. Sometimes an impoverished father could not contemplate the provision of an adequate marriage portion for his daughter, and so endowed her with a smaller amount which would maintain her in a nunnery. A widow might prefer not to remarry, but stay in old age in reasonable comfort.[13] Nunneries were not necessarily places of discreet and spiritual behavior. A bishop inspecting a foundation in his jurisdiction reported a nun "who on Monday did pass night with Austin Friars at N'hampton and did dance and play lute with them in same place till midnight and on night following passed night with Friars Preachers at N'hampton, luting and dancing in like manner."[14] Whatever the deportment of the residents, the abbess could exercise considerable authority, depending on whether or not she was exempt from the local supervision of a bishop. Many abbesses, especially in Spain, owed their jurisdiction directly to the pope, who did not always exercise stringent control.[15] Consequently monastic institutions for women offered to the nobly born an alternative to the perpetual protection of a feudal lord, and opportunities for running estates and businesses, for each foundation was supported financially by its own endowments, which had to be managed. Nuns also enjoyed widespread respect and admiration and could gain recognition for their spiritual interpretations and writings.

In the twelfth century the church experienced a spiritual revival. Some new monastic foundations, like the Cistercians, emphasized retreat from worldly affairs and a concentration on the traditional contemplative rule; others wished to identify more immediately with the rural and urban populations and preach to them directly of Christ; and the Dominican and Franciscan friars followed a rule which emphasized poverty even more than obedience.[16]

Women responded to this revival in religious feeling in ways parallel to those of men. Some became benefactors of new foundations. A new Cistercian foundation attracted an endowment from a Spanish countess who wrote: "I fear the pains of hell and I desire to come to the joys of paradise, and for the love of God and his glorious Mother, and for the salvation of my soul and those of my parents, I give to God, Saint Mary, and all the saints my whole inheritance in Retoria."[17] Others traveled on pilgrimages, often far distances, to Rome, to the Holy Land, or to shrines where miracles or visions had occurred. Chaucer's *Canterbury Tales* relate the stories with which a group of pilgrims, men and women, entertained each other en route.

But many women wanted to participate more directly in a new *vita apostolica*. Like the usual inhabitants of convents, many were of noble birth, but by no means all. New convents were founded, following the rules of the new orders who initially welcomed them. Overwhelmed by applications, the orders' leaders changed their acceptance and in fact forbade the establishment of further houses. Jacques de Vitry, protector of a group of religious women from Liège, bluntly wrote his view of why the Cistercians, for example, changed their tune. "It was not thought desirable that the female sex submit itself to such rules of austerity and approach such summits of perfection."[18] After 1227 the pope established a policy whereby female branches of the male orders were created, against the wishes of the Dominican and Franciscan leaders themselves, primarily in order to retain supervision over these women, and forestall them from going their own way.

This was no imaginary threat. At the beginning of the thirteenth century two remarkable movements of religious women were found all over Europe, especially in the towns: the Beguines, and the Poor Clares. The Beguines had no named founder, and submitted to no specified rule, nor had they irrevocable vows. They kept chaste, and they renounced worldly goods. They lived by their own manual labor and they brought the gospel in their way to urban populations. In 1243 the chronicler Matthew Paris wrote of their proliferation throughout Europe and said over two thousand were in Cologne and surrounding cities, for example.[19] The Poor Clares looked to Clare, a noble lady converted to the *vita apostolica* by Saint Francis in 1212, who had given away her property and wealth in order to live a cloistered life in the church of Saint Damian in Assisi, maintaining herself and her followers on alms or bequests, rather than on their own labor. Their example encouraged women with spiritual leanings. Both nuns and laywomen were disappointed at the cold shoulder offered by the established orders, exemplified by a late-thirteenth-century Cistercian record explaining why women could not be admitted into the order:

> . . . that the iniquity of women surpasses all iniquities which are in the world, and that there is no wrath greater than the wrath of a woman, that the poisons of vipers and dragons are healthier and less harmful for men than familiarity with women . . . we shall receive under no condition more sisters for the increase of our perdition, but rather we shall avoid accepting them as if poisonous beasts.[20]

Saint Clare, dispensing alms

Nor was it surprising that some women turned to an experience with the heresy of Albigensianism, or Catharism, which displayed many of the Gnostic ideas purged from the orthodox church nine hundred years before. Unfortunately Catharism was basically no more sympathetic to women than orthodox Christianity. Its religious elite of *parfaits* had to abstain from both meat and women, and no woman could herself become a *parfait*.[21] Within Christianity, women, however spiritual and devout, were tarred with the brush of Eve.

The Virgin Mary and the Saints: Images of Holiness

Most women were tainted, that is, save one: the Virgin Mary. Along with the establishment of the Cistercian monasteries in the twelfth and thirteenth centuries went the image of founder Saint Bernard's beloved. His order was dedicated to the Virgin, her image was on its seals, monks wore white for her purity and set up special chapels in their churches. The Virgin was depicted in prose, poetry, and painting not only as the pure mother of God, but also as his bride, and the bride of the church. She was Queen of Heaven. In Saint Bernard's own work she was celebrated as the object of Solomon's *Song of Songs* in all its sensual and erotic splendor.[22] She even replaced the troubadours' images of *midons*. When Occitania was pronounced under the sway of Albigensian heresy by Pope Innocent III in 1209, the area was conquered by northern French Crusader lords who consummated their victory by marriage with Occitanian heir-

Saint Wilgefortis   *Fifteenth-century martyrdom of Saint Barbara*

esses. The heiresses swiftly lost their previous economic landholding status and coincidentally their aesthetic position as the object of the troubadours' affection.[23] Those poets who continued to write now addressed themselves to the Virgin Mary: the madonna image displaced the disturbing *midons*. As such she became less the lover and more the mother, but a mother unstained by carnal love.[24] The adulation bestowed on Mary as a virgin only served to emphasize ordinary women's uncleanness and basic weakness but the development of her worship, particularly when she was associated with human qualities of pain and bereavement, could at least give laywomen the image of a female advocate with the masculine deities of God the Father and God the Son.

In a similar way, laity could invoke female saints to be their familiars, intercessors, and comforters. Sensational stories of their legendary asceticism and ability to perform miracles doubtless helped Christianity to maintain its blanket of faith over all Europe. An example of one nonspiritual benefit to be obtained from the cultivation of a female saint is the custom which surrounded worship of Saint Wilgefortis, whose story is all the more interesting since it was totally invented: as a person, she never existed. Some early-twelfth-century crucifixes depicted Christ fully clothed and shod, wearing a beard. It became the later convention to show Christ naked on the cross, and so the earlier figures were presumed to show a gowned woman. The beard caused her to be known as Virgo Fortis, or strong virgin. The story then grew up that she was a septuplet of a pagan king of Portugal. With her siblings she converted to Christianity, and took a vow of virginity. Her father wished her to marry the king of Sicily, so she prayed to God to make her unattractive. A beard, mustache, and whiskers appeared on her face, thus deterring her suitor, and her father had her crucified. On the cross she prayed that all who remembered her passion should be liberated from all encumbrances and troubles. She became known by a variety of names (Liberata, Liberatrix, Kummerniss, and in English, Saint Uncumber) which refer particularly to her ability to dispatch unwanted husbands. In sixteenth-century England, Thomas More described the custom whereby English women placed oats around her statue "because . . . they reckon that for a peck of oats she will not fail to uncumber them of their husbands."[25]

The Christian views of women are important because a medieval woman, or man, met these images everywhere—in the Sunday sermon, in the preachings of itinerant friars in the marketplace, in the iconography of church buildings, in the shrines set up by the wayside, in the hagiography and worship of female saints, in the communities of holy women, in the dwellings of hermits and anchoresses. All women too were subject to the law. The laws which particularly affected women were inheritance laws and the church canon law regarding reproduction—marriage, divorce, and sexual matters generally, for even in a Christian society, a woman's main value was still as the procreator of future protectors of property.

Women and Property

Indisputably some women owned both real estate, in land and buildings, and personal estate, in movable property. Stenton has drawn attention to the number of English place-names derived from an association, probably of ownership, with a woman, and has also remarked on the large number of women's wills bequeathing property.[26] Herlihy has noted the connection between women as owners or managers of land and their status as measured by the use of matronymics among their sons: approximately 12 percent of land alienated in the five centuries before 1200 in continental Europe was done by women.[27] Customs varied in time and place. There was frequently a distinction made between realty and personalty, with women prohibited from ownership of realty altogether, for example, in the Salic Law. The ninth-century Thuringians also made it difficult for a woman to inherit land.

> Down to the fifth generation the males in the paternal line shall succeed. After the fifth, however, the daughter shall succeed to everything coming both from her father's and mother's side; not until then does the inheritance pass from the spear to the spindle.

The Visigothic code, on the other hand, allowed women to inherit property without priority being accorded to brothers. "If a father or mother should die intestate, sisters shall succeed without any hindrance to the inheritance of their parents' wealth, sharing it equally with their brothers."[28] Court proceedings testify to the frequency with which women, often widows, were able to fulfill their obligations as tenants to their lords.[29]

For the edification of the wives of property owners, noble or bourgeois, advice books were written. One such was composed about 1394 by the Ménagier de Paris, a wealthy man, over sixty, recently married to a well-born orphan of fifteen, apparently fond of his new wife. His book indicates the scale of values, and the pastimes, of a lady of such rank. The two most important things were the salvation of her soul, and the comfort of her husband, and he instructed her how to achieve both. She was to be loving, humble, obedient, careful, silent regarding her husband's secrets, and patient if his thoughts strayed to other women. To reinforce his teaching, he related several morality tales including the fearful one of Petrarch's patient Grizelda whose craven marital obedience even encompassed standing by while her child was abducted from her and supposedly killed. He also described to her every detail of household management, which included instructions on gardening, how to manage servants, how to get out grease spots, and how to catch fleas. There was a cookery section with menus and recipes and a section, doubtless with a view to his future, on cooking for invalids. He then described her likely pastimes: indoor parlor games, riddles, and hawking. Only the hawking treatise survived. Throughout the book he helpfully gave her examples to clarify his intentions, and in one of the most illuminating he described at length a pet dog, with its loyalty, obedience, and cheerfulness even after chastisement. In the same way, his wife must be "very loving and privy" with her new husband.[30]

Demography: From a Deficit to a Surplus of Women

Most women were not the wives of men of property, and most people lived in the countryside. For peasant women, there was no time and little inclination for falconry. The problem of survival, literally, was paramount. Calculations of demographic patterns are impossible without comprehensive statistics, but it is noteworthy that the sex imbalance noted in ninth-century rural France was reversed five hundred years later in urban Germany. A census designed for the administration of a large, twenty-six-hundred-household monastic estate in the early ninth century near Paris has revealed a distinctly unequal proportion of men and women in the population. The number of males was considerably greater than the number of females, both children and adults. Possibly the clerical recorders underreported females. Possibly the excess of males was due to single men migrating in to work on the monastery's farms. Possibly young adult women died in childbirth. Maybe others worked as servants in the monasteries rather than on the estate farms. One factor which contributes to an explanation is the likely practice of female infanticide, which avoided the reduction of a family's limited resources by requiring a dowry when the girl married later.[31] By the time of a census taken in the city of Frankfurt in 1383, for every thousand adult males there were eleven hundred adult women.[32] In the meantime there had been several technological innovations improving agricultural productivity, and it is possible that the increased use of the three-field system, the greater cultivation of former forest and waste

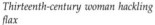

Thirteenth-century woman hackling flax

Woman with spindle feeds poultry, fourteenth century

land, and the introduction of the iron plow enabled the land to support both an increased population and an increased proportion of females.[33]

David Herlihy has drawn attention to this demographic change occurring between the early and late Middle Ages. He has also observed concomitant developments in marriage customs which bring to mind the analyses of Whyte and Goody concerning simple and complex preindustrial societies. Using scattered but consistent data from the eighth and twelfth centuries, Herlihy concludes that a bride was then normally the same age as her spouse at the time of first marriage. After the twelfth century, the situation changed. As women became more numerous—as more women survived—they married younger, and the age gap between them and their grooms grew. Men delayed marriage while accumulating capital in resources which became scarcer under pressure from the increasing population. The families of marriageable daughters engaged in "competitive bidding to attract reluctant grooms," and another significant change occurred: the bride's family offered a dowry to enhance her marriageability. This was in contrast to the custom in the early Middle Ages when the groom brought property or money to the marriage— the bride price phenomenon described by anthropologists. Herlihy, like Whyte and Goody, also notes that with the increased number of women and the eventual preponderance of the dowry custom noted in prehistorical complex societies, "the social position of the medieval woman seems in some ways to have deteriorated."[34]

Heretical Peasant Women

Historian LeRoy Ladurie notes the demographic imbalance of females, among other phenomena, in his recreation of the society of an early-fourteenth-century village in Montaillou in the French Pyrennees. The local bishop of Pamiers conducted an inquisition into the Albigensian or Cathar heresy in his diocese which continued there long after its suppression elsewhere in Occitania. The bishop in his register reported verbatim the examinations of suspected heretics, both the male elite *parfaits* and their men and women supporters. The respondents' replies provide a rich and unusual picture of peasant life at the time: besides describing the particular sheep-rearing economy of the village, they also furnish information about their traditional practices and assumptions, which were probably more universal than specific.

As elsewhere, women's work was centered on the dwelling. While men plowed, harvested the cereals and dug up turnips, and minded the sheep, women were in charge of the water, the fire, the vegetable garden, cooking, and gathering kindling. They ventured further from the house to weed the crops, tie sheaves, and assist with the harvest. Since most animals apart from the sheep were stabled in the dwelling during the winter, women were involved in their care too. The people of Montaillou were fully conscious of the supreme value attached to the care and guardianship of their household (*domus* or *ostal*), which comprised the domestic group of coresidents and involved a composite of elements: the kitchen hearth, goods and land, children, and conjugal alliances. The well-being of the domus was paramount. Individuals were valued only insofar as their domus prospered and was respected. In the accumulation of respect for their domus, women had a crucial role. Their chastity and marital fidelity were appreciated but were not of overriding significance.

Sixteenth-century church carving of two women plucking a chicken

Affairs and liaisons with both married men and the shepherds, who because of their poverty were generally bachelors all their lives, were common. Marriage for a woman was inevitable: no woman was single all her life. The *parfait* Bélibaste expressed the Cathar view of sex in a way similar to the orthodox Christian:

> the sin is the same, to know one's own wife carnally or to do the same with a concubine. This being so, it is better for a man to attach himself to a definite woman than to fly from one to another like a bee among the flowers: the result in the latter case is that he engenders bastards; moreover, when a man frequents several women, each of them tries to lay hold of something, and between them all they will turn a man into a pauper. But when a man is attached to one woman, she helps him to maintain a good *ostal*. As for incest with women of one's own blood or related through marriage, that is a shameful act, and I in no way advise believers to indulge in it.[35]

With peasant families, the well-being of the two parental households and the resultant new domus in a marriage was as important as it was for noble families. The amount and the nature of property clearly were different, but the idea, the paramountcy of the family's interest, was the same. It seems too that there was a place in peasant marriage for love, but while the evidence in Montaillou has instances where a man was in love with his wife, it is silent on a woman's love for a husband. When married, a wife could expect to be beaten and oppressed, but as she grew older (if she did not die in childbirth or epidemic) she became revered as a mother and aunt and could expect to survive the earlier death of her husband. As a widow, normally living then in the domus of her married son or son-in-law, she would continue to inspire respect.

Women were responsible for the material (not the spiritual) care of the dying and then prepared the dead for burial and preserved locks of hair and nail parings from the corpse, since they were thought still to contain life. At social gatherings, which were the prime vehicles for the reinforcement of heresy, when a visiting *parfait* would talk, women cooked and served, sitting to eat separately from the men. Women were friends, sitting in the sun outside their homes and talking, and relating news heard from acquaintances and tradeswomen who traveled from one village to another selling cheese. Women took wheat to the mill to be ground, fetched water, reaped corn together, and deloused each other and their menfolk. Since their lack of formal education was totally matched by the men's, there was little to differentiate their gossip from their menfolk's. Despite their economic value, as reproducers and producers, and their rough equality in poverty with the men, women were nevertheless considered inferior, and the jobs they performed—cooking, gardening, water carrying, child rearing—were thereby considered inferior too. Spiritually, the Cathars were crushing about women's souls. Insulting a local woman, a strong Cathar remarked: "the soul of a woman and the soul of a sow are one and the same thing—in other words, not much," and the *parfait* Bélibaste thought "a man is worth nothing if he is not his wife's master."[36]

Urban Women

In the countryside there was a flexible division of labor, with women, widows especially, often performing work which traditionally belonged to men. In the towns also women could be seen in jobs where men predominated but had not exclusively appropriated the work. Trade guilds of craftsmen often forbade single women from a certain occupation but still expected wives and daughters to assist, and they occasionally expressly allowed widows to continue in the trade of their dead husbands. Women therefore as partners or widows were engaged in a wide variety of occupations. They were merchants, often in large capital ventures like shipping or the wool trade, as well as artisans. Also, women, either unmarried or working separately from their husbands, worked as businesswomen or at a trade. As girls, they were apprenticed, and a general English statute of 1407 assumed that parents apprenticing a child would do so for a son or a daughter. Female apprentices were considered to be under the care of the master tradesman's wife, but the kind of skills they learned were sufficient to set themselves up in business at the end of the long, usually seven-year, training period. If qualified, and not excluded by guild or corporation regulations, a woman, even if married, could be considered for business purposes a *feme sole*. In Lincoln,

> if any woman that has a husband use any craft within the city, whereof her husband meddles not, she shall be charged as a sole woman as touching such things as belongeth to her craft. And if a plaint be taken against such a woman, she shall answer and plead as a sole woman and make her law and take her advantage in court by plea or otherwise for her discharge.[37]

A *feme sole* designation meant that a husband was not liable for his wife's debts or contracts. Unlike a *feme couverte*, she could therefore operate her business in her own name, and the husband was not responsible for her protection. All over Europe women worked in towns in skilled and unskilled labor. In mid-fifteenth-century Strasbourg, for example, named women were licensed to work in the capacity of blacksmith, gardener, goldsmith, wagoner, grain dealer, tailor, and cooper. In thirteenth-century Paris, about one hundred fifty trades and crafts were licensed by the city, and in six of these, women predominated, especially in textiles and spinning.[38] The commonest form of occupation for wage-earning women was domestic service, and the other two areas in which women were most usually found were textiles, and jobs connected with food, drink, and hospitality. Women often made and sold charcoal, traveling from village to village. Retail merchants of a variety of goods often were women, at daily or weekly markets. Women's wages were always less than men's.[39]

Crime: Fewer Female Felons

Medieval women had as much motivation, and as much opportunity, to engage in crime as men. Motives revealed by jail delivery rolls include desperation, acquisitiveness, and vindictive reprisal, the same motives as men. However, not as many women as men were accused of crimes, and of those that were, a lower percentage was found guilty and punished. The treatment meted out to convicted female felons was the same as to male, except that a pregnant woman sentenced to death was able to defer execution until after the birth of her child. The kind of crime women did was similar to what men were involved in, with one exception: a higher percentage of women were found guilty of receiving stolen goods, probably because most married women were in no position to refuse access to the family dwelling to other members of their family who had stolen goods in their possession.[40] One crime which, because it covered sexual matters, was regulated and punished by the church courts was prostitution. In this, the medieval canonists prescribed a greater punishment for the prostitute's clients than for the prostitute herself. She was thought to be acting in accord with a woman's basically sexual nature, and therefore less culpable than her customer. Moreover, she retained ownership rights over her fee, not only on the grounds that she had performed a service, but also because medieval canon lawyers thought her presence was more useful than her absence.[41]

Side by side with the idealized figure of the *midons* love-object of the troubadours, the Virgin Mary, and the weak and wicked temptress of the clerks were working women oblivious of the stereotypes utilized by the literate imagination. "When Adam delved and Eve span, Who was than a gentleman?" Women's labor was of prime importance to the household economy and as members of a household women had status commensurate with that of their family. Even without a husband, widows, if they inherited or could acquire a minimum of economic resources, could hold status and respect. The cloister offered some women an alternative to that provided by a husband or hard and underpaid work. The story of Joan of Arc is a morality tale of how a woman could deviate in medieval Europe and at what cost.

Joan inspired the political cause of the French dauphin Charles VII against the English claimants to the French succession and also, through her prophecies and leadership, directed much of his military strategy before her execution by Anglo-Burgundian forces in 1431. She was a peasant girl who captured the imagination of contemporaries and still serves not only as a symbol of French national resistance but also as a mythical champion of women: suffragist parades in the early twentieth century were frequently led by martial figures dressed as Joan. She was one of a handful of women ever to achieve public power in Western society before modern times, and did so without benefit of dynastic connection to a ruling family. Joan's success was due to the peculiar combination of her acceptance and rejection of contemporary stereotypes. She overcame prejudice against a woman's self-assertion in two ways: she remained a virgin and she wore men's clothes, thereby renouncing the world of the flesh and of female subordination. She acted within conventions of chivalric romance and she also claimed divine inspiration. However, she neglected to secure approval from the church hierarchy before accepting advice from Saints Michael, Margaret, and Catherine; and her transvestism contained its own nemesis, for the ecclesiastical authorities could cite Deuteronomy 22:5 against her: "The woman shall not wear that which pertaineth unto a man." They could also insinuate that her voices came not from God but from the Devil. Joan was never able to neutralize clerical unease and churchmen contributed enthusiastically to her downfall. When she was burned at the stake it was as a witch and heretic against acceptable codes of belief and behavior.[42] Some women, however, survived nicely despite official powerlessness. Chaucer had his Wife of Bath end her tale, whose moral was the inevitability of women's mastery over men, with the chilling invocation: "And Jesu hear my prayer—cut short the lives Of those who won't be govern'd by their wives."[43]

Suggestions for Further Reading

Bogin, Meg. *The Women Troubadours.* New York, 1980.

Herlihy, David. *The Social History of Italy and Western Europe 700–1500.* London, 1978.

Ladurie, LeRoy. *Montaillou: The Promised Land of Error.* New York, 1978.

Power, Eileen. *Medieval People.* London, 1950.

Power, Eileen, and Postan, M. *Medieval Women.* Cambridge, 1975.

Southern, R. W. *Western Society and the Church in the Middle Ages.* London, 1978.

Warner, Marina. *Alone of All Her Sex: The Myth and the Cult of the Virgin Mary.* New York, 1976.

———. *Joan of Arc: The Image of Female Heroism.* New York, 1981.

CHAPTER 7

Spirit in the Female

The Renaissance and the Reformation together forged modern Europe from medieval times, and their impact on women, both contemporary and modern, has been considerable. In comparing the influence of the Renaissance on women as distinct from men, though, one historian has asked whether women had a renaissance at all.

The rebirth of classical ideas, scholarship, and curiosity was displayed in the painting, architecture, and sculpture of the Italian cities and in the writing and philosophy of the western European universities, exemplified in the publications of Erasmus. Manuscripts chronicling the Golden Age of classical Greece and the heyday of imperial Rome were reexamined and an immense joy in the human spirit and the human form emerged as one of the more momentous developments from medieval art and thought. Nor was this an ephemeral movement with only immediate impact. The Renaissance "created an image of man, a vision of human excellence, that still lies at the heart of the Western tradition."[1] The emphasis on human potential and its fulfillment also contributed to a more individualist outlook and sense of personal responsibility. Delight in human activities was matched by an appreciation of worldly pleasures in all their variety. The image of the Renaissance prince was a model for the exceedingly numerous heads of state to adopt. The notion of good, preferably excellent, multiple interest and performance encouraged the patronage of artists of all sorts as well as creating a taste for intellectual disputation, political theory, and clever conversation. Wealth was displayed by conspicuous consumption in the plethora of princely courts all over western Europe as well as in the rich bourgeois households of major cities.

Did this celebration of the human spirit affect women in the same way as men? Women—some women—could not help but receive new ideas and new outlooks from Renaissance achievement. The number of receptive vessels was necessarily few. Even with the development of the printing press, and the consequent spread of ideas and reading matter, literacy was still low and confined largely to the noble and wealthy. Within the elite, were women affected in similar ways as men of the same group and class?

Artists: Talented Relatives

Women as patrons of artists did not appear too numerous, and women as artists themselves were few. Patronage required independent wealth. Isabella d'Este, wife of the duke of Mantua, was one of the few women who possessed both wealth and the control over it to have the opportunity to commission works of art.[2] As artists, many nuns in the cloister had copied and illustrated medieval manuscripts, and some gained a reputation for their skill. Embroidery and tapestry were almost exclusively female forms of art, but such works were largely anonymous. Professional painters in Renaissance Italy were required to undergo a long apprenticeship and education, studying newly important areas such as perspective and human biology. Despite the novelty of providing extended artistic training for girls, some women painters did appear whose opportunities were contingent on relatives. Those who are known were related to professional artists and could study and practice in their workshops with less difficulty. One painter, Artemisia Gentileschi, the "magnificent exception" of great genius among women artists, avenged her own rape by a family acquaintance in her picture, "Judith beheading Holofernes," painted about 1620. The violence and power of Judith and her female assistant sawing at the victim's neck while blood spurts around is impressive. Gentileschi enjoyed noble patronage from all over Italy and personified the female equivalent of an Old Master. Only exceptional women had the talent, opportunity, or bravado to pay Gentileschi's price, which Germaine Greer describes as the rejection of a conventional feminine role for a revolutionary female one.[3]

A Renaissance Woman?

Few of the typical activities of the would-be Renaissance man were available to women. Martial pursuits, rehearsed many times during wars over religion, territory, and power, were for men. Overseas exploration and adventure were for men: settlement of European colonies was not yet a feature of foreign exploration. There was, however, one broad area to which women were not only admitted, but were indispensable, and in the Renaissance lexicon it was a central form of activity for the influential and wealthy. This was attendance at court, and involvement with its rituals, etiquette, and entertainments.

Women had always had a primary role to play in the planning and executing of marriages for their children, and in family politics, hospitality was paramount. The novelty about Renaissance courts was that any man with a reputation to make or keep was required to assume gentility. The art of conversation was a skill which was required of the warrior and hunter and regarded as at least equally significant. And men were expected to talk not just to each other, but to court ladies as well, who were expected to talk back, not merely provide flattering expostulation.

In order to help both men and women in this strained activity, rule books were issued, of which the first and most famous was Castiglione's *The Courtier*. The book appeared in 1528 and included a detailed description of the role of the woman at court. It clearly identified the qualities a woman should share with a courtier—prudence, magnanimity, continence, for example—along with characteristics any noble woman should have: kindness, discretion, the ability to manage her husband's property, household, and children, and all maternal graces. Additionally, a lady at court should have

> a certain pleasing affability . . . whereby she will be able to entertain graciously every kind of man with agreeable and comely conversation suited to the time and place and to the station of the person with whom she speaks, joining to serene and modest manners, and to that comeliness that ought to inform all her action, a quick vivacity of spirit whereby she will show herself a stranger to all boorishness.

Castiglione recognized the difficulty of observing the parameters of appropriate behavior, and recommended an extensive education for girls likely to spend adult life at court. "I wish this Lady to have knowledge of letters, of music, of painting and know how to dance and how to be festive." One of the characters in *The Courtier* remonstrated at the futility of a woman's being educated, on account of her natural weakness and inferiority, but Castiglione firmly stated: "women can understand all the things man can understand and . . . the intellect of a woman can penetrate wherever a man's can." He then adduced evidence from history, ancient and modern, to give examples of women fighters, rulers, philosophers, poets, women who "prosecuted, accused, and defended before judges with great eloquence," and declared that women's skill in "manual works" was self-evident.[4]

The Renaissance accorded a public and highly approved pastime for wealthy and noble ladies and moreover reinforced this by everlasting discussion on the true nature of woman, the *querelle des femmes*. Essays intended for the entertainment and later discussion of learned men on the subject proliferated. They differed from the diatribes of most earlier writers in that the experts on Renaissance women were laymen rather than clerics, and their writings were intended to stimulate thought and discussion rather than be accepted as blueprints for behavior backed by the sanction of the church. Some of the Renaissance authors were themselves women, and drew inspiration from an exemplary court woman of a century earlier, Christine de Pisan.

Education: More Books for a Few

Christine de Pisan was the daughter of an Italian astrologer and physician at the French court, and engaged in literary controversy on several counts. Hailed later as one of the first feminists, she wrote a book called *The City of Ladies*, in which she described all the activity of a city being conducted by women rather than men.[5] In her book she stressed, in the same vein as all feminist writers after her, the importance of education and intellectual development:

> If it were customary to send little girls to school and to teach them the same subjects as are taught to boys, they would learn just as fully and would understand the subtleties of all arts and sciences.

Christine de Pisan presenting her book, City of Ladies, *to Queen Isabeau*

She acknowledged that contemporary women understood less than men, but thought that was because of their more restricted opportunities, for "there is nothing which teaches a reasonable creature so much as the experience of many different things."[6]

The purpose of education and study for women was not to compete with men in public life. Rather it was to broaden a woman's knowledge and capacity for enjoyment, that she might be a more virtuous and useful mother and a more entertaining companion in marriage, as well as a more interesting person for other people to talk to. Obviously there is the assumption of continuing economic dependence on men, together with the notion that any shaping power in all aspects of life, including social and family life, would continue to rest with the man. It was the intensification of this underlying lack of control which prompted Joan Kelly-Gadol's conclusion that Renaissance women experienced a "contraction of social and personal options" in contrast to such women's medieval "position of power and erotic independence."[7] That power and independence had been available to very few—some noblewomen of twelfth- and thirteenth-century Occitania, for instance. Among sixteenth-century authors, the notion of women having a classical education similar to that received by men perplexed those who felt threatened by a woman who might talk back. Erasmus in his *Colloquies* reflected in a humorous way the conservatism of an abbot who rather inarticulately felt that "learning does not become a woman." The abbot's sparring partner, Magdala, got him to admit that a woman's business was to look after her family and instruct her children. This could not properly be performed without wisdom, and he agreed that study of good books could generate wisdom. But he balked at women reading

81

books in Latin. His reason (because it contributed nothing toward the defense of their chastity) doubtless recalled erotic poetry whose consequences were familiar to the clerical community.[8]

Intelligent conversation, thorough attention devoted to the raising of children, and enough familiarity with a husband's problems to discuss them helpfully—the Renaissance woman was supposed to be educated with these three objectives in mind. There were some writers who radically asserted that "the only difference between man and woman is physical," but neglected to follow up the revolutionary implications of that remark. Along with modern advocates, traditionalists still prospered, and often dominated even court conversation. Alberti's ideal woman, for example, would confine herself to management of the household, and leave smart talk and philosophical advice to others.[9] Indeed, when the lives and writings of major Protestant reformers are examined, it becomes clear how very small was the circle of women who had the opportunity to take advantage of expanded intellectual and social options. A king who wrote in 1599 advice for his son on governance included advice too on marriage, and displayed ideas untouched by Renaissance courts. "Treat her as your own flesh, command her as her Lord, cherish her as your helper, rule her as your pupil, and please her in all things reasonable," he allowed,

> but teach her not to be curious in things that belong her not; ye are the head, she is your body; it is your office to command, and hers to obey; as willing to follow, as ye are to go before.[10]

Here was the traditional view of the subordinate wife, tempered perhaps by kindness and the possibility of her becoming the "helpmeet" partner. Outside the exotic atmosphere of Renaissance courts, this familiar view was elaborated most often during the sixteenth century.

Reformation and Counter-Reformation: "Women Shall Prophesy"

The Protestant Reformation, though, changed many traditional aspects of life. The Lutheran split began with total rejection of certain corrupt practices of the Roman Catholic church, and developed into the different versions of creed, theology, organization, and practice of Protestantism. Two of the more visible signs of the revolution were the abolition of monasticism and of clerical celibacy by the Protestants. Among ordinary laity the Reformation led to a close scrutiny of daily life and habits in individual attempts to live a righteous life, and here too, in family life, women were critically affected. On the surface at least it seemed as though women could not but benefit from the changes. When Luther announced that every man was his own priest, and could enjoy a direct communion with God, the traditional interpreters of God's word were jettisoned. If religious hierarchy could be set aside, why not political hierarchy? or social deference? or sexual subordination? Had not Saint Paul written, "In God there is neither male nor female, for ye are all one in Jesus Christ"? Had not the prophet Joel prophesied, "And it shall come to pass, that I shall pour out my spirit upon all flesh, and your sons and your daughters shall prophesy"?[11]

These were two texts invoked repeatedly during the sixteenth and seventeenth centuries. Spiritual equality in the eyes of God had from the beginning been part of the Christian message, but insofar as women were concerned, it had been overridden by insistence on subordination and inferiority in this present material world. Mary Cary, a "servant in Jesus Christ," wrote in 1651 *A New and More Exact Map or Description of New Jerusalem's Glory*, and anticipated the time when Joel's prophecy would be fulfilled. "Not only men, but women shall prophesy; not only aged men, but young men; not only superiors, but inferiors; not only those that have university learning, but those that have it not; even servants and handmaids."[12]

In continental Europe there were many indications that indeed women were already more involved in religious matters than formerly. In 1523, a noblewoman, Argula von Grumbach, wrote to the faculty of the University of Ingolstadt protesting their treatment of a follower of Martin Luther. She anticipated criticism from the Pauline doctrine that women should be silent in the churches, but she took comfort, she wrote, in the words of the prophet Isaiah, "I will send you children to be your princes, and women to be your rulers." Described by Luther, with whom she corresponded, as "that most noble woman," she was denounced as "an insolent daughter of Eve, a heretical bitch and confounded rogue" by the university, but she maintained her support of Luther despite family opposition.[13]

Katherine Zell of Strasbourg made a political statement by her marriage, for her husband was a priest supporting Luther. "Good works," of which clerical celibacy was one, were denounced by Luther as inadequate substitutes for true faith. Celibacy was a gift from God, bestowed only occasionally, and Luther warmly supported clergy who married, sending a congratulatory letter to the Zells in 1523. On the staff at Strasbourg cathedral, Matthew Zell together with his wife led the Lutherans of the city in worship and in their many fights with the Roman Catholic hierarchy. Her role was not confined to providing hospitality for those seeking refuge in her house. She also published letters she wrote to the families of refugees from villages evacuated during the Peasants' War; at the death of her husband she addressed the congregation; and in 1558 wrote her own commentary on the Lord's Prayer. She wrote children's hymns which she published in cheap editions. Her works contain no hint that she found her own role of helpmeet for her husband in the effort to interpret God's message unduly constraining, nor did she enjoin other women to step outside their traditional roles.[14] Some education and understanding on a woman's part were required, but the spiritual infusion of a family could be done within the traditional role allotted to women.

When Luther himself married an ex-nun named Katherine von Bora in 1525, there is nothing to suggest he or his wife was unhappy with that traditional role. According to his *Table Talk*, anecdotes culled from his domestic conversation by friends and acquaintances, he was satisfied with his wife "because other women have worse faults, and she is true to me and a good mother to my children."[15] He had married her in the first place, he said, to please his father, to rile the pope, to make the angels laugh and the devils weep, and because marriage would symbolize his rejection of good works and clerical celibacy. Like Katherine Zell, Luther's wife furnished hospitality for perpetual visitors, a task of critical importance reinforcing support networks among religious rebels taking immense risks.[16] Unlike Katherine Zell, Katherine Luther left no evidence of separate action interpreting the scriptures.

Sects and Sex: "Love My Neighbour's Wife as Myself"

In mid-sixteenth-century Europe, and a hundred years later in England and colonial America, there flourished a multitude of Protestant sects taking certain texts in the Bible more literally than the Lutherans or Calvinists. Both these major Protestant groups tended to concentrate on the grand matters of transubstantiation in the Eucharist, on predestination and the notion of a universal church of all believers, and on the importance of a laity educated to interpret the Bible directly. Anabaptists were no less concerned about these affairs, but additionally believed in adult baptism—entry into the church when an adult understood what sort of a faith he or she was joining. They also declared their separation from a world of popish remnants, which included attendance at churches where much of the service of worship retained phrases and doctrines from the highly corrupt Roman Catholic church. Anabaptists too took heart from millenarian prophecies that the end of the world was at hand and the establishment on earth of the Kingdom of Heaven was nigh. Within Anabaptist groups it appears as though women shared with men the responsibility of acting as God's vessels. The Anabaptists made several nontraditional declarations about women: that divorce was appropriate if one partner in marriage was an unbeliever, that property belonged to all members of the community (occasionally including women in the definition of property), that polygamy was acceptable. Demonstrations by naked men and women, particularly in Munster in 1535, linked the Anabaptists with shocking and unnatural behavior. Yet examinations of Anabaptists for heresy suggest that they could be sensible, clever, and devout people seriously trying to live according to God's will. In the American colonies, Anne Hutchinson daringly usurped leadership of the Boston church in Massachusetts, and led most of the congregation to her own church before final banishment for heretical and presumptuous behavior.[17]

During the Puritan revolution in England, women were again most prominent. This was no novelty: since the Henrician reformation women had been leaders of radical religious communities.[18] What was new in the 1640s was that their ideology was now more likely to be egalitarian, although this fluctuated, particularly in matters of sex. One woman in 1658, absent from a Baptist meeting, gave the excuse that her husband had not let her attend. She was rebuked and reminded that there were limits to what a husband could properly authorize.[19] A woman preacher in London, Mrs. Attoway, practiced what she preached in terms of divorcing, by declaration, her nonbelieving husband and going to live with another man. While they all professed to believe, with Samuel Torshell, that "the soul knows no difference of sex," few could imagine the notion of an independent woman in control of her own worldly destiny.[20] The one group which approximated most nearly was the Quakers.

Margaret Fell, who later married the founder of the Quakers, or Friends, George Fox, gave him advice which in its sexual as well as social context was simply revolutionary: "Be not afraid of man. Greater is he that is in you than he that is in the world." The Quakers emphasized an individual conscience as the ruler of every person, man or woman. A few other sects claimed similar "parity, equality, community" in order to establish "universal love, universal peace, and perfect freedom," like the Ranters, who flourished around 1650.[21] What came to distinguish the Quakers was first, an orderly commitment to a community of worship which at the same time preserved individual self-discipline, and second, a serious regard for a single sexual standard. However much groups like the Ranters and even the Baptists professed to allow freedom to women, allowing women preachers and prophets, it was hard for them to avoid seeing women as a form of exploitable property providing lusty pleasure for men. As Abiezer Coope wrote, "external kisses have been made the fiery chariot to mount me into the bosom of the King of Glory. . . . I can kiss and hug ladies, and love my neighbour's wife as myself without sin."[22] This was understandably interpreted as a paean to promiscuity. The Quakers achieved the remarkable feat of realizing both sexual equality and sober responsibility within the limitations of mid-seventeenth-century English society.

Quaker men refused to doff a hat in deference, and they insisted on calling all persons "thou" with no title, but their belief in the equality of all souls went deeper than surface customs. Spiritually, all Friends moved by the Spirit of God, men or women, could speak out: they "are helps meet, Man and Woman, as they were before the Fall."[23] Both men and women were spiritual leaders. Over twenty Quaker women, most of them single, traveled to America between 1656 and 1663 and preached, risking imprisonment and death. Two women traveled as missionaries to Barbados in 1671, and women were the first Quaker preachers in London, Dublin, and at the English universities. Margaret Fell wrote a tract justifying the ministry of women and organized the Fortnightly Women's Meetings on a national basis.[24]

The Quakers required an ideological commitment to equality and parity, not just between men and women but also between and among all classes and groups in society, regardless of birth and wealth. In early modern Europe such commitment required imagination as well as great courage. Some women were able to benefit from the Protestant Reformation without having to make such an effort. At the time of Luther's protest, many women were able to see in the Protestant faith an opportunity to participate directly in their own spiritual affairs, and those of their family, without reference to priests whose orthodoxy was to condescend to women. As one traditionalist wrote:

> to learn essential doctrine, there is no need for women or artisans to take time out from their work and read the Old and New Testament in the vernacular. Then they'll want to dispute about it and give their

opinion . . . and they can't help falling in error. Women must be silent in church, as St. Paul says.

As Protestants, on the other hand, women were encouraged to read and talk about the Scriptures, and were important agents in the religious instruction of their families, husbands as well as children. Others too published their own comments, like Marie Dentière, expelled from her convent for heresy, who married a pastor and brought the Protestant word to other women. She defended her actions by appealing to the notion that God could work through women as well as men: "Is it not foolishly done to hide the talent that God has given us?"[25]

Theoretically the Protestant Reformation brought new opportunities to women. Their self-esteem was improved by the public declarations of spiritual equality, their energies were harnessed to participation in the ministry of some churches, and their directing role in enabling the family to lead a godly life was recognized. But how important were these developments, and did they represent only positive gains for women?

The theory of spiritual equality was almost invariably diluted, in the clear distinction made between life in this world and life in the world to come. In the Protestant Anglican church, for example, ministers were enjoined to read the homilies in lieu of sermons, and the eighteenth homily, issued under Elizabeth I's authority as governor of the church in 1562, was "of the state of matrimony." This was the image of woman delivered most often from the pulpit:

> for the woman is a weak creature not endowed with strength and constancy of mind; therefore they be the sooner disquieted, and they be the more prone to all weak affections and dispositions of the mind, more than men be; and lighter they be, and more vain in their fantasies and opinions.[26]

Consequently it was the misogynist Pauline statements of which the congregation was reminded, of obedience, silence, and subjection, rather than the liberationist call for parity. Indeed, it would appear that the wife's spiritual development was now more under the control of her husband than it had been under the Roman Catholic church, since she now had no authoritative priest to countervail her husband's opinion, and a wife was repeatedly reminded of her lack of autonomy.[27] A seventeenth-century preacher, William Whately, wrote two popular tracts on marriage which were reprinted until the nineteenth century. His description of the wife's duties insisted that "firstly she must acknowledge her inferiority. Secondly she must carry herself as an inferior," and concluded that she should chant this in her soul: "Mine husband is my superior, my better; he hath authority and rule over me."[28] These incessant reminders would lead an observer to suspect that wives' behavior was not always as subordinate in practice as Whately would have had it be.

In terms of activity within the church, as preachers and governors, this was very limited. Katherine Zell discounted her own presumption by insisting she was not John the Baptist nor was she rebuking the pharisees. "I do not claim to be Nathan upbraiding David. I aspire only to be Balaam's ass, castigating his master." At her husband's funeral she denied she was usurping the office of preacher or apostle. "I am like dear Mary Magdalene, who with no thought of being an apostle came to tell the disciples that she had encountered the risen Lord."[29] As for women theologians, after Marie Dentière published her religious epistles, no book by a woman was printed in Geneva for the rest of the century. The Calvinist authorities differentiated carefully between the establishment of spiritual equality and the continuity of social conservatism. A woman must not speak in a Christian assembly; her role was confined to instructing her children when young.[30] The Quaker women were exceptions to this tendency. They neither apologized for their activism nor were they restrained within the ministry. But even in the Society of Friends, Margaret Fell was outstanding for few other women were nearly as active.

During the Puritan revolution in England many blueprints for a new society were considered, discussed, and attempted. They had little to offer women. Women were considered total dependents, and therefore ineligible for political rights, and the most they could anticipate from a new society was elementary education comprised of reading, sewing, knitting, and spinning— scarcely to be distinguished from what they could already have. The Quakers, and occasionally others, recognized the importance for the economically dependent woman of a single sexual standard. As Gerrard Winstanley, leader of the Diggers, wrote, alluding to sexual "freedom,"

> the mother and child begotten in this manner is like to have the worst of it, for the man will be gone and leave them, and regard them no more than other women after he hath had his pleasure. . . . By seeking their own freedom, they embondage others.[31]

In matters of sex, Calvinist ideology was often as harsh with men as with women. In England during the interregnum, a Sabbatarian Protestant code was substituted for the previous Catholic canon followed by the Anglican church, and equal punishments were prescribed for equal offenses.[32] In sixteenth- and seventeenth-century Geneva, the Consistory, the institution responsible for the moral supervision of adults, dispensed "evenhanded justice for sexual misdemeanors" and also tolerated the widespread use of contraception.[33] The commonest forms of punishment in both societies were measures involving ridicule and humiliation: public whippings, serving penance in the marketplace stocks, as well as fines and, for serious offenses, excommunication.[34] Protestants could not provide a more egalitarian secular life to women immediately after the Reformation, but in some communities offered a taste of equality in both the theory and practice of religion.

Family Mainstay

All over Europe women did what they could to keep their families and property together during the wars and civil disruptions of the sixteenth and seventeenth centuries. As they always had in similar circumstances, they provided partisan support for their men, and tried to hold the fort on the home ground. This did not go unremarked. Some "divers well-affected women" from London petitioned parliament on behalf of their menfolk who had been arrested by the parliamentary army. Turned away by the Puritan parliament, and told to go back to their housekeeping, they responded the next month by repeating their petition, this time prefacing it with an appeal to the Puritan rhetoric:

> since we are assured of our creation in the image of God, and of an interest in Christ equal to men, as also of a proportional share in the freedoms of this Commonwealth, we cannot but wonder and grieve that we should appear so despicable in your eyes.

From the other side, "women were never so useful as now," remarked a royalist in 1646, noting wives' activities in safeguarding estates.[35] This owed little to either the Renaissance or the Reformation.

On balance, was the image or role of women much different at the end of the seventeenth century from what it was at the beginning of the sixteenth? There had been a few female heads of state, not without detractors, but at least one, Elizabeth of England, had survived magnificently. This had little effect on other women. Protestant lay women could act privately as their own spiritual interpreters, but only if they could read. Protestant women could no longer pray to female saints, nor were they supposed to regard the Virgin Mary as an interested female intermediary. On the other hand, they could now sing hymns and psalms alongside men during the church service, and depending on the enlightenment of the preacher, a Protestant wife had the chance of a higher domestic profile than before.[36] Within the precious atmosphere of European courts, an intelligent woman had more chance to show off her wit and more interesting subjects to talk about. The Protestant abolition of convents, however, excised in Protestant countries one of the few alternative life-styles for a single adult woman. These groups were directly affected by the changes brought about by the Reformation, but the vast majority of women were individually unconcerned by the cultural ideas of either Renaissance or Reformation. They were probably more affected by the survival into the early modern period of a phenomenon as old as the hills—witchcraft.

Witchcraft: Diabolical Power

With few exceptions, most people at this time would know of at least one person who could be described as a witch or a wise woman, the terms being generally synonymous. Witches were almost always women, and had by the sixteenth century two distinguishing features. They were capable of doing damage (maleficium) which could be explained satisfactorily only by reference to the occult; and they were supposed to owe this power to the Devil.[37] The latter characteristic was a recent notion, advocated particularly by the Roman Catholic church and culminating in the papal bull against witches issued in 1486. The church had waged an intense campaign against these relics of pagan Europe and by 1488 was able to publish a handbook for persecutors, *Malleus Maleficarum* (*Hammer of the Witches*), to help in the efficient prosecution of persons accused by either secular or church officials. The age of humanism and religious reformation (1450–1640) saw more prosecutions, convictions, and punishments for witchcraft than any other time in European history. The crime of witchcraft was the single capital offense of which women defendants were most often accused, and it is interesting to identify the witch craze with the continuing misogyny of European culture, dramatically juxtaposed to the more sophisticated ideas of cultured society.

Certainly the church's agents specializing in witchcraft accusations and trials made telling points of the greater susceptibility of women to the work of the Devil. The natural explanation was that a woman "is more carnal than a man," and the more attracted to satanic copulation and the lure of incubi. Every month women were supposed to be

> filled full of superfluous humors, and with them the melancholic blood boils; whereof spring vapors are carried up, and conveyed through the nostrils, and mouth etc. to the bewitching of whatsoever it meet. For they belch up a certain breath, wherewith they bewitch whomsoever they list.[38]

Many people may have believed this, particularly monks raised in the severe tradition of the early church fathers, and it was they, rather than village neighbors, who were the first to lead the witch-hunts. The use of torture encouraged confessions and almost invariably led to convictions. The number of subsequent burnings is not accurately known, but in Switzerland an estimated five thousand were executed and approximately seven thousand in southern Germany. In England, where torture was normally prohibited, there were fewer: under one thousand between 1559 and 1685.[39]

It is difficult to assess the significance of the fact that most witches were women. Victims of witches were men, women, children, and animals; and when accusations became popular, women as well as men testified against them. If there was an antifemale relish in their persecution, it was conversely a testimony to one of the few occupations in which a woman could enjoy power and reputation as well as risk a miserable end.[40] Marginal women at both edges of the medieval scale were acknowledged by one Elizabethan authority on witches. Alluding to the pope, Reginald Scot wrote: "He canonizeth the rich for saints and banneth the poor for witches."[41]

Witches had their renaissance; court ladies and Quakers benefited from the new ideas; but the vast majority of women had to wait another four or five hundred years before their options broadened in a re-formed society.

Suggestions for Further Reading

Chadwick, Owen. *The Reformation*. London, 1977.

Davis, Natalie Zemon. *Society and Culture in Early Modern France*. Stanford, 1975.

Greer, Germaine. *The Obstacle Race: The Fortunes of Women Painters and Their Work*. London, 1979.

Hill, Christopher. *The World Turned Upside Down*. London, 1975.

Kelly-Gadol, Joan. "Did Women Have a Renaissance?" In *Becoming Visible: Women in European History*, edited by Renate Bridenthal and Claudia Koonz, pp. 137–64. Boston, 1977.

Monter, E. William. "Pedestal and Stake." In *Becoming Visible: Women in European History*, edited by Renate Bridenthal and Claudia Koonz, pp. 119–36. Boston, 1977.

———. *Witchcraft in France and Switzerland: The Borderlands During the Reformation*. Ithaca, N.Y., 1976.

———. "Women in Calvinist Geneva, 1550–1800." *Signs* 6 (1980):189–209.

Stone, Lawrence. *The Family, Sex and Marriage in England 1500–1800*. London, 1977.

CHAPTER 8

Court and Salon

The *Age of Reason* and the *Enlightenment* are two labels describing eighteenth-century Europe. Just as there is doubt whether women had a renaissance, so there is also a question whether reason and enlightenment were translated into theoretical or material benefit for women.

Such a sour note invariably appears with respect to the vast majority of the population which was poor—those persons who survived among the fine distinctions of subsistence, poverty, and indigence. Within the ranks of the poor, it was the women who carried much of the responsibility for the family survival, let alone welfare.[1] Not until the industrial growth of the nineteenth and twentieth centuries was much inroad made into the intractable problems faced by so large a proportion of Western population. From any angle of vision, it is hard to see an improvement in their lot brought about by philosophes, or even by the French Revolution. But for women who by birth or by chance lived among the ranks of the economically secure, the eighteenth century saw some favorable developments.

Women Rulers: Pragmatism Enthroned

Women were prominent at the political courts. Never ministers of state, they nevertheless contributed a measure of polite society with their presence at balls, receptions, gambling, and theatrical events and used their opportunities to further the careers of men connected with them. The most visible women, to contemporaries and, above all, to historians, were those few who were themselves rulers: queens and empresses. Once at the apex of public power, they generally experienced the same executive authority as a man in the same position. Monarchy was limited by convention and occasionally by law but was still a vehicle for the will and personality of the incumbent. Women's rule was different from that of men only in the way that one individual differed from another. In very few instances is it possible to explain the policies or even the styles of queens as an attribute of gender.

The very fact that a woman became a monarch, despite the universal custom of male inheritance, could always be explained by reference to the family interests of the dynasties who controlled the thrones of Europe. Allowing a woman to succeed in her own right, in default of heirs male, was the last resort of a family which did not wish to lose its hold on the monarchy solely because of the reproductive whimsy of one generation. The particular women who became rulers, however, were not simply prisoners of their family. Most of them displayed highly developed political skills coupled with willful determination to rule according to their own vision, but without that umbilical family proximity to the crown, no woman could ever have made herself ruler.

Several women were monarchs before the eighteenth century. Outstanding was Elizabeth I of England who for forty-five years kept her throne and stabilized her country's government at a time when most other European states experienced civil wars of succession and religion.[2] In the Age of Reason, the careers of two women rulers illustrate the importance of the family connection, and also the opportunity for individual action afforded to its few practitioners by the institution of monarchy. Barely discernible is any peculiarly feminine dimension exhibited by either Maria Theresa of Austria or Catherine II of Russia.

Although the Hapsburg emperor Charles VI had no son, he made no particular effort to prepare his eldest daughter to become ruler. Maria Theresa's education included no instruction in history, politics, or economics, and she served no apprenticeship by attending to government business. After her marriage in 1736 Charles made some attempt to train her husband Francis in government, making him a member of his highest advisory body: Charles hoped to live to make a grandson his heir under the protection of Francis. But Charles died in 1740 before Maria Theresa bore a son, and at the age of twenty-three she determined to rule herself, with Francis as coregent.

Empress Maria Theresa

Maria Theresa's aims were to ensure the survival of Austria as a power, to strengthen her territories, to ameliorate the lives of her subjects, and to further the interests of her children, aims indistinguishable from other rulers of the time. Nor were the methods she employed particularly innovative: she increased the size of the army and paid for this by a new land tax on previously tax-free noble land; she started the codification of peasants' dues and prohibited noble encroachment on land worked by peasants; she initiated an ambitious scheme to bring universal, primary, secular education to all; and she followed prevailing mercantilist philosophy by encouraging industrialization in selected areas of the empire. At the outset of her reign she was the victim of Frederick of Prussia's seizure of Silesia, and Austrian forces were engaged in war for several years in a vain attempt to recover this lost territory. However, toward the end of her reign she more than compensated for the loss by her participation, with the same Frederick and with Catherine of Russia, in the First Partition of Poland in 1772.

Certainly in some of her speeches she used her femininity to provoke a chivalric response of loyalty. "I am only a woman," she said at her coronation in 1741, "but I have the heart of a King." Contemporary observers ascribed to her some hypocritical regret at the dismemberment of Poland: "she carved territory out of Poland with one hand, and used her handkerchief with the other."[3] Her reign, however, can in no way be characterized as feminine. Until her husband died in 1765 Maria Theresa was almost perpetually pregnant, bearing sixteen children in nineteen years, but it is impossible to argue that her gender had any material effect on her domestic policy or diplomatic relations, policies which showed she was capable, concerned for the welfare of her subjects, and internationally amoral.[4]

Catherine's accession to her throne was less assured than Maria Theresa's. There were no less than three women rulers in Russia since Peter the Great died in 1725, and as a young bride, Catherine lived in the household of the empress Elizabeth (1741–61). Catherine was the daughter of a minor German prince and married Elizabeth's nephew and heir, Peter, in 1745, when she was sixteen. For the next seventeen years Catherine was an intimate observer of the Russian court intrigues. Bored by her infantile husband, she was involved in several liaisons and also cultivated leaders of the European intelligentsia: Voltaire called her the "north star" and she became the correspondent of Diderot, editor of the *Encyclopedia*. She read widely in philosophy and politics and even before her husband, Peter III, succeeded as tsar she determined to pursue her "own interests as far as the Russian people were concerned in order that the latter would see in me the savior of the nation."[5] A year after Peter's accession she conspired with a clique discontented with his militaristic, Lutheran, German sympathies to replace him as ruler herself. One of Catherine's lovers murdered Peter in July 1762 and in September she crowned herself monarch, acknowledging her authority not from the nobles, or the people, but from God alone.

Catherine was admired by the Enlightenment philosophes as an enlightened despot, and made a few moves in that direction. She started the codification of laws, reorganized provincial government to allow closer supervision of the noble officeholders by central government appointees, and initiated state-sponsored education for boys and girls. By 1796 her schools were teaching 16,200 boys and 1,100 girls, out of a population of approximately 36 million. However, she later released the nobles from the service obligations introduced originally by Peter the Great and allowed them unlimited power over their serfs, a measure contrary to Enlightenment preference for serf emancipation. Like Maria Theresa she participated in the First Partition of Poland, and later acquired not only more Polish territory along her western boundary but also territory in the south formerly belonging to the Turkish empire bordering on the Black Sea.

Catherine, like Maria Theresa, was hard-working and administratively well organized. She personally conducted much domestic and diplomatic business, and chose good advisers. She rewarded her lovers with money, status, and occasionally power but rarely allowed affection to cloud political judgment. She also energetically pursued a wide range of interests—she wrote several plays, mildly satirizing contemporary behavior and credulity, and adapted Shakespeare's *Merry Wives of Windsor* for a court performance. She also wrote history, and a dictionary of comparative linguistics. Among intimates she could use lewd language, and felt no particular bond with Maria Theresa, whose piety she mocked. Both monarchs overcame contemporary prejudice for masculine rulers by extraordinary competence, and exercised public power like other forceful, perceptive, pragmatic despots.[6]

The Salon: Woman as Impresario

If the politically ambitious congregated in royal courts, the arbiters of fashion and the intelligentsia flocked to the glittering and stimulating life concentrated in the capital cities, Paris in particular. For several months each year, an entire household would leave its country house or chateau and reside in a house in the city which they owned or rented for the season. Polite society in France tended to be divided between attendance at the king's court, at Versailles, and residence in Paris. In England, London attracted many during the parliamentary sessions but other towns—Bath, for example, and other minor spas—also harbored families away from their principal residence for months at a time. The income of these families was derived primarily from land and property rented to others, but alternative sources of supply frequently occupied the men: investment, trade, and government service either military or administrative—even sinecures—required some time. Rising professional men—lawyers, medical men, the higher clergy—also emulated the lifestyle of the very wealthy, which above all was leisured. Taking time to secure one's livelihood was not a regular feature of the day. Instead there was time to read, to talk, to interact socially with others of one's class. Gambling was a favored pursuit, but just as in the Renaissance courts there was a social premium on conversation, so there was an obligation for the prototype noble or landed gentry family in the eighteenth century to engage in talk.[7] And women could talk as well as men.

Women did much more than talk. It was largely women who stage-managed and produced the environment within their houses where so much social intercourse took place. Already in seventeenth-century France, women had been the focal point of an intensified continuation of the Renaissance *querelle des femmes*. In her analysis of French writings on women, Carolyn Lougee found that protagonists in the literary debate were considering matters of social as well as intellectual importance. These writers took one of two fundamental positions with regard to whether or not women should play a public role in French society. Those authors who considered women should, were known as the feminists; those who took the opposite side were the antifeminists. Feminists were more than champions of women's abilities to conduct salons, which essentially was the particular kind of public role women filled. While different social groupings vied for political and social status at the early-seventeenth-century French court, the salon functioned as the forum where upwardly mobile men and women could legitimate and further develop their social ambitions. Feminist writers welcomed this aspect of the hostesses' activities. Antifeminists deplored it, and severely criticized women's role in acting as solvent of previously rigid distinctions among the ranks of the nobility.[8]

The women who frequented and organized the salons were themselves beneficiaries of the social fusion which was hastened by and reflected in salon society, but not without a price: they were caricatured for posterity as précieuses in Molière's *Femmes Savantes*. But such treatment was a tribute to their impact on the upper echelons of French society. In the seventeenth century their overriding significance was to inculcate aristocratic habits in the bourgeoisie who were newly ennobled through marriage, purchase, or office. They enabled a newcomer "to have his cake of bourgeois success and eat it in aristocratic company."[9] In the following century women salon hostesses acted as catalysts of a different sort, serving to undermine, rather than consolidate, the ancien régime.

This was especially so in France. In Paris, the major salons were regular weekly events: Madame Geoffrin entertained artists on Mondays and the literary world Wednesdays, giving direct financial support to the Encyclopedists and pensions to men she judged in need. Madame Geoffrin's impact was sufficient for her to be treated as royalty when she traveled elsewhere in Europe. Madame du Deffand, whose salon was coterminous with Geoffrin's, from about 1740 to 1780, made her way from a convent education through marriage with a dull military marquis to be mistress of the regent, Philippe d'Orleans, who supported her with a large allowance. She became friendly with Horace Walpole, English wit and man of letters, who wrote of her:

> I have heard her dispute with all sorts of people, upon all sorts of subjects, and never knew her to be in the wrong. She humbles the learned, sets right their disciples, and finds conversation for everybody.

A third salon leader was Madame d'Epinay who hosted many of the Encyclopedists as well as diplomats, and Rousseau, to whom she became a patron.

Like other hostesses, she wrote books—novels, memoirs, treatises—and took a vigorous part in the discussions she set up.[10]

In England sophistication and elegance were never so polished. One woman, Mrs. Elizabeth Montagu, started by giving literary breakfasts and later moved into evening conversation parties. Horace Walpole frequented these, and met there actors, artists, conversationalists like Dr. Samuel Johnson, and some of the more intellectually inclined nobility. Other women directed salons in a similar way, and the women and their guests became known as the bluestockings. The English women, like the French, wrote too: Mrs. Catherine Macaulay was a historian, a radical who considered the regicide and Protector Oliver Cromwell insufficiently radical and a traitor to the republican cause; Elizabeth Montagu, Dr. Johnson's "Queen of the Blues," defended Shakespeare against Voltaire in print; Hannah More was a poet, dramatist, and educational theorist; Mrs. Thrale chronicled Dr. Johnson's wise remarks; and Fanny Burney wrote novels.[11]

What distinguished these parties from enjoyable but precious forums for flirting and small talk was the intellectual content as well as the style of the conversation. Especially in France, and to a lesser extent in England, the institutions of the ancien régime were being critically examined, and found wanting, socially, economically, and politically. Straightforward treatises together with short articles in Diderot's *Encyclopedia* and periodical magazines, and lightly disguised fiction, were the media for the propagation of Enlightenment ideas, but the salons of the Parisian society leaders were the hothouses. There readings were given, ideas were formulated and exchanged, and mutual criticism informed smart society. There aristocratic and monarchical government was mocked and undermined, and a few writers carried the analogy over into social structure and family organization. If divine right government by virtue of birth alone was considered neither true nor useful nor permanent, if the established church was seen to promote false and harmful ideas, if it was wrong and foolish to exclude from public service the prospering members of the Third Estate, could not these hypotheses be examined also with relation to the legal and civil subjection of women?

Only a few writers were concerned with this topic. Possibly they did not consider that the women they met at the salons or at the courts were materially or socially underprivileged. Those who systematically addressed the issue of women—that is the nature of woman, her true role in life, her education, her contribution to society—were of two minds. Both emphasized the immense importance of the environment, and the need to alter existing customs if women were to be given their just deserts, but the single assumption produced divergent images of women. Rousseau saw women as a gender with functions totally separate from men, with no overlap of activity. Condorcet saw women sharing identical rights with men.[12] Other Enlightenment writers alluded to women, often directly. Montesquieu, for example, could satirize the hypocrisy and unfairness of the sexual double standard, but the extent of his enlightenment was in his promotion of divorce reform.[13] With respect to the education, civil rights, or legal status of adult women, most philosophes showed no conception that women should be other than what the ancien régime allowed them to be—wives, mistresses, mothers, and society impresarios.

Rousseau: Consort for the Noble Savage

Rousseau's message was not without its contradictions or ambivalence, but it was highly significant because it was his view of woman, rather than Condorcet's, which engaged the imagination of the following generations of women as well as men. In the context of the rational Enlightenment it was rather a shocking message. While the standard view of mankind was that it was progressing to a more perfect understanding and control of the environment, becoming more sophisticated, cosmopolitan, and humane, Rousseau's view of woman predicated a return to nature. Voltaire derided Rousseau's noble savage crawling around on all fours, and sceptically caricatured Rousseau's new woman in her fanciful prelapsarian wooded retreat.

In *Emile*, Rousseau expressed dislike for the salons of Paris (even though, or perhaps because, he enjoyed the patronage of one of the most splendid salon hostesses, Madame d'Epinay) and wistfully preferred

> a homely girl, simply brought up, than a learned lady and a wit who would make a literary circle of my house and install herself as its president. A female wit is a scourge to her husband, her children, her friends, her servants. [P. 371]

Rousseau considered that the behavioral differences he observed between men and women derived from women's different nature which was deliberately designed to flower domestically. Confinement to the home, there to be personally involved not only in household management, but, most importantly, in the rearing of her children, was woman's lot in life. Here she would guard her chastity and her modesty and find her limited abilities flourishing, untaxed by exorbitant demands that by nature she would be unable to fulfill. Her education as a girl was to equip the adult woman for this role. Essentially she was to be taught not at school but at home by her mother; she was to wear no artificially restricting clothes; she was to run around in the countryside, cavorting with nature. Her mother was to teach her that women were made for the delight of men and that their justification in marriage was to personify delectability, and also to provide their husbands with children. She must not be taught about religion, as her husband would teach her all she needed to know about God when she became adult. Information on Rousseau's ideal woman was contained in book 5 of *Emile*, whose other sections described the education of the man who was to become the ideal citizen able to handle freedom and responsibility. Rousseau harked back to classical Greece and Athenian democracy not only in his political designs, but also with respect to the upbringing of women. The seclusion of women, the age difference whereby the husband was old enough to be his wife's father, the management of the woman by the patriarchal, more educated, experienced man: it appeared that Rousseau felt a need to stack the deck thoroughly against the natural woman. Rather he rhapsodized on her purity and moral supremacy.[14] This was predicated on her total dependence on man. It was no coincidence that the festivals and parades of the French Revolution embodied as their centerpiece Greek-costumed nymphs who were daughters of the friends of the revolution.[15] Rousseau's indignant opener to the *Social Contract*, "Man is born free but everywhere is in chains," found no parallel in his examination of the relationships between men and women. Thirty years after the publication of both the *Social Contract* and *Emile*, women pamphleteers used Rousseau's stress on their moral superiority, and their destiny for oasislike marriages, to justify demands for legal safeguards and appropriate educational opportunities.[16]

Condorcet: Political Equality for Women

Condorcet wrote in the late 1780s and during the early years of the French Revolution. His ideas on women were more consistent with the major themes of the Enlightenment. He agreed that women were different physically from men, and hence should not be soldiers; he agreed too with Voltaire that women had not displayed artistic genius. He did not see that these lacks justified the withholding of civil rights, notably citizenship and the right to vote or hold governmental office. These should be accorded to women who were otherwise eligible to vote, through ownership of property. Six years later, in 1793, he was prepared to support the new constitution which destroyed the property, but retained the sexual qualification for suffrage. Before his death, however, he wrote *Progress of the Human Mind*, and noted that perfection required total equality of the sexes and universal education.[17]

Perhaps the reason why Rousseau's ideas on women predominated over more egalitarian views was that articulate eighteenth-century women could more easily empathize both with the notion of a superior moral status and with the glorification of what they did anyway, that is, maternity. It was gratifying to have their side of the double standard recognized as an accomplishment. It could be rewarding to find public acknowledgment of the value of raising children. Some women, especially Mary Wollstonecraft, chafed at these limits, but there were few like her because it was not easy to translate Condorcet's ideas into a realizable way of life.[18] Presiding over one's own salon required wealth as well as wit together with a certain indifference to the church's view of morality. Apart from this role, there were pitifully few other occupations besides those of wife and mother for noblewomen and richer bourgeoisie. At least with Rousseau a woman could feel she was appreciated. If she followed Condorcet, she would risk the ridicule Molière accorded to *Les Femmes Savantes* and not every woman would enjoy the company of clever men arguing over church and state.[19]

Mary Wollstonecraft: Enlightenment Feminist

Mary Wollstonecraft was a unique courageous woman of undoubted, though delayed, influence. Her own life illustrates the difficulties faced by a woman of integrity in the late eighteenth century. She was born in 1759 in

London, daughter of a silk weaver, but spent her childhood in various places where her father tried unsuccessfully to farm to support six children. At nineteen she left home to be companion to the widow of a London merchant, whose life was divided among houses at Bath, Southampton, and Windsor. At twenty-one she nursed her mother through a final illness, then went to live with the family of a childhood friend. Then she lived with her sister Eliza, encouraging her to leave her violent husband. Together they borrowed money to establish a boarding school for girls at Newington Green, where many radical frequenters of the London bluestocking crowd lived and worked. The school was not a financial success, and Wollstonecraft lived briefly with her friend again, now married to a man in the Portuguese wine trade. After her death, Wollstonecraft returned to England at the age of twenty-seven, unmarried and without financial means of support. She wrote a brief book, *Thoughts on the Education of Daughters,* in which she emphasized the importance of training the intellect, then took a job as governess to an Irish peer to earn money to repay debts. In a letter to her publisher she remarked, "A state of dependence must ever be irksome to me. . . . I have most of the comforts of life, yet when weighed with liberty, they are of little value."[20] Returning to London, she supported herself for the next five years by literary hack work: book reviews, translating, and stories designed for the expanding market of subscribers to locally based lending libraries all over the country.[21] In 1792 she published *A Vindication of the Rights of Woman,* the work which earned her feminist reputation and sufficient money to visit France to experience the French Revolution firsthand. In Paris she enjoyed a series of love affairs, apparently her first passionate relationships; after an American she lived with abandoned her and their daughter, she attempted to commit suicide. In 1796 she renewed an acquaintance with the philosopher William Godwin, who like Wollstonecraft respected freedom, individual dignity, and the power of reason and agreed with her on the critical function of a proper education. With him she came to know a relationship she had idealized in *Vindication:* the voluntary association of independent adults based on deep friendship and mutual respect. They married five months before the birth of their daughter Mary (later to write *Frankenstein*) but the mother died from an infection in September 1797.

Mary Wollstonecraft's life-style was a measure of the enormously limited opportunities for economic support available to a single, intellectual woman of principle, even when she had the company of persons who were of a similar frame of mind. Nevertheless she went far in living a righteous life by her own standards, and it is in this practical application of the ideas set out in *Vindication* that she showed her courage. *Vindication* was provoked by Talleyrand's report on education to the French Constituent Assembly in 1791. He called for free education, but made no reference to education for girls. She dedicated *Vindication* to Talleyrand in the hope he would revise his report and supervise the establishment of a proper universal system of education in France. *Vindication* owed much of its form to polemic against theorists of girls' education: Rousseau especially, but also Dr. James Fordyce, who had written *Sermons to Young Women* in 1765, Dr. John Gregory, author of *A Father's Legacy to His Daughters* (1774), Madame de Staël, who had welcomed Rousseau's adoration

of natural woman, and Lord Chesterfield, whose *Letters to His Son* contained advice of an "unmanly, immoral system."[22] Wollstonecraft opposed writers who urged the separate education of women in subjects designed to prepare them for a subordinate, decorative adult role, which she summarized as an education "only useful to a mistress." She urged an education which would create an adult woman who "will become the friend and not the humble dependent of her husband." Drawing inspiration from Catherine Macaulay, whose *Letters on Education* she had praised a year earlier, Wollstonecraft argued that a girl, like a boy, should attend coeducational day schools provided by the government, and learn botany, mechanics, astronomy, reading, writing, arithmetic, natural history, and "simple experiments in natural philosophy"; she would enjoy "gymnastic plays in the open air," and learn, through socratic conversation, religion, history, and politics.[23] At the age of nine, children should be separated according to ability, and the clever ones, girls and boys still together, should learn dead and living languages, elements of science, history, and politics, and "polite literature." Those children "intended for domestic deportments, or mechanical trades" should continue to share education in the mornings, while in the afternoons, the girls only should learn "plain work, mantua-making, millinery etc." This scheme, Wollstonecraft believed, would create her ideal women: "rational creatures, and free citizens," who would "quickly become good wives, and mothers; that is, if men do not neglect the duties of husbands and fathers."[24]

A woman, Wollstonecraft thought, should not be taken out of her family. Her supreme fulfillment was as a companion wife and a teacher mother, and sound intellectual training was necessary in order to allow a woman to carry out these responsibilities. She assumed that a man would continue to be an adequate breadwinner. She hoped that a double sexual standard would no longer operate, because a man married to such a wife would have no reason to seek diversion with prostitutes, and she considered that there was no need to contemplate the notion that women educated like men would shirk domestic responsibilities.

> Would men but generously snap our chains, and be content with rational fellowship instead of slavish obedience, they would find us more observant daughters, more affectionate sisters, more faithful wives, more reasonable mothers—in a word, better citizens.[25]

Together, men and the new women would advance civilization from the base of a "dignified domestic happiness." A role outside the home was also envisaged, in the sense of assisting neighbors, and all women, married as well as single, should have some civil persona and protection at law. In a brief passage, Wollstonecraft explored further her notion of independence. Women could become physicians as well as nurses, study politics, and pursue business. Government should "provide for honest, independent women, by encouraging them to fill respectable stations." This line of thought, however, was not developed. She saw an adult woman as an economically dependent wife and mother, rather than as a self-supporting entity. Governmental action was required to provide education and a legal identity and protection. Wollstonecraft's analysis of a woman's moral independence did not posit an underlying economic sufficiency.[26]

After Mary Wollstonecraft, feminists developed much further than she the notion of individual independence. The constant message in all her writing was that women had the same intellectual and moral capacity as men, and that education ought not to be denied them. The newly developed person ought then to devote her sensibility to creating the ideal setting for the raising of virtuous children and the cultivation of a mutually rewarding relationship with her husband. Wollstonecraft was vague about the economic means for subsistence. To her, the "happiest as well as the most respectable situation in the world" was to be "raised sufficiently above abject poverty not to be obliged to weigh the consequence of every farthing they spend," and to indulge "a taste for literature, to throw a little variety and interest into social converse, and some superfluous money to give to the needy and to buy books."[27] Economic independence was left to later nineteenth-century writers to emphasize.

Wollstonecraft's ideal life, it seemed, was a scaled-down version of the splendid French salons of the ancien régime. In *Vindication*'s preface, she remarked admiringly that "in France there is undoubtedly a more general diffusion of knowledge than in any part of the European world, and I attribute it, in a great measure, to the social intercourse which has long subsisted between the sexes."[28] She was scathing in her contempt for aristocratic households where the women, "a set of silly females," conversed alternately about matrimony and dress.[29]

The Single Woman

Jane Austen, a single woman who wrote her novels at about the same time as *Vindication*, chronicled this kind of society, and made explicit the tragedy of women whose needs were not satisfied. "You know we must marry," remarks Elizabeth Watson, in *The Watsons*. "I could do very well single for my own part. A little company, and a pleasant ball now and then, would be enough for me, if one could be young for ever, but my father cannot provide for us, and it is very bad to grow old and be poor and laughed at."[30] For women of the nobility and country gentry, their only means to respectable survival lay in marriage, or, occasionally, in a rich father who could afford to support a single daughter for life. It was hardly surprising therefore that so much effort was devoted to arranging advantageous marriages for the young women of this class, and that women spent so much time in their attempt to appear irresistible. The stakes were high. Self-interest required that a woman avoid remaining single, for then she would be dependent on the kindness of friends. As Austen herself, just before her death, wrote to a friend: "If I live to be an old Woman, I must expect to wish I had died now; blessed in the tenderness of such a Family, and before I had survived either them or their affection."[31] If Rousseau's Sophie was the victim of the need to educate the new rational virtuous man, able to handle political freedom, then the single woman was doubly the victim of the enlightened age. The single woman was free from the imperative of Rousseau, who wished women "to please, to be useful to us, to make us love and esteem them, to educate us when young, and take care of us when grown up, to advise, to console us, to render our lives easy and agreeable" with respect to a husband;[32] but her dependence on others, without the expectation of reasonably secure economic support in return, meant the single woman would likely have to dissemble more, and with less dignity, than a wife.

Unenlightened despotism in the political sphere was deplored by the philosophes, and social aristocracy was criticized vehemently. As Figaro, in Beaumarchais's play *The Marriage of Figaro*, asks the Count: "Nobility, fortune, rank, position. How proud they make a man feel! What have *you* done to deserve such advantages! Put yourself to the trouble of being born—nothing more!"[33] In the home, few were prepared to forego the theory of male domestic supremacy. When Abigail Adams, wife of a member of the Continental Congress and a future president of the United States, asked her husband in 1776 to "remember the ladies" in a new American constitution, and warned, "do not put such unlimited power in the hands of the husbands. Remember all men would be tyrants if they could," he teased her in reply and noted, "Depend upon it, we know better than to repeal our masculine systems."[34] It was a knotty problem. Even the indignation and perspicacity of Mary Wollstonecraft were insufficient to frame a realistic theory of a free relationship between the sexes. She came near, in her insistence on moral independence, but many years passed before that was extended to include economic independence too.

Suggestions for Further Reading

De Madariaga, Isabel. *Russia in the Age of Catherine the Great.* New
    Haven, 1981.
Flexner, Eleanor. *Mary Wollstonecraft.* Baltimore, Md., 1973.
Graham, Ruth. "Rousseau's Sexism Revolutionized." In *Woman in the
    Eighteenth Century and Other Essays,* edited by Paul Fritz and Richard
    Morton. Toronto, 1976.
Lougee, Carolyn. *Le Paradis Des Femmes: Women, Salons, and Social
    Stratification in Seventeenth-Century France.* Princeton, 1976.
Macartney, C. A. *Maria Theresa and the House of Austria.* London, 1969.
Wollstonecraft, Mary. *A Vindication of the Rights of Woman.* Edited by
    Carol H. Poston. New York, 1975.

CHAPTER 9

Liberty, Equality, Sisterhood?

In July, 1794, Mary Wollstonecraft wrote from France that she sickened at the thought of a revolution which cost so much blood and bitter tears.[1] Yet in 1789 she had welcomed the fall of the Bastille; in 1791 she had defended both the revolution and its English supporters in *A Vindication of the Rights of Men;* and after *A Vindication of the Rights of Woman* was published, she traveled to Paris to experience firsthand a society in which many traditions had been overturned. For women, the French Revolution brought some changes. It brought opportunities to participate in cataloging grievances, in demonstrations, in debates, clubs, and pamphlet warfare, in the pageantry and drama; but there was also participation in the suffering provoked by any major political dislocation. Their participation was both egalitarian, as befitted the call to liberty and equality, and at the same time Rousseauesque, for it embodied a masculine appeal to fraternity.

Women's Grievances: Bourgeois Marriage and Market Women

When the Estates-General were summoned to meet in Versailles in May, 1789, lists of grievances (cahiers) were drawn up by local districts, cataloging their preoccupations with matters in need of reform. A handful of women were involved in debates giving rise to the cahiers: some women in religious orders in the Second Estate, and some noblewomen in the First Estate, were entitled to send representatives; but on the whole women were not specifically included in the intense politicizing process induced by the financial crisis and economic distress of the old regime. Nevertheless some cahiers included grievances strictly concerning women, and some pamphlets listed reforms which women authors desired. One was an outright request for women representatives: a noble could not represent a commoner in the Estates-General, so why was it presumed that a man could represent a woman? Political rights were demanded, but a more frequent demand was for a broader education, and for a single, rather than double, standard of sexual morality. A network of paid midwives should be made available to all women, and indeed women should be assured of respectable means of livelihood without being obliged to turn to prostitution, which was deplored. Condorcet supported the call for political rights, asking "Why should people prone to pregnancy and passing indispositions be barred from the exercise of rights no one would dream of denying those who have gout or catch cold easily?"[2] The few feminist demands requested were primarily those which would enhance the life of economically secure bourgeois women. When jobs for women were called for, it was not so much to provide an alternate option to full-time motherhood as it was to provide an alternative to prostitution for poor women who might otherwise threaten the sanctity of the middle-class home. The notion of the home as a solace, an oasis, where the gentle loving wife devoted her life to the care of her husband and children, struck a responsive chord with these women as well as with their men.[3]

A rather different catalog can be seen in the cahier of the complaints and grievances of the "Ladies of the Markets" of Paris, dictated at the *grand sallon des Porcherons* the first Sunday in May, 1789, for presentation to the Estates-General. This is the closest to an authentic voice coming from women workers. They complained at the lack of protection from winds in the open market, and at the conditions under which they were obliged to work; they objected to the tax collectors at the entrance to the city; they complained of the hospitals, where four people died in one bed and where children contracted disease and learned vice. They thought rich grain speculators who had benefited from the starvation of the poor should be punished; they were against the bishops for leading selfish, luxurious lives but sympathized with poor parish priests who, they thought, should be allowed to marry; and they criticized the king's ministers for deceiving him.[4] These women took for granted the fact that they worked for money, and resented people growing rich through the exaction of taxes by virtue of privilege while their own lives, and those of their dependents, were in jeopardy despite the hard physical work they did every day. The ostentation, idleness, and wealth of the minority were galling. Unsurprisingly they agreed with the Enlightenment philosophers who had drawn attention to the injustice of a society perpetuating inequality of rank and wealth. In short, the interest of these women was with their men, the sansculottes, before it was with the would-be heroines of the home.

Women from this group, the market women, formed the six thousand strong demonstration marching from Paris to Versailles on 5 October 1789 after they learned that there was no bread supply in the capital. They were accompanied by armed National Guardsmen. A delegation of the women entered the National Assembly to complain about grain hoarding and argue in favor of a fixed price for bread; six other women were received by the king who promised that Paris would get its bread.[5] The women stayed overnight and the following day their presence strengthened the arguments of members of the National Assembly who persuaded the king and the royal family to leave Versailles, the king's court, and make the symbolic gesture of returning to Paris, the nation's capital. On the return journey the market women were joined by some of the society women who had watched the debates in the National Assembly from the gallery. Among them was a salon hostess, Théroigne de Méricourt, who was rumored to have dressed as a female Amazon. The following spring, a police enquiry into the march was held and as a result, Reine Louise Audu, "queen of the markets," was imprisoned for a year.[6]

Bourgeois Feminists

Bourgeois feminists in the capital continued to agitate for reforms which drew their inspiration from both the egalitarian and the primitive strands of the Enlightenment. Tactics were muted in comparison to the march on Versailles, but they were nevertheless radical in the context of male-dominated politics. Pamphlets and letters to the editors of newspapers and magazines were printed, while delegations were sent to the National Assembly and to the many political clubs. Speeches made in these forums were also printed later for wider circulation. Demands for a broader education for girls coupled with a more liberal divorce law predominated: both could be seen as consistent with Rousseau's image of a woman fulfilling herself within a secure family. Divorce was necessary in order to protect the woman whose husband failed to provide for her economically, or whose sexual morality was an insult. Increasingly, demands for political rights were made, and it was necessary to go to Condorcet and the mainstream Enlightenment thinkers who had advocated rights for men in order to support these claims. A Dutch woman who had resided in Paris since 1774, Etta Palm d'Aelders, petitioned the assembly and spoke in clubs in favor of women's education, a legal identity for women at age twenty-one, political freedom and equal rights, and divorce legislation. A Frenchwoman from the Beaurepaire section in July, 1793, addressed the convention noting that "women count for nothing in the political system. . . . As the Constitution is based on the Rights of Man, we now demand the full exercise of those rights for ourselves."[7]

One of the most dramatic pamphlets appeared in September, 1791, "The Rights of Woman," a statement closely copying the Declaration of the Rights of Man which had been decreed by the National Assembly in 1789. The author was Olympe de Gouges, a playwright. She was a royalist and dedicated her "Rights" to the unpopular queen, Marie Antoinette. De Gouges's "Rights" paralleled those of 1789, and she attached a "social contract," echoing Rousseau's phrase but defying his philosophy. Hers was a marriage contract, by which a couple were united for the duration of mutual affection under specified conditions. Property was held in common and if there was a separation, the property should go to the children, including children of another parent; and children had a right to the names of the parents who acknowledged them. De Gouges's thought was inclined toward sexual and economic independence and an egalitarian society, which was rather at odds with her admiration of the monarchy and her condemnation of the sansculottes. She suffered for her refusal to abate criticism of Robespierre in 1793 when she died on the guillotine. The semiofficial newspaper commented: "It seems the law has punished this conspirator for having forgotten the virtues that suit her sex."[8]

Many Parisian political clubs admitted women as members, at least one (the Société Fraternelle des Jacobins) had a woman officer, and feminist issues were debated. Initially the clubs functioned as educational interchanges rather

Marie Antoinette on her way to the guillotine

than political pressure groups. One, the Cercle Social, was sponsored by a society advocating women's education, the Amis de la Vérité: it generated both debates and pamphlets advocating more rights for women, rights which tended to secure their position as mothers of families as distinct from independent persons taking part in public life. Besides societies with descriptive titles, like the Société fraternelle des patriotes de l'un et de l'autre sexe, many clubs were formed around neighborhood churches, which no longer functioned as religious institutions, or within the sections into which Paris was administratively divided. By 1791 these groups, comprising radical, educated bourgeois and artisans as well as sansculottes, became more politically active. They protested against several laws impinging on their interests—for example the prohibition against professional or workers' associations—and were also involved in a large-scale demonstration in July, 1791, on the Champ de Mars. Several women, including d'Aelders, were arrested for their participation at that time.[9]

Street Politics

Some of the most decisive revolutionary activity undertaken by women occurred in the streets rather than in meeting halls. In early 1792 a sugar crisis provoked taxation populaire, a device repeated many times before the revolution was over. In the French Caribbean islands, civil war between royalists and patriots was interfering with the steady supply of sugar, and speculators were hoarding colonial products in anticipation of increased profits. Women found the prices rising and took petitions of complaint to their local government offices. When nothing was done, crowds seized stored merchandise, distributed items at a "just price" determined by the participants, and returned the proceeds to the shopkeeper. The following year, in February, 1793, the execution of the king and the mobilization of the Revolutionary Army put pressure on the supply of grain, flour, and bread, and the women again petitioned both municipal and national government offices in an attempt to effect an economy planned by the government rather than controlled by hoarders. In the face of official delay, they resorted again to taxation populaire incidents, and by the end of February the National Convention had responded to their requests.[10]

Club Women

During 1793 the most respected and feared of the women's clubs, the Citoyennes Républicaines Révolutionaires, came into existence. It was founded by a chocolate maker, Pauline Leon, and an actress, Claire Lacombe, who identified with the sansculottes: "Our rights are those of the people, and if we are oppressed, we shall be able to resist oppression," declared Lacombe.[11] They wore the tricolor cockade, which they wished to make mandatory for all women, and also the bonnet rouge, a red knitted liberty cap worn by men as well.[12] Their program emphasized economic claims, notably cheap food, and they advocated fixed prices.[13] They became more radical during the summer and developed differences with the Jacobins in power, who accused Lacombe of being manipulated by the counterrevolution. A Jacobin deputy exploited the notion of women's susceptibility to the influence of others to conclude that they had neither the political nor the moral education to use rights responsibly. The Citoyennes Révolutionaires supported the idea of the Maximum, a law passed in September, 1793, regulating prices on forty commodities, but in doing so found themselves at odds with the market women, who by now considered government price fixing against their interests. The market women allied with the Jacobins in a violent altercation with the Citoyennes Révolutionaires, and the government found this a propitious time to decide the issue of extending rights to women generally.[14] All women's clubs were suppressed, to the accompaniment of the remarks of the procurer of the Paris commune, Anaxagoras Chaumette, who said he thought every sansculotte had a right to expect his wife to run his home while he attended political meetings.[15] Two years later the government further suppressed any collective action by women, announcing that women on the streets in groups of more than five would be dispersed by force and then held under arrest. This was less in reaction to feminist calls to arms than to the bread riots precipitated by a reduction of individual rations to only two ounces of bread a day, coupled with the closing of the workshops which for five years had furnished a livelihood for workers unemployed by the demise of aristocratically patronized trade.[16]

Outside of Paris women's clubs performed a different function. Dijon bourgeois women, for example, formed a Club des Amies de la Vérité et de la

Bienfaisance in 1791 which performed for a few years the same work which aristocratic women had done before the revolution. They collected voluntary alms to bring some relief to the poor. This was allied with appropriate bourgeois revolutionary gestures. The wives of department and district authorities, and of town officials, met each Sunday after attending mass given by a priest loyal to the revolution; they boycotted merchants who favored nonjuring priests (priests who would not swear allegiance to the civil constitution of the clergy); and ran lotteries to help poor families. By 1792 some of the provincial women's clubs anticipated the attempts of the Citoyennes Révolutionaires of Paris by urging fixed prices as a policy, and they also mobilized local efforts in support of the army after France was at war in the spring of 1792. They collected household linen for use as bandages, jewelry to help amortize the national debt, and kept vigilant watch for traitors among the local population, children as well as adults.[17] But when the Besançon Club urged the convention to extend the suffrage to women, it was forced to withdraw the request by local ridicule.[18] Neither feminism nor female political activism was any longer viable.

Propaganda and Pageantry: Woman on a Pedestal

During the revolutionary years, people from all ranks periodically took loyalty tests to the current regime, no empty gesture during the Terror when enemies of the revolution were guillotined with dispatch. The commonest test was participation in the many festivals designed to celebrate the latest victory or accomplishment, and one of the earliest was taking a collective oath of loyalty to the nation. Yet many pageant organizers and government officials were bewildered as to whether women might legitimately take the oath because they did not possess political rights. One woman from Lanion wrote the assembly in 1790 urging clarification of this in favor of women taking the oath, and a member of the Cercle Social argued that at least all married women of respectable conduct be permitted to swear.[19] The issue was shelved.

At ceremonies where people gathered to make the symbolic affirmation of loyalty, women were certainly involved. The use of pageantry and art in the service of the revolution reached an apogee during the Jacobin rule, 1793–94. Politicians commissioned artists to depict two kinds of virtue: the grand and heroic, and the humble and domestic. In both, women figured prominently. The heroic contained mythological figures crowned by the female trinity of Liberty, Equality, and Fraternity. Divinities to replace Christianity were portrayed also as women: Virtue, Innocence, Force, Probity, Truth ("normally nude and holding a mirror"), Victory, Reason, and Nature. These found their way onto playing cards, medals, letterheads, and anywhere decorative art could find a place. Similarly, Robespierre recommended the glorification of frugality, conjugal faithfulness, paternal love, motherly affection, hard work, and agricultural labor.[20] Throughout France local administrations commissioned works of art which could both demonstrate their own loyalty and help propagate revolutionary ardor in the breasts of those who saw them. It appeared as though women were safer relegated to marble or canvas, or in choirs dressed in Greek tunics singing secular revolutionary hymns, than considered as real citizens who could swear the oath of loyalty like a man. Some artists managed to include in their work suggestions of the irony. The artist David was able to convey bitterness, despair, and a sense of tragedy in his "Woman of the Revolution." He was also able to make a powerful comment in his picture of Marie Antoinette en route to the guillotine, reducing her to a caricature of a market woman.

Poor Women

Despite the fact that poor women were everywhere, historians know little about their attitudes toward the revolution or their experiences in it. In prints women carried banners announcing that they had given so many children to the republic, as soldiers in the war, and there is Charles Dickens's *tricoteuse* Madame Defarge, the grim "hag knitting stockings for the war effort as the internal conspiracy is annihilated before her eyes," who, although fictional, is "undoubtedly real."[21] One aspect which has been documented, in addition to the brief mentions of market women and bread rioters, is the failure of the revolutionary regimes to provide poor relief. Under the ancien régime, poor relief was the responsibility of the church. From the tithe and voluntary contributions church authorities gave alms to the poor and simultaneously some hope of salvation to the rich. Enlightenment philosophes were bitterly anticlerical, however. They berated the hypocrisy of a society which perpetuated the existence of the poor in order to earn a reduced stay in purgatory for the rich, and they provided good arguments for opponents of the ancien régime to nationalize the church and rationalize its charitable functions. There were attempts to provide an integrated system of state-supported employment and relief, but by 1792 such attempts had broken down, and "the traditional methods of according relief were destroyed without any substitute."[22] The consequence was that when women were unable to work or obtain bread they and their families went hungry, for women's wages were central to the family economy. The revolution brought a hiatus in employment provided by rich society women who no longer fueled the demand for the lace and labor-intensive clothing industry which had been predominantly staffed by women. The abolition of the gabelle, or salt tax, also ruined the livelihoods of those involved in smuggling salt.[23] Unemployed women were therefore dependent on private philanthropy in the absence of public poor relief.

Voluntary charity was spasmodic and subject to political caprice, like the existence of the provincial women's clubs whose object had originally been to alleviate the distress of poor families. When babies cried, they were given rags dipped in water, and did not take too long to die. It was women and children who died before the men, and in 1794 some women in Masannay demanded the annihilation of people over sixty years of age in order to increase the amount of food available for the young.[24] Poverty was not introduced into France by the revolution, but it was exacerbated by poor harvests, the absence of any system of poor relief, and by political developments of revolution and war which interfered with the distribution of food, particularly bread. By 1795 poor women, who formed a considerable proportion of the population,[25] could assess the legacy of the revolution in terms of children aborted, stillborn, or dead; in terms of their own ill health and likely sterility; by the disappearance of any assets (such as household goods) they may have owned, pawned for food; and by failure to sustain a family economy at all.[26] If some of these women earned a living at a market, or participated occasionally in the march to Versailles or the festivals of the revolution, that was scant compensation.

Revolutionary Legacy

Women with more economic security benefited more from the revolution. Women achieved a legal majority and the right to be witnesses in civil suits in 1792. Inheritance laws were changed to guarantee equal rights to female and male children. Divorce legislation was promulgated which allowed mutual consent, marital incompatibility, and desertion as grounds for divorce, and in 1794 allowed divorce to couples who had been living apart for six months. Primary education, which was not compulsory, was made available for both sexes, who were taught separately. Women teachers were to receive two-thirds the pay of men teachers. Such reforms were short-lived. The only legal reform which survived Napoleon's law codification and the restoration was the law allowing equal inheritance rights to daughters as well as sons, of no mean significance when there was property to inherit.[27] The ethos of the Napoleonic Code was expressed in Article 213: "The wife owes obedience to the husband."

As it turned out, women's most pervasive legacy from the French Revolution was the internalized image of domesticated romanticism epitomized in the novels of Madame de Staël.[28] Rousseau provided a theory which was consistent with the existing economic reality. Women were defined in terms of men because without a man the grim reality was that few women, rich or poor, could survive. Rousseau elevated this necessity into a virtue. Few women could afford, intellectually or financially, to ignore that imperative. Still, there were working women who lived outside this Rousseauesque imagery. They had a different, more subversive legacy: they had become politicized by political and economic hardship and had pressed to the limits their title of *citoyenne* in pursuit of demands for subsistence and security for their family economy. On the whole, Rousseau's theories reinforced patriarchy with cultural and educational overtones which thoroughly permeated the consciousness of Western society. At the same time, future politicians could not ignore the pivotal role of food purchasers and food retailers, so many of whom were women, at a time of volatile political instability.

Suggestions for Further Reading

Abray, Jane. "Feminism in the French Revolution." *American Historical Review* 80 (1975):43–62.
Graham, Ruth. "Women in the French Revolution." In *Becoming Visible:*

Women in European History, edited by Renate Bridenthal and Claudia Koonz, pp. 236–54. Boston, 1977.

Hufton, Olwen. "Women in Revolution 1789–1796." *Past and Present* 53 (1971):90–108.

Levy, Darline Gay; Applewhite, Harriet Branson; and Johnson, Mary Durham, eds. *Women in Revolutionary Paris, 1789–1795.* Urbana, Ill., 1979.

CHAPTER 10

Industry and Husbandry

The notion that a woman ought not to work would, for thousands of years, have been considered extraordinary by the vast majority of people. Work was what people did during the day, and occasionally during the night, six days of the week, when work was to be had. Individual ablebodied persons who on the whole wished to work rarely sought limitations to regular and constant employment. The economic system, however, could only offer work subject to the fluctuating vagaries of market forces, climate, and technological bottlenecks. Before the agrarian and industrial revolutions of the eighteenth century, each family unit sought to maintain its livelihood by work. Work could be translated into services or goods, and rewarded either in kind, by reciprocal services or goods, or in money, by wages or cash for goods sold. For centuries women, along with children and men, participated fully in this system.

Production and Reproduction

"Women's work is never done" was a rueful comment on the particular nature of women in labor. Women produced certain sorts of goods and services in the same way men and children did. In addition, their exclusive biological function in childbearing and primary social function in child rearing meant that women never ceased to work in one capacity or another. Before the eighteenth century these three generic occupations—production, childbearing, and child rearing—were accepted as intrinsic parts of the life-style of most women. The few who were not involved in all three were generally regarded as deviant, not necessarily through any fault of their own. Perhaps they were sick, or infertile, or too poor to maintain dependents directly. Perhaps they had not married. Or perhaps they were rich enough to employ other women to do the labor. The point was that a woman's life normally included responsibility for production as well as for reproduction.

In reproduction, women's options were wide ranging since men's responsibilities for child rearing were indirect. Yet there was by no means total segregation. In a sense, the community as a whole collectively shared responsibility for the regulation of family size, for example, since before the nineteenth century a general expectation was the late age of first marriage. The normal

113

length of marriage was quite short. This had the effect of limiting the number of children which could be born. Although child rearing was a top priority for a woman, it was never exclusively her sphere. After a child was weaned, its social training was shared among family, kin, and neighbors. Children's socialization familiarized them with traditional expectations and with customary occupations and livelihoods. Formal schooling was at best very elementary.

Before the industrial revolution a woman was expected to contribute to the family livelihood directly as well as by domestic labor and management. Within a largely agrarian economy most women lived in agricultural communities, but women who lived in towns had occupations derived from their place of residence too. The one occupation universally applicable, in town and country, was housewifery, containing the several reproductive tasks of cleaning, cooking, and rearing children. Even Mary Wollstonecraft remarked

> No employment of the mind is a sufficient excuse for neglecting domestic duties, and I cannot conceive that they are incompatible. A woman may fit herself to be the companion and friend of a man of sense, and yet know how to take care of his family.[1]

This basic responsibility was carried out personally by the vast majority of the agrarian population.

As always one must distinguish between those with an adequate income and those without, between those who "increased the wealth of the kingdom" according to Gregory King in 1688, and those who decreased it, or, according to the French historian LeRoy Ladurie, between those who owned a plow and those who did not.[2] Women in the first, more fortunate, group changed their life-style after industrialization from one of work to one of predominantly leisure. Women in the second group changed their life-style from work located in and around their rural dwelling to work separated both in function and location from their home.[3]

John Robey in 1843 compared the lot of the gentlemen farmers to that of their forefathers a century earlier:

> 1743: Man, to the Plough
> Wife, to the Cow
> Boy, to the Barn
> Girl, to the Yarn
> And your rent will be netted.

> 1843: Man, Tally Ho
> Miss, Piano
> Wife, Silk and Satin
> Boy, Greek and Latin
> And you'll all be gazetted.[4]

Like so many other families of the middle and entrepreneurial groups, these families changed from essentially units of production to units of consumption.

Farmers' wives before industrialization took an active share in the management of the household and of the farm as a business operation. Often it was the farmer's wife who kept the accounts and also ran the dairy, poultry, and orchard components. This involved helping select stock—the calves, pigs, and cows—and selling them; it meant organizing, supervising, managing, and actually working in the dairy. On an English farm with thirty cows, milking would have to be done twice daily, and the cows would be visited in the fields for milking. The milk then had to be transported back to the farmhouse for making into butter, cheese, and cream. The hens had to be fed, looked after, and the eggs collected. Fruit and vegetables had to be grown and processed at harvest time. The produce which was a surplus for maintenance of the household had to be marketed. At harvest time the farmwife helped in the fields, and at other times during the year might have to help with seeding and hoeing. If her husband died, the farmer's widow was usually able to take over full responsibility for the entire operation as she already had extensive experience and versatile training. Besides her unpaid work, agricultural publicist Arthur Young estimated that frequently the cash earned by the wife's surplus goods amounted to over one and a half times the rent of the property.[5]

This life was filled with hard manual labor and required managerial skill. On top of work directly connected with farming, the farmwife still had her children to rear and her household to clean and cook for. Even with large households of ten to twenty people, division of labor was relatively primitive, and the farmwife, like the farmer himself, had to be able to turn a hand to most tasks herself, even if a servant was available to help.

Female servants in husbandry came from the large group of nearly landless rural inhabitants who had few rights in law. Despite their legal insecurity and the squalor of their dwellings, their garden plots were often tolerated and on such property could be grown cabbages, potatoes, some wheat and turnips to feed a pig, and pigs, poultry, and bees could be kept. In other words, food for a family could be produced because such families lived in rural areas without too much pressure of population. The husband earned wages as a day laborer when work was available, as did the wife, and in addition, the wife took into her home textile work, mainly spinning, which made her an essential part of the domestic system of the woolen industry. Cash flow was always a problem. The work needed to provide money wages to buy what the family could not itself produce was not always available when the family needed it, and such families were already at risk because of their lack of legal as well as economic security.[6] This latent insecurity became a reality toward the end of the eighteenth century in Britain when engrossing and enclosure changed the landscape.

Agrarian and Industrial Change: Producers and Consumers

During the eighteenth century several inventions (new methods of draining, seeding machines, stock breeding), together with an increase in the selling price of wheat, encouraged farmers with extensive holdings to experiment in the interest of efficiency. They engrossed contiguous properties, and they also enclosed fields to accommodate single crops rather than the scattered crops and management methods intrinsic to open field strip farming. Those who owned agricultural land were compensated for what they sold, but those without legal title—the squatters—were turned off the land which had provided them with nourishment and often with work. Large landowners came to own more land, small landowners sold their equity and became dependent on their labor for income, and often the rural poor became destitute.[7] The last two categories also provided part of the migratory labor force for factories which were initially located near water power, in the countryside. Later, as steam power became the preferred form of energy, factories were built nearer coal mines or railway termini, and hence in urban areas.

Obviously the transition from independent farmer to propertyless laborer is a dramatic simplification of the economic and social effects of the agrarian and industrial revolutions. The time period involved is over a hundred years (1750–1850). During that time the population increased all over western Europe, adding further incentive for improving the efficiency of food production and also providing industrialists with vast numbers of workers and, of course, consumers. But viewed in retrospect, for both men and women, the change in life-style was dramatic.

Industrial structural change was only one of several determinants of the way women divided their time among tasks associated with production and reproduction. Clearly, the changeover from the household to the factory system was of paramount importance. Other developments also influenced women's work: opportunities for employment in any particular region; demographic changes in birth and death rates and the consequent different age distribution of the population; significant changes in the economic value of children; a general increase in the real wages earned by male heads of households; and a change in the relative importance accorded to a mother's domestic work. The relationships between industrialization and these other economic and demographic trends, which in the West took place largely in the nineteenth and twentieth centuries, are highly complex. Underlying them are the unquestioned assumptions that women rather than men should take primary respponsibility for the rearing of children and that men rather than women should take primary responsibility for earning wage income. These assumptions require that the household circumstances of women, as well as sex-based differences in a capitalist economy, be examined in any study of women's work.

Before the industrial revolution, most women worked most of the time for all of their lives. Agriculture-related jobs, together with textile-related piecework, were generally integrated with the work of child care and the maintenance of the family dwelling. Similarly in the towns, small trades and businesses operated by women shared time with the care of house and children.

Segregation of Family and Job

Industrialization changed the pattern of expectations for the majority of the population, that is for the 70 percent dependent on wages for its subsistence.[8] The single most significant difference was in the physical separation of the work place from the home. A woman had to leave her family home for regular, specified long periods each day if she was fully employed. This was not entirely unknown before the industrial revolution. Women in the Middle Ages and after worked in a variety of trades: in rurally based mining and extractive industries;[9] peddling strawberries, milk, fabric, crabs, mops, washcloths, socks, and biscuits, for example;[10] as retailers, and in hospitality industries (tavern keeping, waiting at table, keeping accounts);[11] midwifery;[12] and in the oldest profession of all, as prostitutes, driven less by moral degeneracy than by economic necessity.[13] But when the factory, employing often hundreds of operatives of large and expensive machines, became the standard unit of production, the separation of wage work and home also became standard. In some areas of France especially, smaller units of production, both industrial and agricultural, continued to predominate. There, the physical integration of workshop and dwelling continued to be an important factor in the work of adult women.[14] In the areas where factories predominated, new decisions had to be made by women with two newly differentiated imperatives: family care, and the need to contribute cash to the family economy.

Women's Work

Family-related work depended on the size and the structure of the family itself. Feeding, clothing, and caring for a household with all of its children too young to work themselves was different from providing household support to a family of wage earners or to a family where sickness was prevalent. Family size and structure was not at all uniform during the nineteenth century. National trends illustrate changes which developed in individual families.

First, life expectancy lengthened by over ten years: in 1800 a baby girl's life expectancy in Britain was about 30 years, whereas by 1850 it was 42.8. The age at first marriage tended to fall: in a factory town a couple could substitute their joint wage-earning power for access to property assets of a rural plot of land. Adult females therefore were married for a longer time before their own death or the death of their spouse, and had a longer period of time in which to bear children. During the nineteenth century infant and child mortality declined a little, but was still high, so if parents wished to ensure that children survived into adulthood, the mother would have to use her fertility to good measure.[15] Birth rates were high, reflecting the expectation that several children would die before maturity, but also the expectation that for those who survived there would be adequate employment opportunities: children represented a future wage-earning investment for the benefit of the family economy. The reproductive work that the mother had to do was a realistic economic activity, but there were costs attached.

The main cost was that a woman would lose her own wages in the latter stages of pregnancy, and likely would continue to lose them after the child was born. This could be offset by having in the household an older person whose economic contribution was made by minding the children while the mother maximized her wage-earning capacity;[16] but this in turn represented a further cost, in that the household was then a larger unit for the mother to manage.

Until the end of the nineteenth century, generally speaking, families living in industrialized urban centers experienced a continuous struggle to balance the subsistence needs of their members with the cash income produced by their wage earners. The provision of housing, clothing, and above all food were managed by the mother, who additionally earned wages herself if there was an imbalance and if the local industry offered job opportunities. In the precarious situations of capitalist expansion and depression, of family members' uncertain health and with some likelihood of having to meet extraordinary expenses like funerals, budget balancing was difficult. Without the substructure of essential welfare services which the twentieth century brought to Western states, a great many families existed "under the pressure of chronic want."[17] When a man's wages were low, this pressure could be permanent. When the family did not have an adult man's wages, through illness, death, abandonment, or other reasons, the responsibility on the mother could be overwhelming. The requirement to earn money to buy food necessitated the subordination of child care. Babies would be set with indifferent minders, and would more frequently die, which in turn would mean the mother would lose a potential wage earner eight or nine years hence, and her own life would likely be curtailed because of its harshness. Rowntree's investigation in York and Booth's in London concluded that 30 percent of the population lived in poverty.[18]

The nineteenth-century proletarian woman differed from her predecessors primarily in where she lived. Not only did the factory system necessitate the separation of wage and household work, but it also involved living in urban centers. This did not necessarily involve a separation from the important kin networks which could be so important as a thin welfare cushion and an introduction to alternate employments and ways of coping, for often members of the network moved together.[19] But urban living did imply that a poor family no longer had access to the rural market garden which had provided so much sustenance in the preindustrial age.[20]

By the beginning of the twentieth century conditions were stabilizing. Men's real wages increased. Consequently, the reserve potential represented by a mother's wage-earning capacity had to be utilized less often for subsistence reasons. Mothers worked for wages, less to avoid poverty than to improve the family's standard of living.[21] Medical progress and the provision of clean water supplies finally had an impact on child mortality, thereby reducing the number of pregnancies a mother must take to term to ensure enough live adults. Social insurance and welfare provisions were gradually introduced, thereby widening the margin between tolerable conditions and disaster, and actually reducing the strictly economic value of children within the family structure. Industrialization eventually revolutionized women's reproductive as well as productive behavior, and brought in its wake profound societal changes. Modifications of attitude slowly followed.

Before industrialization, at all levels of society including the top, women made a continuing and necessary contribution to the livelihood of the family unit. After industrialization, approximately a third at least of the population lived in families which required wages from more than one adult wage earner, so mothers also earned wages. Elsewhere a woman's work revolved around her family within the home. This economic division was paralleled in public life by a solidification of assumptions on woman's proper place being in the home, and only in the family.[22] Not all women were part of an economically viable family unit, and those who were, were not always satisfied with their exclusively domestic role. As early as the middle of the nineteenth century, some women were translating dissatisfaction into attempts to change society's expectations and the opportunities available for women.

Suggestions for Further Reading

Clark, Alice. *The Working Life of Women in the Seventeenth Century*. New York, 1968.

Ladurie, E. LeRoy. "Peasants." In *Companion Volume to the New Cambridge Modern History*, vol. 13, edited by Peter Burke. Cambridge, 1979.

Pinchbeck, Ivy. *Women Workers and the Industrial Revolution, 1750–1850*. London, 1969.

Tilly, Louise A., and Scott, Joan A. *Women, Work, and Family*. New York, 1978.

CHAPTER 11

Working Women

There were two prime determinants of whether women worked in the nineteenth century and, if they did, what kind of work they performed. These were class and marital status. Upper-class married women had servants to perform any necessary labor, whether productive or reproductive. To a large extent upper-class single women shared the work experience of their married sisters, but two additional factors helped determine their working status: family wealth, and energy. An ample private income could remove any need to work from their lives, but a single woman's individual energy, imagination, and intellectual capacity might inspire her toward activity in a plethora of reforming societies, many of which were designed to improve the work opportunities for middle- and upper-class women. Middle-class married women were occupied in their domestic, reproductive labor; middle-class single women had difficulties. They had neither the economic security which upper-class single women derived from family wealth, nor the educational training which their brothers used as a preliminary to professional and business work. Working-class married women, like middle-class married women, were considered primarily responsible for managing the household economy. Unlike middle-class women, they had no servants nor did the level of their family income allow the purchase of many domestic appliances. Because the income provided by working-class husbands was sometimes insufficient to meet basic family needs, many working-class married women were engaged in paid work as well. Working-class single women participated in the work force as a matter of course if they were young; and if they never married, or were no longer married, as in the case of widows, continued to work to support themselves and dependents. Family resources, age, and marital status helped decide the productive work experience of working-class, middle-class, and even upper-class women. The kind of work women did varied both regionally and chronologically.

Industrialization introduced for women the separation of reproductive and productive labor, but it also brought other changes which were highly significant, including the development of government bureaucracies and services industries. By the beginning of the twentieth century a discernible pattern of women working was emerging. The personal and social features of class, age, marital status, and family economic resources helped predict whether or not women would be involved in productive work. The numbers of women working in the new white-collar occupations were increasing at a pace faster than the numbers of men: whereas in England and Wales in 1881, 12.6 percent of women employed were working in middle-class occupations, by 1911 almost twice that proportion, or 23.7 percent of employed women were classified as middle-class. (These occupations comprised the census categories of teachers, nurses, shop assistants, clerks, and civil servants.) Still, in 1911, over three-quarters of the women who worked were employed in jobs requiring manual labor; and 8.5 percent of working women were widows, while 14 percent were married.[1] Over three-quarters were single, most of them young. While the predominant profile of the working woman is that of a young, working-class single person, who ceased to work in the labor force after marriage, there were nevertheless many other kinds of working women in the nineteenth century.[2] The proliferation of these images helps dispel some of the popular tradition which confined women totally to the canon of domesticity.[3]

Domestic Service

Young, single women worked in a wide variety of occupations in the area where their family lived, and occasionally apart from their family. For those appreciating familiarity even in different geographical surroundings, domestic service was often a first preferred step away from a childhood setting, and it remained the largest single occupation for women even in the early twentieth century. In Paris in 1901, 45 percent of all working women were servants, and in England in 1911, over 90 percent of the 1.3 million domestic servants were women.[4] More than two hundred years earlier, in England in 1688, Gregory King estimated that servants comprised a tenth of the total population of five and a half million.[5]

In larger households, the cook would be a woman: Dean Swift's *Directions to Servants* published in 1713 declared that "because my Treatise is chiefly calculated for the general run of Knights, Squires and Gentlemen, both in Town and Country, I shall therefore apply myself to you, Mrs. Cook, as a woman."[6] The cook was assisted by a maid who might also be expected to do housework as well, and who often had to contend with the sexual advances of male members of the household. Diarist Samuel Pepys was habitually tempted by his wife's waiting women and his wife was perpetually dismissing them for his transgressions.[7]

Conditions of work were severe, yet there were compensations. By law, a servant, male or female, was constrained to obey all legal demands of the employer, and although wages were supposed to be paid quarterly, the servant had little redress if the employer fell into arrears. Yet food, clothing, and board were provided, as was shelter, and this payment in kind provided an inducement to many. In return for expected obedience, employers were obliged to offer succor and protection. Only limited free time was given on a regular basis, yet the continual shopping and message carrying gave opportunities for a change of scenery and a meeting with friends. Traditionally, servants of long standing inherited some money at their employer's death.[8]

Industrialization paradoxically intensified both the advantages and the drawbacks in domestic service as an occupation, and in the long run also ensured the virtual disappearance of the servant class.

In the nineteenth century, several elements undermined the economic conditions of service and the attitudes of master, mistress, and servant. In England, the number of middle-class people (defined as families with incomes of between £200 and £500 per annum) doubled between 1851 and 1871, even though the total population increased by only 13 percent.[9] These newly rich desired the trappings of their newfound status, including a servant, even though their financial resources were often strained. In Lyon in 1872, only a third of the city's servants worked in households where more than one servant was employed; in London in the 1890s, 27 percent of the servant-employing households had one servant and an additional 35 percent had only two.[10] By the beginning of the twentieth century, the social status attached to servant keeping was diminishing, for economic and ideological reasons: keeping a servant cost money; there was an increasing emphasis on housewifery as a respectable occupation for middle-class women; there was also a tendency to insist that they should look after their own children; and new technological appliances like washing machines and vacuum cleaners reduced muscular drudgery.

One significant feature of nineteenth-century service was its transient character. Urbanization concentrated the expanding bourgeoisie in the towns, so the demand for servants was concentrated there. Many servant recruits came from rural areas, particularly in France. A considerable proportion of women moved great distances in search of jobs, even when alternative, industrial employment was nearby.[11] Service was a familiar route for rural residents wishing to leave a crowded slum home. Besides the comfort of familiarity, rural women choosing to go into urban service had other benefits. "It is good training for married life." With no other expenses, they could save money for a dowry. A servant received room, board, clothing, occasional tips, and wages. In the capital cities wages were higher than elsewhere. In comparison with wages paid for work which was open to women of comparable age, social background, and training, both English and French estimates suggest that the total compensation of a servant exceeded the purely monetary wage of a factory worker.[12] This was not the case with male workers and servants by the end of the century: men could earn more in factories, and this helps explain why there were fewer men, and more women, in domestic service by the end of the century. For semiskilled women in England in 1906 an interesting comparison indicates the relative advantage of the woman servant:[13]

Occupation	Annual Wage
Cotton frame tenter	£50
Clothing machinist	34
Shop assistant	50
Laundress	30
Domestic servant	49

Those women servants who were dissatisfied with their work could use their household as a base while seeking other work in the town.

For most women servants, service was a temporary period in their lives between living in the parental home and their own marriage, as indeed was most wage-earning work for most women. After service, the next largest occupation for women was work in the textile industry—spinning and weaving the cloth and sewing garments in the factories, or doing piecework as outworkers in their homes.[14] Women's experience in this occupation varied from that of the fairly well paid Lancashire mill workers to the abysmal sweatshop conditions of the large cities.

Textiles

A Lancashire cotton mill, prototype for spinning and weaving factories elsewhere in the industrialized world, housed several distinct processes by which the bales of raw cotton went through carding and blowing to spinning and then to beaming and winding through sizing to weaving. By the end of the nineteenth century women were not involved in the spinning, nor in the sizing—two of the most highly paid trades, at about forty-two shillings per week. They were involved in all the other activities, and although the wage rates were not directly based on sex, the particular jobs the women worked in tended to be rated as less skilled than the men's and they therefore took home less pay. In the cardroom, for example, where the raw cotton was cleaned and disentangled, the men averaged twenty-five shillings per week but the women earned between sixteen and nineteen shillings. In the weaving shed, the men weavers again averaged twenty-five shillings per week, and the women weavers twenty-one. Women in other industries, however, averaged only thirteen or fourteen shillings per week.[15] "Round about a pound a week" (twenty shillings) was the total income of a large number of families: the median wage in 1906 was calculated at twenty-nine shillings and four pence (approximately seven dollars and fifty cents).[16] Lancashire mill girls had the most plentiful work opportunities among British working-class women. They had steady, full-time employment, they were well paid, and many of them were also unionized. But their work was physically hard and monotonous; the fluff in the air could give rise to asthmatic conditions, and the noise in the weaving shed could be deafening.[17]

Women involved with the garment industry experienced fewer opportunities and lower wage levels than those of the Lancashire mill workers. Their average wage was under fourteen shillings and many beginning workers earned less than eight shillings paid on a piecework basis, which divided the workers in competition.

> Imagine the scene . . . a table with at least fifty girls on and around it. Lay a dozen garments, probably not worth more than 7 shillings in all to us. These girls all clamoring, with arms outstretched, for a share of it, say a shilling's worth. . . . I have seen the youngest hands literally fight and scramble for garments, for which 2 pence each is paid. . . .

Women at shoemaking benches

Glasgow cotton spinning mill

Scotch fisher lassie cutting herrings

Workers in a pottery

wrote a correspondent to the *Crewe Chronicle* in 1894.[18] Many women welcomed the chance to take tailoring piecework to do at home, and experienced times of frantic activity alternating with involuntary idleness when work was not available.[19] Taking in laundry was also an ill-paid option available for mothers who needed to mind their children but who also needed money for the family income, as was taking in boarders, and charring, or cleaning offices and houses.[20] Charles Booth found that most married women who worked out of their home did so in order to raise their family income to subsistence level.[21]

An attempt to create a more romantic version of the Lancashire mill experience in an American setting was made in the years after 1813 in the northern states. Francis Lowell copied the textile machinery he had observed during a tour of Britain in 1810–12, and established a factory at Waltham, Massachusetts. He and his partners, the Boston Associates, eventually spread their operations throughout New England. Like the Lancashire manufacturers, they were concerned to keep their costs low, and achieved this partly by attracting women workers with handsome wages which were still half the scale of male factory workers' wages. The unique but temporary feature of Lowell's experiment was the provision of dormitories for the "girls," together with employer-sponsored educational and recreational pastimes. Visitors found the Lowell mills a "philanthropic manufacturing college" while the rural parents of the first generation of mill workers were reassured that their daughters enjoyed moral supervision and had their little leisure time spent in uplifting pursuits.[22] The mill girls edited and produced their own house organ, the *Lowell Offering*, during the 1840s, in which they praised their jobs—"it is easy to do, and does not require very violent exertion, as much of our farm work does"—and the paternal guardianship of their employers. The magazine also contained utopian sketches of what life in general, and factory life in particular, could be like, if only people would follow egalitarian cooperative principles in the fashion of the early French socialist Charles Fourier.[23]

Not all the workers were satisfied. Even writers in the *Lowell Offering* complained about dirt and overcrowding in the dormitories, and the poor ventilation and long work day of thirteen hours in the mills. In 1834 and 1836 the workers went on strike against wage cuts and during the 1840s joined the widespread agitation for a ten-hour day. They also spearheaded the first trade unions for industrial women: the Female Labor Reform Associations.[24] By the 1860s the philanthropic features of Lowell mills had largely disappeared. The dormitory system was abandoned in the 1850s. The mills no longer employed a majority of native-born women, fresh from the farm—by 1860, about 60 percent of the workers were immigrants, mainly Irish.[25]

Immigrant women increasingly dominated the female labor force in nineteenth-century America. By 1860 about 10 percent of white women aged ten years or older were engaged in paid labor. Black women in the southern slave states had no choice but to work for free. Most of the white working women, as elsewhere in Western society, worked in domestic service, but those who were not servants tended to be concentrated either in textiles or in textile-related work like the garment industry where in 1850 women comprised about half the number of people employed.[26]

One trade which serviced the garment industry was the collar laundering business located in Troy, New York. Employees worked up to fourteen hours per day in enclosed space under intense heat. They needed strength, endurance, and skills acquired after about three weeks of intensive training. During the 1860s the predominantly female laundry workers formed a union, struck successfully several times for higher wages, and generated enough money in their union fund to donate large sums to fellow workers either on strike or locked out. They were not strong enough, however, to withstand joint action on the part of their employers with the collar manufacturers, and were forced to dissolve their organization after an unsuccessful strike in 1868. Effective union activity by women remained as sporadic in America as in Europe.[27]

The wages earned by working women were not pin money, but necessary for their own support or as a contribution to their family income. Those wages were less than men's for similar work. Other grievances they shared with men: the haphazard ways in which state factory acts were enforced, resulting in a wide variety of poor working conditions, the general practice of making individual workers responsible for faults developed in the machinery, and the petty irritations of having wages docked for tea money, whether or not the worker wanted the tea.[28] The way to resolve such grievances was through a union, argued Emma Paterson in Britain in 1874.[29] Paterson's Women's Trade Union League was a loose federation of women's associations and its central and regional boards were almost exclusively composed of upper- and middle-class women. Paterson urged that legislation would provide for women's particular working conditions to be inspected by female factory inspectors and she also argued that both sexes should work together through trade union organization. By 1893 a woman factory inspector had been appointed, but Paterson's appeal to women to work through trade unions was not enthusiastically heeded. Although trade union membership among women increased, it represented less than 10 percent of women workers at the beginning of the twentieth century in Britain, and under 4 percent in the United States.[30] The existing male trade unions had an ambivalent attitude toward women members, seeing them as possible undercutting competition, while women workers clearly had doubts about the efficacy of the Women's Trade Union League, for example, with its preponderance of organizers who had never had to work for a living.[31] The overwhelmingly temporary nature of a woman's employment, together with her added domestic shift if indeed she remained at work after marriage, meant that few women had the energy for effective trade union involvement even if they saw their interest served by the unions at hand.

Ladylike Occupations

Nineteenth-century working women had an interest in well-paid employment which did not require too long an apprenticeship, so that a young single woman could build up money to bring to a marriage. Thereafter her preference was for her husband to earn enough to sustain the family, while she could manage the family budget. Since older single women with or without dependents were in a minority, and since widows and older spinsters were scarcely regarded sympathetically by popular culture, the interest of all working women was identified with a teenager who contributed to either her parents' or her own future household.[32] She was not regarded as an individual, nor as the sole support for dependents. This image of a working woman as a supplementary economic contributor was satisfactory only if a woman, on marriage, acquired a husband whose income could sustain an appropriate standard of living.

Middle-class attitudes toward dependent daughters reflected an awareness of their own economic circumstances. Their girls were educated "not to be wives, but to get husbands," according to an educational reformer of 1871, but part of the problem was that many did not marry.[33] Moreover, many families who considered themselves too genteel to allow their daughters to work in factories or as domestic servants nevertheless did not have the financial resources to support adult daughters living at home until their mid-twenties. Young middle-class single women therefore had to find an occupation which would not detract from their marriageability. Older middle-class single women, who had concluded that they would never find a man to look after them, had to use their own resources for financial support. By the middle of the nineteenth century the search for respectable employment, and for a suitable education, became a preoccupation for a large number of middle-class women, not only in England but in America and other Western countries too.

Teaching

Before the spread of business and government services opened up new and expanding employment opportunities in the late nineteenth century, middle-class women who had no means of family support considered only the occupation of governess or teacher as appropriate for their station in life. The socialization of children was traditionally women's work, and teaching in schools or a private family was but one aspect of this. A book published early in the century noted the ubiquity of schools for middle- and upper-class English girls.[34] Its author noted that a strange kind of conversational French was taught, along with dancing, needlework, singing, and music—accomplishments a lady hoped to use after her marriage. Teachers were women, usually the owners, with little training themselves. (Mary Wollstonecraft had started a girls' school in 1788.)[35] Toward the end of the eighteenth century some women became involved in various schools designed to educate not girls from their own class, but boys and girls of "the poor." Sunday schools were designed to instill religious principles and orderly habits into children and incidentally to teach them to read and write.[36] Frequently the tracts or primers used were written by women, particularly by Sarah Trimmer who also issued *Instructive Tales* to instill virtue. Hannah More, one of the bluestockings, between 1795 and 1798 issued 114 *Cheap Repository Tracts,* simple moral tales designed to teach children to read and how to behave.[37]

The curriculum at both the ladies' schools and schools for the poor was not academic. For the teachers it was a way of making income consistent with the idea that the rearing of children was women's work. Teaching was one area which nineteenth-century feminist reformers were anxious to upgrade while retaining its accessibility to women. By the middle of the century there were over twenty-one thousand female teachers and governesses and their usual pay was estimated at about £25 per year.[38] When they were too old or sick to work, they were destitute. The plight of these pathetic women, highly visible to middle- and upper-class families, led to the establishment of the Governesses' Benevolent Institution in London in 1841. Philanthropists behind this venture extended their concern to providing education for governesses in houses adjacent to the institution, and two educational establishments were founded: Queen's College, and Bedford College.

The impetus for a much broader examination of work and educational opportunities for women came from an article written by Harriet Martineau in the 1859 *Edinburgh Review*. She drew attention to the problem of "redundant women," the half-million more women than men revealed by the 1851 census. "The supposition was false," insisted Martineau, "that every woman is supported . . . by her father, her brother, or her husband."[39] Recognition of this demographic imbalance, bolstered by an acute sense of unfairness, and fortified by the prevailing middle-class liberalism, led a group of intelligent and well-connected women to found a magazine, the *English Woman's Journal*, and a Society for Promoting the Employment of Women in 1859. The journal became a forum for the dissemination of sexually egalitarian ideas: "Let a woman be permitted . . . to enter into any calling the duties of which she can adequately discharge. . . . We must acknowledge an independent self-nature in woman as in man, and a common responsibility, because a common dignity, in both." The Langham Place group, named after the location of the office of the journal and the society, argued that education, and appropriate employment, for middle-class women would benefit society at large and also enable women to be "in a better sense than they have ever been before, companions and helpmeets to men." The society sponsored a few businesses giving employment to women—the Victoria Press, for example, employing women as compositors—but hoped to encourage others to open up jobs for women, partly by pointing out, in an argument contradicting much of the *Journal*'s rhetoric, the benefits of hiring women—the most telling one being that women would accept lower wages.[40] The Langham Place ladies accomplished much in their work to improve middle-class education. Their achievement in opening up employment for middle-class women must be seen as a sequel to better educational opportunity. It was also a consequence of their educating middle-class opinion as to the respectability of women leaving the house to work for money.

Writing

One of the few other respectable jobs open to middle-class women was writing, convenient for the very reason that it could be combined with work of a domestic nature.

Even in the fifteenth century, at least one woman, Christine de Pisan, was able to earn her living through writing. One of the first early modern women who wrote for money was Aphra Behn, who lived in Restoration

London, wrote seventeen licentious plays, and was buried in Westminster Abbey in 1689. Behn's plays were performed at court, on the public stage, and in courtiers' private houses. Of mysterious parentage, she used her "handsome voluptuous countenance" to gain the patronage of King Charles II and wrote poetry in the Restoration vein:

> Down there we sat upon the Moss
> And did begin to play
> A thousand amorous tricks, to pass
> The heat of all the day.
>
> A many kisses he did give
> And I returned the same
> Which made me willing to receive
> That which I dare not name.[41]

One of the commonest outlets for women writers during the eighteenth century was the periodical. The first woman's magazine was the *Ladies' Mercury* (1693), whose publisher promised to answer "all the most nice and curious Questions concerning Love, Marriage, Behavior, Dress and Humor of the Female Sex, whether Virgins, Wives or Widows." The publisher, John Dunton, employed many women to write articles and poems, and to make translations. Titillation and sensationalism were not unknown. One series of articles was described as "Six Night Rambles of a Young Gentleman through the City, for the Detection of Lewd Women."[42]

Topics considered suitable reading for women were love, marriage, beauty, behavior toward servants, and advice on those matters. Some women's magazines reached the high circulation of six or seven thousand a year: women not only wrote for these and other magazines, but also became editors and booksellers. Dean Swift's successor as editor in 1711 of the *Examiner*, a Tory weekly, was Mrs. Mary Manley, whose political broadsides in the previous two years had led her into a much-publicized libel action. Women writers provided much of the romantic pulp serial fiction that was so attractive to the young ladies of Jane Austen's novels. This was given a boost by the establishment, around 1740, of circulating libraries or book clubs.

One of the most prominent women authors was Mrs. Radcliffe. Her *Mysteries of Udolpho* published in 1794 made £500; her next novel, *The Italian*, made £800.[43] Gothic romanticism, with wild scenery, craggy mountains, haunted medieval ruins and castles, and strange night ceremonies, riveted her readers. Henry Tilney in Austen's *Northanger Abbey* confessed to Catherine Morland,

> I have read all Mrs. Radcliffe's works, and most of them with great pleasure. The Mysteries of Udolpho, when I had once begun it, I could not lay down again; I remember finishing it in two days, my hair standing on end the whole time.[44]

Women also wrote religious tracts, and treatises urging moral reform. They were playwrights; there was little they did not do as hack writers and novelists. This occupation required a modicum of education. Many of the women writers were related to publishers who could give them employment. Several spoke out for a new perspective on women, pleading for equal recognition for women's minds and potential, and this was reflected in the proposals for girls' education in the late seventeenth and eighteenth centuries. But most women writers were simply writers, earning money and writing to please their mainly female audience. Changed economic circumstances by the middle of the nineteenth century led many of the formerly acquiescent women readers to seek both employment and education for themselves. The mode of working changed little. By the end of the century, as earlier, women writers were able to dovetail their writing into domestic work.

Work in the Service Sector: Schools, Hospitals, Shops, and Offices

By the end of the century there were many more occupations than governess or writer for the middle-class woman who by then was also able to acquire an adequate education: teaching in elementary schools had increased the number of women teachers in England, for example, by 862 percent between 1875 and 1914 (the number of men teachers increased by 291 percent). More women also taught in secondary education. The number of nurses tripled between 1861 and 1911 to seventy-seven thousand. By 1914 women shop assistants numbered half a million, the largest single group of white-collar women workers, and women clerks in government offices numbered forty thousand. In all these areas, the pay of women workers was less than men's, and varied according to previous training. In 1914, for example, a qualified woman teacher in England earned an average of £92 while her male colleague earned £127. A qualified woman head teacher earned £122, and a man in the same position £176. Nurses received about £30 per annum, with free room and board. Women shop assistants, helped by union activity, earned 75 to 80 percent of men's pay, and had wages of approximately £1 per week. Clerical pay rates varied over the country in both government and private offices, and according to the level of responsibility and skill, but for women they were generally about 70 percent of men's pay. By 1910 the average salary of women government typists was £52–68 per annum and of women telephone operators £44–67 per annum. The sex differential was greater for the few women in higher-level positions: in 1914 the women factory inspectors earned £300–400 per annum while their male counterparts earned £600–750. Some middle-class occupations therefore were remunerated at about the same rates as factory work. Nursing and shop work were not highly paid, nor was less-skilled office work. Teaching and skilled secretarial work provided higher wages for women than manual work, and offered the added benefit of greater security and regularity. In all areas, though, men's pay scales were higher than women's, and in many jobs, for instance teaching and government service, a marriage bar was in effect which prohibited married women from work.[45]

Work opportunities for single middle-class women expanded both with the extension of secondary and higher education and with the employment demands of increased governmental and industrial activity. Bureaucratic and service industries offered work for people with basic literacy and some mathematical skills. Writing continued to provide an occupation for talented women, as did other areas of the arts. Acting, for example, was regarded with ambivalence: as a possible step toward high-class prostitution as well as an exciting and rewarding professional activity.[46] Education, which by the end of the century was compulsory in most Western countries, added a means for upward social mobility to the standard one of marriage.

Identical trends were at work in the United States. By the end of the century, over 75 percent of all teachers were women, and teachers accounted for 90 percent of all professional women. Women writers were highly visible: Nathaniel Hawthorne remarked of his competition in 1855, "America is wholly given over to a damned mob of scribbling women." Women were admitted after long and frustrating struggles by intrepid pioneers like Elizabeth Blackwell in the 1840s to the practice of medicine: women's admission was a question that had been settled, wrote Dr. Mary Putnam Jacobi in 1891, even though only 115 women had in fact qualified as doctors by then. By the same date, there were two hundred women lawyers, and although many states still confined legal practice to "white male citizens" the notion of a woman practicing a profession was not totally exotic. As in Britain, women continued to work in domestic service and factories but additionally entered office work on a large scale. The 1900 census showed seventy-four thousand women employed as bookkeepers, accountants, and cashiers while one hundred thousand were stenographers, typists, or secretaries. As elsewhere in Western society, working women were predominantly single and their wages were invariably less than men's.[47]

Women as productive wage earners were more numerous in the years before World War I than ever before. However, their wage scale, the existence of a marriage bar, and their preponderance in work which required minimal training merely reinforced the widespread assumption that women's work was secondary to men's in the national economy and that their wages were only supplementary in the household economy. If the notion of women working was accepted, even by the middle class, there was still the assumption everywhere that a woman's prime responsibility was domestic, and that other functions should be subordinated to motherhood. A woman could be defined only within the context of a family. She was a daughter, a wife, a mother. Very definitely, she was not a person. This assumption was very tenacious. It was held by feminist reformers as well as by unreconstructed patriarchs. Consensus could not be reached, however, on the issue of women's sexuality. If some people were disturbed by more women in the work place, many more were agitated by women's claims for equal consideration in human relationships.

Suggestions for Further Reading

Branca, Patricia. *Silent Sisterhood: Middle-Class Women in the Victorian Home.* London, 1975.

Foner, Philip S., ed. *The Factory Girls: A Collection of Writings on Life and Struggles in the New England Factories of the 1840s.* Chicago, 1977.

Holcombe, Lee. *Victorian Ladies at Work: Middle-Class Working Women in England and Wales, 1850–1914.* Hamden, Conn., 1973.

McBride, Theresa M. *The Domestic Revolution: The Modernization of Household Service in England and France 1820–1920.* London, 1976.

Meacham, Standish. *A Life Apart: The English Working Class, 1890–1914.* London, 1977.

Scott, Joan W., and Tilly, Louise A. "Women's Work and the Family in Nineteenth Century Europe." In *The Economics of Women and Work,* edited by Alice H. Amsden. London, 1980.

Stearns, Peter N. "Working Class Women in Britain, 1890–1914." In *Suffer and Be Still: Women in the Victorian Age,* edited by Martha Vicinus. Bloomington, Ind., 1973.

CHAPTER 12

Love and Duty

Women's sexuality was an explosive issue in the nineteenth century. Middle-class advocates of women's rights used the rhetoric of equality to justify the access of middle-class women to the educational and occupational world of men. Insofar as they considered sexuality at all it was to deplore the double standard and to hope that sometime men too would observe premarital celibacy and monogamous purity. "True Womanhood" was prone to veer away from the subject altogether: an ideal woman's attributes of piety, purity, submissiveness, and domesticity scarcely allowed her to acknowledge the existence of other female qualities.[1] Marriage was still the standard shelter for women. Education and work beforehand were hard-won options, but an educated woman would use her experience mainly to be a better mother. At marriage her love was due to her husband. Legislation by the end of the century was to help protect the woman whose husband violated his marital duties, economic or sexual. Most women saw their sexuality served by marriage with a faithful provider.

However, it was impossible to avoid the subject altogether. Darwin after all had propagated the biological determinism of the survival of the fittest, and his ideas were ventilated thoroughly in discussion societies, newspapers, and magazines. By the time John Ruskin offered his romantic medieval and Rousseauesque vision of woman in the 1860s, feminists were quick to oppose it.[2] Most early feminists adopted the finite, though substantial, goal of removing the legal and formal impediments to woman's participation in public life. Toward the end of the century, however, many writers were additionally concerned about the quality of women's, and men's, private sexual relations. They discerned an essential connection between women's emancipation in public life and control over their own bodies in private relationships. The questions of prostitution, free love, birth control, and sexual pleasure were all closely related to women's reproductive role, yet open discussion and action were still penalized, either by middle-class public opinion or literally by court action.

133

Reform of the Contagious Diseases Act: Successful Activism

The unease of middle-class feminists in Britain was thrown into relief by the campaign to repeal the Contagious Diseases Acts of the late 1860s, a campaign which successfully ended in their suspension in 1883 and repeal in 1886. The acts were designed to check venereal disease within the British armed forces by providing for the compulsory surgical examination of women thought to be prostitutes in the vicinity of barracks, and the detention of those women found to be diseased on the authority of the examining surgeon rather than by order of a magistrate. At the end of 1869 an association was formed of a large proportion of Quaker women and a few others who had already made a mark by outstanding individual achievement: Mary Carpenter, who had pioneered in the treatment of juvenile delinquency, for example, and Florence Nightingale, who had become a folk hero through her nursing work in the Crimean War. The campaign leader was Josephine Butler, wife of the principal of a boy's public school, who had a reputation as a reclaimer of fallen women in Liverpool, and had also been involved in educational reform, the suffrage movement, and efforts to change the law regarding married women's property. The campaigners argued that certain women were robbed of civil rights only by the judgment of the policeman taking the women into custody; that the state regulation of vice implied state support for vice; and that only women, rather than their male customers too, were being regulated. The campaigners were not as much concerned by the existence or spread of venereal disease itself.[3] Butler used the occasion of the Colchester by-election in 1870, where a strong supporter of the acts was a government candidate, to visit the constituency with her reformers, address gatherings, and canvass. The result was a defeat for the government candidate, and a royal commission was established to investigate the working of the acts. Butler's testimony there was most impressive, and after further agitation the acts were suspended in 1883. Her main achievement was to destroy the hold of the double moral standard on "thoughtful and serious people," and "the position of women in regard to sex questions began at last to improve."[4] Butler's success was singular because it involved direct political action both at the constituency level and in parliament. By contrast, most of the middle-class feminists eschewed contacts outside their class and assigned low priority to any discussion of sexuality.[5]

Sex and Socialism: Parity and Priorities

This inhibition of upper- and middle-class women suffragists, anxious not to alienate respectable public opinion, was not at all shared by members of radical and socialist groups drawing inspiration from Robert Owen, William Thompson, Charles Knowlton, and Marx, Engels, and Bebel.[6] All these writers undermined the notion of the passive dependent woman as the natural female. They argued that women were products of an unfavorable environment and that when the environment changed, so would the women. Owen was not against marriage, but felt that a marriage should last only so long as love between the partners. A woman should have access to a means of livelihood, and children's support should be provided by the community. Divorce would then be a realistic prospect for women, as well as men, who no longer wished to live with their spouse.[7] His son Robert Dale Owen similarly wished to provide a sound basis of mutual respect and enjoyment for marriage, by his advocacy of birth control; William Thompson urged birth control as a means to relieve the dependency of women on men, and Charles Knowlton helped publicize in America some of the specific birth control methods that Richard Carlile in England had advocated in 1826.[8] Later socialists were much more inclined to advocate exclusively economic change as a means to change the status of women. They considered that the public oppression of the workers was paralleled by the private oppression in the family of women, and that the private oppression could only be remedied when economic changes in the ownership of the means of production had changed the distribution of power in the state. Engels in 1884 wrote in *Origins of the Family, Private Property and the State,*

> the determining factor in history is . . . the production and reproduction of the immediate essentials of life. This . . . is of a two-fold character. On the one side, the production of the means of existence, articles of food and clothing, dwellings and of the tools necessary for that production; on the other side, the production of human beings themselves, the propagation of the species.

He, like Marx, considered that the patriarchal monogamous family was the result of the private ownership of property, and that this type of family would disappear when private property disappeared. "The predominance of man in marriage is simply a consequence of his economic predominance and will vanish with it automatically."[9] August Bebel, in *Woman Under Socialism*, first published in Germany in 1879, concurred that man's oppression in the work force and women's in the home were two aspects of the same problem, but in two respects he was more practical than Marx or Engels. First, Bebel suggested how women's domestic oppression might be transformed: through provision of communal kitchens and nurseries, for example. Second, he did not assume that domestic subordination would automatically vanish when appropriate economic changes occurred. "Women have as little to hope from men as the workmen from the middle classes." Bebel considered that women themselves had to take responsibility for their own liberation. Their reward, like men's, would be life in a socialist society where all activities, including lovemaking, would be between free equals.[10]

Communes: Experimental Living

The idea that cooperative communal living arrangements would benefit all people, women as well as men, was a theory which was tested in practice many times during the nineteenth century. Utopian communities were found in all countries, but over five hundred flourished in America, where there seemed endless room for the pursuit of happiness. In his textile mills at New Lanark, near Glasgow, industrialist Robert Owen had already attempted to create a model environment for his employees and families by promoting education and social welfare, but he moved to the United States in order to spread the benefits of new social arrangements to a wider community. He bought a village and twenty thousand surrounding acres on the Wabash River in Indiana and named it New Harmony. He advertised for settlers sympathetic to his ideas of living in freedom from traditional institutions. Nine hundred responded. On 4 July 1826, Owen delivered "A Declaration of Mental Independence" and identified three main enemies of the happy life: "private or individual property, absurd and irrational systems of religion, and marriage founded upon individual property." Owen's solution was to redefine marriage. At his community's early marriage ceremonies, the couple stood, held hands, and declared, "I, A.B., do agree to take this man/woman to be my husband/wife, and declare that I submit to any other ceremony upon this occasion only in conformity with the laws of the State." The woman did not promise to obey the husband and neither party vowed to love until separation at death. Divorce was possible after a trial separation and child support was the responsibility of the community.[11]

New Harmony was regarded by Owen as only a halfway house toward his ideal community, which promoted communal living and working arrangements accommodating "scientific associations of men, women and children . . . arranged to be as one family" in groups ranging from four hundred to two thousand. Architectural plans were drawn in the manner of a self-sufficient medieval castle. There was a single continuous structure containing gymnasiums, schools, a library, ballrooms, theaters, museums, a brewery, a bakery, and laundries, as well as living quarters. Each couple would occupy a lodging room and have no more than two children, who would live with parents until aged three, when they would live in the community nursery. This requirement was put into effect at New Harmony. People ate in the communal dining hall and domestic tasks were performed collectively. Sarah Cox later wrote of her childhood experience that she saw her parents only twice in two years. Owen had to admit failure after three years. "Families trained in the individual system, founded as it is upon superstition, have not acquired those moral qualities of forebearance and charity for each other which are necessary to promote full confidence and harmony among all the members, and without which Communities cannot exist."[12]

Owen was concerned to banish the notion that a woman was the private property of a man, and Owenite communities were frequently attacked for promoting free love and promiscuity. Such charges were usually founded more upon the writings of the leaders than on the actual practice of residents, but there was one famous settlement where sexual experimentation was actively engaged in for more than thirty years. Oneida in New York state was founded in 1847 by John Humphrey Noyes, an enthusiastic modifier of Fourier's ideas of communal living. Noyes did not advocate promiscuity. Although his invention of "complex marriage" at Oneida theoretically regarded each male as married to each female, sexual intercourse was firmly disciplined and regulated. Only Noyes, as leader of the community, could designate which couples could cohabit and when. Women could initiate requests. In other areas of Oneida's life women and men worked at all tasks side by side. "Loving companionship in labor, and especially the mingling of the sexes, makes labor more attractive." Children were given the father's surname if it was known. Visitors were impressed by the health and happiness of both old and young members of the community, which was singular not only in allowing a real measure of sexual equality, but also in Noyes's experiments in controlled breeding.[13]

Fellowship of the New Life: Comradeship

Utopian communities were elite laboratories for new social and sexual arrangements; artists too were showing how a new woman might live. Karl Marx's daughter Eleanor translated Ibsen into English, and *A Doll's House* was read by enthusiasts along with Olive Schreiner's *Story of an African Farm* and the plays of George Bernard Shaw. One London society providing a forum for discussions of women's sexuality was the Fellowship of the New Life, which wished to promote "a perfect character in each and all, through the subordination of material things to spiritual."[14] Hannah Mitchell, a working-class suffragette, eventually a city councillor and magistrate, wrote in her autobiography that it was the "newer ideas which were being propounded by the Socialists" which impelled her to marry in 1895. She remembered that "men and women were talking of marriage as a comradeship, rather than a state where the woman was subservient to, and dependent on, the man."[15] Socialist activists however were not always anxious to divert energy from the strictly political objectives of either revolution or parliamentary representation. H. M. Hyndman, founder of the Marxist Social Democratic Federation, was opposed to women's rights and his associate Belfort Bax was antifeminist enough to be a member of the Men's Anti-Suffrage League.[16] Still, other members of the Social Democratic Federation were strong feminists, like Annie Besant, and it was generally within the socialist organizations that much of the debate on the subject of women in a new society took place.[17]

Such discussion drew extensively on the new publications of Havelock Ellis. Ellis, founder member of the Fellowship of the New Life, was a doctor who worked through many organizations for a more enlightened attitude toward sexual matters. He wrote numerous popular and encyclopedic reference books to further his cause. He stressed the value and importance of sex in people's lives, and the pleasure to be derived from it, for both men and women. Ellis's assertion that "the female responds to the stimulation of the male at the right moment just as the tree responds to the stimulation of the warmest days in spring" was the basis for Marie Stopes's later plea for a husband to stir his "chaste partner to physical love."[18] Stopes's *Married Love*, published in 1918, was a remarkable book, not least in being written by a thirty-eight-year-old virgin, and was considered one of the most influential books of the early twentieth century.[19] The message of *Married Love* and its two sequels, *Wise Parenthood* (1918) and *Radiant Motherhood* (1920), was that a woman, no less than her husband, experienced sexual desire which should be gratified within marriage independently of procreation. At the same time, motherhood was a glorious experience which no suitable woman should miss.

Birth control should be used for two main purposes: to reduce the dangers of excessive childbearing for the individual mother, and for "the creation of a New and Irradiated Race."[20] Eugenics was both an inspiration for, and a deliberate outcome of, Stopes's advocacy of birth control.

Eugenics and Birth Control

Eugenics was a cause which some of the middle-class feminists could support. Its creator, Francis Galton, cousin of Charles Darwin, believed in selective breeding for the human race. He and other supporters, including Ellis, argued that eugenics would work fruitfully to solve the problems of feeblemindedness, criminality, and even unemployment.[21] Nineteenth-century free love advocates were strong supporters of eugenics, believing with the American free lover Lilian Harman that the state had hitherto "barred the way of evolution" since it had rendered "natural selection impossible, by holding together the mismated."[22] John Humphrey Noyes systematically directed selective breeding in his Oneida community. The resultant "stirps" (named from Galton's designation of the raising of offspring of matched parents as stirpiculture) were later interviewed by an anthropologist who believed them physically and intellectually superior, and generally happy.[23] Marie Stopes wrote that a child "conceived in beauty" where both parents had an "ardent and wonderful experience" would have a physical advantage over children born of "blind" or "coerced" motherhood.[24]

Because of the early identification of birth control with eugenics, socialists regarded contraception with suspicion. Guy Aldred expressed his opposition to birth control this way:

> An economic disease (poverty), its remedy is not individual, but social; not racial, but class; not a question of birth-rate, but one of wealth distribution; not lack of production, but fluctuation in existence.[25]

The standard socialist view was that birth control was proposed by the capitalist establishment as a preferred alternative to redistribution of wealth, or social reform. Socialist energies should be channeled to the acquisition of higher wages for the male wage earner, so the adult woman need not be involved in productive labor.[26] Changes in woman's status in society could be deferred until after economic reorganization. The presumption of the automatic disappearance of inequality reduced the need for socialists to consider separately the condition of women in society, but many working-class women, socialist and others, did not find this dismissive attitude satisfactory.

Birth control could be interpreted as social control. When Annie Besant and Charles Bradlaugh stood trial for their reissue of Knowlton's 1832 book, *The Fruits of Philosophy,* Besant argued that birth control was indeed a "path from poverty for the poor."[27] But birth control could also be seen as personal control of the means of reproduction. As such it could be attractive to women in the general sense, as an expression of self-determination and autonomy, and in the pragmatic sense of relief from physical strains of involuntary pregnancy and the usual concomitant strains of the domestic management of a larger family. However, both approaches were not universally welcomed by women.

Many nineteenth-century feminists were worried that women might neglect their natural maternal duties if they had the option to decline maternity: they also believed that birth control, through prophylactic devices associated with prostitution, was an unnatural practice from which men, but not women, would experience pleasure.[28] Poorer women frequently saw no sensible alternative to using their reproductive capacity in bearing and rearing several children who would bring wages into the family economy.[29] Not until the twentieth century, with the advent of public social services to substitute for services formerly provided by children, was there more acceptance of birth control as a positive development for women.

Marie Stopes undoubtedly helped promote a less censorious attitude toward sexual pleasure both through her books and her clinic, and through the publicity surrounding the 1923 trial at which she sued a critic who had charged her with "exposing the poor to experiment" for libel.[30] The confusion of so many issues concerning sex—eugenics and social engineering, male sexual indulgence, female sexual pleasure, control over reproduction, the economic value of children, not to mention attitudes of organized churches—retarded the acceptance of birth control within Western society. In predominantly Roman Catholic countries contraceptive information was difficult to obtain even in the 1970s. In the United States, Stopes's contemporary Margaret Sanger experienced similar difficulties. On both sides of the Atlantic widespread knowledge about contraception came only when medical doctors were persuaded to support it and when it was removed from the arena of radical causes and became a measure of planned parenthood within the family.[31] Large-membership voluntary associations as well as charismatic and eccentric leadership helped achieve accessibility of information and devices for women and men, but arguments about reproductive control continued until well after World War II.

The notion that a woman should manage her own fertility through the technology available to her, through contraceptive devices and abortion, was a radical idea at the beginning of the twentieth century. Orthodox medical opinion continued to reflect the Victorian morality which denied positive sexual feelings in women and which required sexual abstinence as the only legitimate birth control. Dr. William Acton's popular medical textbook announced through its many editions that

> the majority of women (happily for them) are not very much troubled with sexual feelings of any kind. What men are habitually, women are only exceptionally.[32]

Professor Anne Louise McIlroy, a gynecologist in London, during the 1923 Stopes trial, advocated abstinence rather than contraception as a means of birth control.[33] Yet there were signs that the medical profession did not totally subscribe to these views, and in addition, signs that women themselves did not take them altogether to heart either.

Female Sexuality: Passive or Active?

The author of *The Physical Life of Woman: Advice to the Maiden, Wife and Mother*, Dr. George Napheys, denounced women who "plume themselves on their repugnance or their distaste for their conjugal obligations" and was convinced that women had sexual feelings which ought to be cultivated rather than suppressed. Over sixty thousand copies of his book were printed after 1869. This alternative view is dramatically reinforced by Dr. Clelia Mosher's work on women's sexuality in the 1890s, when she used detailed information collected from forty-five respondents to gather data about the sexual behavior and attitudes of upper-middle-class American women. These women said they experienced desire for sexual intercourse independently of their husbands' interest; they experienced orgasm "sometimes," "usually," or "always"; and most of them thought love, rather than procreation, was a sufficient justification for sex.[34] It would be as unwise to generalize from this limited sample as it is to draw conclusions from the vast amount of prescriptive literature on Victorian sexual behavior, but this survey is a useful corrective to the pronouncements of male medical authors and middle-class feminists whose interests could not, they thought, be served by any emphasis on the biological functions of women. Doctors on the whole wished to preserve the status quo, with its subordination of women, while the feminists' major concern was to prove the intellectual, rather than the bodily, capabilities of their sex.

The feminists' aversion was also one of priorities. When Havelock Ellis and Marie Stopes romanticized sexuality in women, they also implied, and in some cases explicitly stated, that without a healthy heterosexual sex life a woman would not be fulfilled. Ellis denounced the unemancipated woman as a cross between an angel and an idiot, but saw the new woman only in terms of practicing "conscious eugenics" in the context of a "new reverence and care for motherhood."[35] Stopes's and Ellis's new woman was married. Nineteenth-century feminists were much more concerned about the single woman; although some feminist causes concerned married women, it was generally on behalf of those whose husbands had not measured up. Early feminists, like the socialists, were primarily concerned with the economic and public aspects of existence. It was later generations of feminists, as of socialists, who extended the debate to questions of the quality of all aspects of life, and to what was considered to be the private sphere.

Suggestions for Further Reading

Degler, Carl N. "What Ought To Be and What Was." *American Historical Review* 79 (1974):1467–90.
Gordon, Linda. *Woman's Body, Woman's Right: A Social History of Birth Control in America.* New York, 1976.
Hall, Ruth. *Marie Stopes.* London, 1978.
McLaren, Angus. *Birth Control in Nineteenth Century England: A Social and Intellectual History.* London, 1978.
Muncy, Raymond Lee. *Sex and Marriage in Utopian Communities.* Baltimore, Md., 1974.
Rover, Constance. *Love, Morals and the Feminists.* London, 1970.

CHAPTER 13

Progress and Reform

The idea of progress galvanized many Victorians into action. It encouraged industrialists to search out increased efficiency through new technology and organization. It fired the civic pride of governments, small and large, to provide extensive modern services for their populations. Allied with traditional Christian and humanitarian notions of charity it created an atmosphere of optimism and confidence that a better life was possible through public and private intervention. In the ranks of society susceptible to this enthusiasm, women could share an initial exhilaration which could develop into subsequent bitterness that so much of the benefit of progress was selectively available only to men.

During the nineteenth century there were many attempts, often successful, to reduce the gap between possibility and actuality. Because they were initiated largely by individuals with specific objectives, their results were limited. The most successful attempts to bring the fruits of progress to women were first, those which contributed to a firmer image of the adult woman married to a faithful provider and protector: a woman with superior moral qualities who was able to pass on her virtues to her children. Second, reforms were achieved which helped alleviate hardship among women who, through no fault of their own, suffered from inadequate protection. Efforts to improve education, both in secondary schools and universities, were successful. For women who would marry, their education would help them to be better mothers, and for women without husbands, education would fit them for appropriate nondegrading employment. Similarly, the Married Women's Property Acts allowed married women whose husbands misappropriated the trust placed in them access to their own property and assets. Reform efforts which conformed less obviously to the ideal of a Victorian lady were less successful. The suffrage movement, in a conservative sense, merely gave civic recognition to the virtues of a superior morality permeating the body politic, and in that sense it was not at odds with the prevailing masculine code. On the other hand, it would give a vote to an individual independently of the family structure. The Victorians were not about to surrender without struggle the notion of a woman defined only in relation to her family.

Factory Legislation: Paternalist Concern

Middle- and upper-class women were largely both the participants in and the beneficiaries of the voluntary associations and legislative reforms concerning women in the nineteenth century. However, some reforms were passed also for working-class women whose own reactions were mixed. Two of the most publicized efforts were the protective legislation acts concerning the length of the working day in the textiles industry, which culminated in England in the acts of 1844, 1847, 1850, and 1853, and secondly, agitation concerning the underground employment of women in the mines, which was prohibited by an act of 1842. Lord Ashley (known after 1851 as earl of Shaftesbury) was involved in both reforms. Suffering and cruelty were anathema to him, and he wished to reduce the length of the working day, which before 1844 was twelve or sixteen hours.[1] Concern for the health of the women and children working such long hours, often on a night shift, motivated reformers, rather than the general desire to support the (male) cotton operatives' demand for a ten-hour day. A reduced working day required enforcement by government factory inspectors to ensure that machinery in a factory was physically halted after ten hours. Without these concomitant steps, protective legislation could not be effective. Both points were eventually written into legislation, but not without resistance from the women themselves. In a letter to the local newspaper, "The Female Operatives of Todmorden" responded to a suggestion in 1832 that all women should be excluded from "manufactories":

> It is a lamentable fact, that, in these parts of the country, there is scarcely any other mode of employment for female industry, if we except servitude and dressmaking. Of the former of these, there is no chance of employment for one-twentieth of the candidates that would rush into the field, to say nothing of lowering the wages of our sisters of the same craft; and of the latter, galling as some of the hardships of manufactories are (of which the indelicacy of mixing with the men is not the least) yet there are few women who have been so employed, that would change conditions with the ill-used little slaves, who have to lose sleep and health, in catering to the whims and frivolities of the butter-flies of fashion. . . . We put it seriously to you, whether, as you have deprived us of our means of earning our bread, you are not bound to point out a more eligible and suitable employment for us?[2]

Similarly, women employed in the mining industry were ambivalent about Ashley's legislation. He had urged a royal commission to enquire into children's work in mines and manufactures, but these terms of reference were extended to include the work of all women in mines as well. The report was published in 1842, and was illustrated by sketches drawn of the women and children at work. The pictures and prose together horrified public opinion. The women who worked underground, transporting coal along the passages, were graphically described:

black, saturated with wet, and more than half naked, crawling upon their hands and feet, and dragging their heavy loads behind them—they present an appearance indescribably disgusting and unnatural.

The commission heard many complaints about the work from the women, yet as workers they did not want to be excluded from this work because they had no alternative. In areas where factory, rather than mine, work was available, women preferred that.[3] Civilized society was affronted by the revelations of this report. Subsequent legislation concerning apprenticeship, machine safety, and boys' work was vigorously debated in parliament, but the requirement to exclude women from underground mining work was passed without disagreement. Ashley's appeal in the Commons in 1842 clearly fell on receptive ears:

> they are rendered unfit for the duties of women by overwork, and become utterly demoralized. In the male the moral effects of the system are very sad, but in the female they are infinitely worse. . . . It is bad enough if you corrupt the man, but if you corrupt the woman, you poison the waters of life at the very fountain.[4]

Ashley the philanthropist could not tolerate the horror of the unnatural sight of women miners. Neither he nor the parliamentary majorities considered it their responsibility to improve general working conditions in the mines, nor to provide more acceptable work for the women. He achieved his very specific objective of ending the labor of women and of young children underground.

Factory legislation, however general the agreement on the unsuitability of certain conditions for women, contradicted the Victorian ethos of laissez faire liberalism. It represented state intervention against the freedom of the manufacturer to produce his goods according to a free market.[5] Acts of parliament regulating conditions of work were rare and haphazardly enforced until trade unions and welfare-minded political parties helped change the climate of opinion toward the end of the nineteenth century. The Victorian social conscience preferred to alleviate suffering on the individual level, and in the realm of private philanthropy women both participated and experienced relief.

Philanthropy: Ladies Bountiful

Dispensing charity to the poor had long been an acceptable activity for women. In rural society it was centered on the parish and in Roman Catholic countries it was almost monopolized by the church. In nineteenth-century New England the social life of women revolved around charitable societies designed to sponsor missionaries, for ministers' education, temperance, and later in the century, more secular causes too.[6] In England women were rarely officers in charitable societies, but a network of ladies' auxiliaries was managed by women themselves. Women's involvement was concentrated in charities benefiting women: the Society for the Suppression of Vice, for instance, counted 31 percent women subscribers, and the Friendly Female Society for the relief of poor aged widows and single women listed 88 percent of its five hundred subscribers in 1803 as women.[7] Already in the early nineteenth century, in most church-related charities, women accounted for roughly 12 percent of subscribers and contributed about the same proportion to the funds. In those designed specifically to help women, women too held office, exercising management skills to which John Stuart Mill referred in 1861: "there are few of the administrative functions of government for which a person would not be fit, who is fit to bestow charity usefully."[8] Day-to-day charity work belonged almost exclusively to women—visiting work, establishing soup kitchens, hospitals, lying-in asylums, and so on.

Pity and self-interest combined to promote two kinds of charity work in particular: homes for reclaimed prostitutes, and training schools for domestic servants. In London alone in the 1850s there were about thirty rehabilitative homes for prostitutes, work in which the future prime minister William Ewart Gladstone was directly involved. Societies like the British Society for the Encouragement of Faithful Female Servants attempted to place poor girls in advantageous positions, and other societies like the Invalid Asylum for Respectable Families provided a home for sick servants formerly employed in wealthy families. Involvement in charities gave upper- and middle-class women the opportunity to work away from their families and the chance to meet other women socially, and they could also feel useful in alleviating suffering.[9] So central was this activity for women that Mrs. Beeton's *Complete Letter-Writer* included a standard model letter, "from a lady inviting another to aid a charity."

The prodigal philanthropist dispensing a personal income for particular projects was a common Victorian type. Women too can be found in this role. In 1837 Angela Burdett-Coutts was the granddaughter and heiress of the founder of Coutts's bank at the age of twenty-three. Her fortune gave her an annual income of £80,000 and she chose not to marry young but to make benevolence her life work. In this she had the assistance of Charles Dickens, who advised her on worthy causes, and extended her interests beyond church affairs. Not only did she respond to others' requests, she originated her own activities, and included among her interests education, fallen women, housing, emigration, child welfare, and urban redevelopment. On Dickens's suggestion she patronized the Ragged School Union, a system of day and evening elementary instruction for neglected street children, which by 1861 attracted an average day attendance of twenty-five thousand at its 176 schools. Burdett-Coutts presided over her own Destitute Children's Dinner Society, started as an auxiliary of the Westminster Ragged School, and was a main founder of the 1884 Society for the Prevention of Cruelty to Children. She established a garden suburb in north London, the Holly Village. She assisted unemployed artisans to emigrate to Australia and Canada and helped finance Livingstone's African exploration. She obtained full recognition for this work, becoming a peer in her own right, and given the freedom of the city of London.[10] This remarkable woman who undoubtedly improved the life of thousands of individuals opposed the women's suffrage movement.[11] Like Queen Victoria, who deprecated "this mad wicked folly of women's rights," she acknowledged no inconsistency between her own extraordinary exercise of public power, and her traditional view that other women should fulfill exclusively marital and maternal duties.

Social Work: From Philanthropy to Reform

There were other economically secure and well-born women who pioneered in social service as a deliberately chosen alternative to marriage, including Florence Nightingale and Octavia Hill. Nightingale wrote *Cassandra* at the age of thirty-two, in 1852. She later submitted it for comment to some of the most celebrated male intellectuals of the day, who counseled against publication of such a passionate and heretical document.[12] *Cassandra* is a protest against the society which confined women to the bounds of a family. In her view the family

> is too narrow a field for the development of an immortal spirit, be that spirit male or female. The chances are a thousand to one that, in that small sphere, the task for which that immortal spirit is destined by the qualities and the gifts which its Creator has placed within it, will not be found.[13]

Nightingale herself escaped family boundaries to train as a nurse at a model Prussian hospital at Kaiserswerth and in Paris. She used her family connections in the government to arrange for her appointment to the front during the Crimean War, and afterward spent her career training nurses professionally and working for the improvement of public health.

Octavia Hill learned about housing conditions through her experience with teaching toy making to Ragged School children. Her first venture into urban development came when she persuaded her friend John Ruskin to spend some of his money refurbishing run-down houses for poor families. She considered that an improved environment would lead to an improved character: "I think my particular plan has been that of improving tenants in old houses," she noted in 1882. This was achieved by the additional agency of volunteer rent collectors, women Hill trained to use their weekly rent call as an opportunity for productive social work with the tenants. Hill described in 1877 the value of the visitor:

> You, who know so much more than they, might help them so much at important crises of their lives. You might gladden their homes by bringing them flowers, or, better still, by teaching them to grow plants; you might meet them face to face as friends; you might teach them; you might collect their savings; you might sing for and with them; you might take them into the parks, or out for quiet days in the country, in small companies, or to your own or your friends' grounds, or to exhibitions or picture galleries; you might teach and refine them and make them cleaner by merely going among them.[14]

By the early 1880s nearly two thousand persons were living in accommodations administered by her system.[15]

Both Nightingale and Hill declined to support women's suffrage. John Stuart Mill could not persuade Nightingale to sign the first 1866 petition for it:

despite her private tirade in *Cassandra,* she wrote in 1858 that she was "brutally indifferent" to the rights and wrongs of her sex.[16] Hill opposed suffrage work, because she considered that more pressing, charitable work needed to be done. Hill was alert to the paradox of women being politically active in the antisuffrage campaign: she refused to sign an antisuffrage letter to the press in 1910, pointing out that "the very thing which makes me feel how fatal it would be for women to be drawn into the political arena precludes my signing the letter, and joining in what must be a political campaign."[17]

Contrasting with these exceptional women, who saw no advantage for themselves or their sex in political representation, was the attitude of the American social worker Jane Addams. She, like them, learned of poverty and suffering among people in urban squalor; she, like them, spent a lifetime working to improve social conditions. But Addams used her experience to draw attention to both the justice and the usefulness of women's vote. From 1906 on, Addams's argument was that the modern city performed functions which had formerly been an integral part of women's reproductive responsibilities: the cleaning, feeding, sheltering, educating, and general nurture of the family. The political system needed input from women, who could contribute their long-standing expertise. Further, the women themselves could not properly continue to care for their families if they paid no attention to the officials and institutions who now were responsible for urban design, housing, clean water, proper sanitation, good education, and so on.[18] Possibly the difference between her and the "Lady with the Lamp" was one of generations. Addams once commented that her settlement houses, located in slum areas where novice middle-class social workers lived among the people they wished to help, turned a generation of young Americans from philanthropists to reformers.[19] The difference was also one of attitude toward state action: should the state intervene to promote well-being? Or should the state merely enable individuals to practice self-help and Christian charity?

Education: Universal Elementary and Limited Secondary Expansion

Few of the women who first advocated reforms in women's educational opportunities looked to legislation for help. Rather than have the state provide secondary schools, middle-class reformers chose to establish private schools which could be supported by fee-paying parents and from endowments. By the late 1860s their ideas were coming to fruition, building on the philanthropic foundation of the Governesses' Benevolent Institution of 1841. Frederick Dennison Maurice, a Christian socialist clergyman, considered that training was needed to upgrade the skills of governesses so that they could command improved salaries, and he arranged series of lectures for this purpose. These lectures were frequently given in the evening so that women who worked during the day could attend. The program evolved into the two institutions, Queen's College and Bedford College in London, whose students provided the core of teachers and activists for the next generation. Two graduates of Maurice's lectures, Miss Buss and Miss Beale, founded North London Collegiate School and Cheltenham Ladies' College in the 1850s. Their curricula showed what could be done, and together with Emily Davies, who was concerned to provide university education for women, they arranged for their students to be examined by the same external examiners as boys in secondary schools. In 1871 a trust was established which brought academic secondary education to girls in middle-class suburbs: the Girls' Public Day School Trust (GPDST) was established.[20] These schools became the prototype for other private trusts and academic education for girls at last became a realistic option for thousands of middle-class girls all over England.

At the same time, women's colleges were established at Oxford and Cambridge. Provincial universities admitted women as students. The establishment in 1870 and 1880 of free, compulsory education for all children created large numbers of jobs for these new women high school and university graduates. The admission of women to academic curricula and universities was not accomplished without a struggle. At Oxford, for example, women were not allowed to graduate with a degree, even though they sat the examinations and were evaluated, until 1919.[21] However, the notion of secondary and higher education for women was not totally at variance even with Ruskin's view of woman. The majority of women university graduates married and thereafter confined themselves to domestic tasks, including rearing their children. Most of those who remained single earned their living by teaching children in the classroom. As late as 1977 a historian of women at Cambridge could observe that their education provided "an extension of women's traditional role" in that teaching "has become the kind of accepted pastime that *petit point* was previously."[22] This was what the early campaigners for academic education for girls anticipated. Woman's "inalienable rights and privileges" (which should include a solid education) "are distinct from, and in no wise interfere with, her due observance of the duties arising from the subordinate station she occupies on earth, in relation to men," wrote sisters Emily Sherriff and Maria Grey, two founders of the GPDST.[23] They did not expect that better education would contradict the traditional roles of women. They believed simply that education would equip women to perform those roles in the modern world.

In nineteenth-century America, the spread of educational opportunity for girls was more democratic and at an earlier date. Already by 1787 one leading school, the Young Ladies' Academy of Philadelphia, offered to girls of wealthy parents grammar, arithmetic, geography, and oratory, a curriculum very similar to that offered to boys who expected to be the next generation's leading businessmen and professionals.[24] In the 1820s, other prominent girls' schools offered academic instruction: Emma Willard's in Troy, New York (in a different area of town from the collar factories), and Catherine Beecher's in Hartford, Connecticut. All these schools, which broke with tradition by explicitly training the intellect, were designed for the daughters of wealthy families. A year's study at Troy, for instance, cost two hundred dollars in the 1820s. An equally significant initiative came in 1837, when Mary Lyon inaugurated "an era in female education" by founding Mount Holyoke Female Seminary in South Hadley, Massachusetts. Its distinction was to finance instruction not so much from fees as from endowments drawn from "the Christian public": fees charged were sixty dollars a year.[25] The majority of Mount Holyoke's graduates themselves became school teachers, and public provision for teacher training also proceeded in the years before the Civil War. The new frontier territories and states kept up an increasing demand for teachers in coeducational schools. The swift expansion of elementary education, together with the academic training of teachers to staff the new public schools, was responsible for the dramatic finding of the 1850 census: over 87 percent of all white women in America aged twenty years or older could read and write. There was only a marginal difference in literacy between men and women. This was in marked contrast to prerevolutionary American society, where women were only half as literate as men.[26] Finally, by the 1860s, as state universities were established by legislatures, more often than not they admitted women as students to general courses of study if not to the professional schools. Women however were not made particularly welcome. In the last third of the century several women's colleges were founded (Vassar, 1865; Smith and Wellesley, 1875; Bryn Mawr, 1880) deliberately to attract wealthy students who wished to pursue academically rigorous education undiverted by doubts of its suitability for women.[27]

In the countries of continental Europe, impetus for the establishment and expansion of girls' education came largely from autocratic institutions and governments, rather than from enlightened individuals or advocates of women's rights. Provision of all levels of education was inspired economically by industrialization, and ideologically by nationalism. Education was seen as a necessary preparation for a country's inhabitants to contribute to the power of a nation-state; mechanical skills of reading, writing, and arithmetic were augmented by instruction in elementary vocational skills and in national values as illustrated in the country's history. Compulsory primary education for both sexes was rare at the beginning of the nineteenth century, but by the end was widespread. In the Protestant countries of northern and eastern Europe, education was generally controlled by the state; and in the Roman Catholic countries, the church educated girls in convents. In France, however, governments tended to be anticlerical and suspicious of the political outlook of the church hierarchy, and in 1881 the Ferry government instituted free, compulsory, and secular primary education for girls as well as boys. Secondary education in Europe was confined to the daughters of fee-paying upper-class families, and although higher education was not prohibited to women (indeed, Swiss universities admitted women at the same time as the more progressive American universities: Zurich in 1864 and Berne in 1873) the number of graduates was few. The provision of women's education in America proceeded slowly but there were nevertheless more opportunities there at the end of the nineteenth century than elsewhere.[28]

Legal Rights: Property and Identity

America also furnished the first successful campaign to undermine common law principles concerning the dependence of a married woman. Reformers wished to remedy the hardship which occurred when husbands reneged on their responsibilities. In common law, a husband was supposed to provide material support to his wife and children and to be their legal representative. To enable him to do this, the common law had allowed him to utilize any property his wife might bring to the marriage. He controlled the income from her real property (land), and her personal property (property other than land, including any wages she might earn) became his absolute possession, to dispose of as he chose. Families with large assets were concerned to protect daughters whose husbands used the bride's property irresponsibly. Since Tudor times a legal practice known as the marriage settlement, protected by equity law courts, had become commonplace for the wealthy. Before marriage, a trust would be established whereby real and personal property would be designated as the wife's separate property, relatively free from the husband's common law rights of possession or control. The trustee was generally obliged to carry out the terms of the trust or act according to the married woman's instructions. Nineteenth-century reformers wished to allow married women to own and control in person any property they might have. Further, they sought to make this principle applicable to all women, not just those few whose families were wealthy enough to make marriage settlements in equity worthwhile.

Agitation to let married women hold their own property started as early as 1836 when Ernestine Rose petitioned the state of New York. In 1840 she personally addressed committees of the New York assembly and was able to generate support from reformers in favor of women's rights and also from men who wished to preserve daughters' property from improvident sons-in-law.[29] Minor reforms resulted in 1848 and other New England states passed favorable legislation also. However, a full-fledged campaign did not come until after the 1848 Seneca Falls convention mobilized the opinion of women activists about property laws, and Susan B. Anthony, a recent recruit to temperance work, used her considerable organizing talents in support of women's rights reform. She drew up a petition addressed to the New York assembly advocating control by women of their own earnings, and chose sixty women, one from each county in the state, to serve as "captains" in the campaign to get signatures. In ten weeks during the winter of 1854 they gathered six thousand signatures, women traveling alone, with little or no money and only the flimsiest of social networks to sustain them. The next year Anthony was on the road four months, spending $2,291 and collecting $2,367. Her colleague Elizabeth Cady Stanton addressed a joint judiciary committee of both legislative houses. There was a delayed success. In 1860 a law was passed giving women the right to own property, to joint guardianship of children, to collect their own wages, and to sue in court.[30]

In Britain during the 1850s, reformers wrote books, pamphlets, entertained jurists and politicians, and sent petitions to parliament. They talked of justice for the poor as well as the rich, and drew attention to the deplorable irresponsibility of many husbands who squandered their wives' property or earnings, often on drink. Opponents of the first Married Women's Property Bill of 1857 argued that women themselves did not wish to be placed in a "strongminded and independent position." The bill was dropped at that time, not because of such opposition, but because simultaneously the 1857 Divorce Act was passed. This transferred the administration of judicial separations and absolute divorces from the ecclesiastical courts and parliament itself to a new secular Court of Divorce and Matrimonial Causes. The act included a clause which allowed a separated or divorced woman full possession and control of her own property. Conservatives could now argue that injured wives were adequately protected. Ten years later agitation resumed, this time to allow all wives access to their own property. Full-scale debates in parliament clearly separated the conservatives, who feared this was the thin end of the wedge to promote total independence for women, from the liberals, who cited cases of husbands mistreating wives. The liberals differed in turn from the radicals, who welcomed their view of equality of the sexes in the words of Shaw Lefevre:

> Let them have as far as possible fair play, remove unequal legislation, and women would then speedily find their true level, whatever that might be, for which by nature they were intended.[31]

The Married Women's Property Act became law in 1870, and further acts culminating in 1882 and 1893 refined the principle of separate property. Married women no longer had to wait for widowhood to echo Lizzie Eustace's comment in Anthony Trollope's *The Eustace Diamonds*, that now she was a widow she could do as she pleased. The act also gave married women a legal identity, and the legal responsibility of being liable for the support of their husbands and children. A woman did not get total legal independence: husbands and wives were prohibited from beginning criminal proceedings against each other when they were living together. There were some politicians who wondered what man could be induced to marry a woman with separate interests, free to dispose of her property as she chose, but ultimately general opinion was that, far from weakening the institution of marriage, the acts raised its dignity and stability.[32]

Suffrage: Symbol of the Public Sphere

By the end of the nineteenth century the young middle-class woman had access to intellectually stimulating education, to useful social and charitable volunteer work, and to a marriage which accorded her some recognition, respect, and leeway. Unmarried women of the same class had access to paid work which was not demeaning. Yet women were excluded from the one area to which the Victorians gave pride of place: the public service of the state. No woman could earn fame and glory from politics. Women who wanted to reform the law, or extend it to help solve new problems, had to persuade men to do it for them. Women's political involvement though could not easily be absorbed into the still powerful canon of domesticity. The image of the true woman, in her private sphere, did not accommodate the notion of the woman performing functions which had been exclusively men's. The obvious contradiction of the head of state in Britain being a queen was neutralized by Victoria's own abhorrence of women's rights advocates.[33] Women who wanted the vote had a long and bitter struggle to achieve political recognition.

The intractable nature of the problem made the suffrage fight long and hard in those countries with a rigid, circumscribed image of woman. In more fluid societies where the domestic canon was impossible to impose, votes for women was not so outrageous a cause.[34] Frontier agrarian communities needed adult strength, and when such communities became political entities, adult suffrage was difficult to deny. Economic reality was reinforced by the more open-minded sentiments of adventurous émigrés in New Zealand, Australia, in the western territories and then states of the United States, and in western Canada. In all these areas women's suffrage was achieved before the end of World War I. In countries where the dominant culture was more paternalist, two factors especially retarded women's enfranchisement: the determination of politicians to maintain what they saw as a balanced way of life, and the unclear goals of the women suffragists themselves.

Political resistance to women's suffrage in Britain was muted for a generation after the publication of John Stuart Mill's eloquent brief for suffrage, *The Subjection of Women*, in 1867. The suffragists were regularly able to get a sympathetic member of parliament to introduce a private member's bill granting the vote to women on the same terms as men; equally regularly the bill lapsed through insufficient parliamentary time or through occasional intervention by the government of the day.[35] The suffragists' fair-weather friends were unable to counter the view of the Liberal leader Gladstone, in his fear

> lest we should invite her (woman) unwittingly to trespass upon the delicacy, the purity, the refinement, the elevation of her own nature, which are the present sources of its power.

Nor could suffragists initially persuade a later Liberal leader, Asquith, from his opinion that

> as a student of history and of our own public life, experience shows that the natural distinction of sex, which admittedly differentiates the functions of men and women in many departments of human activity, ought to continue to be recognized, as it always has been recognized, in the sphere of parliamentary representation.[36]

The antisuffragists mobilized in response to increasing suffragette militancy by the formation, in 1910, of the National League for Opposing Woman Suffrage (nicknamed Antis). However, the Antis were undermined when, at the outbreak of war, the radical Women's Social and Political Union totally suspended suffrage work and turned patriot. That, together with a decided shift in public opinion due to women's active role in public life during the war, "gave a very good excuse," in the opinion of a prominent Anti, Lord Balfour, "to a large number of excellent people, who had up to that time been on the wrong side, to change their minds."[37] Politicians perceived that the image of woman had changed during the war, and understood that it would be politically unwise to continue to refuse the vote to women.

In retrospect it is hard to determine whether the suffragists in Europe and North America could have achieved their objective earlier. The fact that

Sketches from Holloway Prison

Women's Social and Political Union membership card

Women's Social and Political
Union design

Illuminated address for released suffragette prisoners

women's suffrage was part of most countries' postwar settlement was an unmistakable tribute to the prewar work of the suffrage societies which had made an issue of political enfranchisement for women. They could not claim mass support: they were mostly vehicles of middle- and upper-middle-class women's political ambition, and did not appeal to the large numbers of working-class women. Moreover, in England, the suffragists at first limited their aim to votes for single, not married, women.[38] Still, some working-class women supported the franchise, notably the Lancashire cotton operatives in the north of England.[39] By 1910, the suffragists were promoting "womanhood suffrage," that is, the vote for all women, without marital or property qualification. They also answered opposition from their most effective competitors, those advocating adult suffrage, by agreeing that adult suffrage was totally consistent with womanhood suffrage. The only distinction was that the women suffragists were prepared to take any concession regarding women rather than insist on total adult suffrage at one fell swoop.

If the objectives of the suffragists could not bring them mass support, the tactics of the militants, the suffragettes, certainly brought them mass attention after 1905. The Women's Social and Political Union (WSPU), run by Mrs. Pankhurst and her daughter Christabel, inspired young, single, mobile, usually well-educated and frequently self-sacrificing young women followers to risk their liberty and even their life for the cause. They spat at policemen, chained them-

153

selves to railings, etched "Votes for Women" on golf greens and cricket pitches, and went on hunger strikes when imprisoned. After 1910 they broke windows and turned to arson, and probably alienated much of the support their tactics had attracted in the previous five years. WSPU members were required to accept autocratic decisions from the leadership, which operated clandestinely from Christabel Pankhurst's headquarters in Paris after 1912. The division of the British movement into a constitutionalist wing, under Millicent Fawcett's National Union of Women's Suffrage Societies, and the Pankhurst militant wing, which in turn generated splits of supporters into Charlotte Despard's Women's Freedom League (1907) and Silvia Pankhurst's East London Federation (1914), reflected the wide spectrum of opinion supporting women's suffrage. Some considered the vote as a facet of a many-sided movement for women's public emancipation; some believed the vote was a means to strengthen trade union legislation and other laws to provide better working conditions for workers; still others argued for the vote in recognition that women, no less than men, had a legitimate interest in a country's political actions.[40]

It is unrealistic to expect a unified political campaign from supporters who accorded different measures of priority to the vote. In the absence of single-mindedness or a single interest on the part of women, it is difficult to envision women's suffrage coming any earlier than it did. In the United States there was a division between those who wished to concentrate on getting each state to pass a measure of suffrage, and those who preferred to work for an amendment to the federal constitution; between those whose priority was the abolition of slavery, or the establishment of temperance, and those who saw the vote as coming first; between those who were more comfortable exerting social pressure at tea and dinner parties and those who wished to utilize WSPU-type militancy; between those who wished primarily to enfranchise middle-class women and those who preferred a mass movement with wider appeal. In most countries with women suffragists, divisions occurred not only over aims, objectives, tactics, and priorities, but also over personalities and leadership style. Undoubtedly these divisions reduced the impact a united front might have exerted, but women in the nineteenth century were no more a monolithic group than at any other time in history. The vote might eventually have come as the trend toward democracy took its course, but there is no question that the political activity of the suffragists was aided by the economic and military dislocations of the war. Women's wartime activities enabled politicians to argue that, as the image and behavior of women had changed, so too must public recognition accord with the new reality. Further, in each European country there were special political conditions affecting the controversy over votes for women, and not all European women were enfranchised. France, Switzerland, Greece, Hungary, and Italy were among the countries which did not give women's suffrage until after World War II.[41]

The franchise was one of many reforms which gave a public personality and role to women; it was a unique symbol of women's entry into the public sphere. Millicent Fawcett saw the nineteenth-century women's movement as composed of

(1) education, (2) an equal moral standard between men and women, (3) professional and industrial liberty, and (4) political status.[42]

Work on all objectives continued in the twentieth century, but there was an important shift in focus. Feminists turned their attention toward the "private" sphere, and, in a sense, helped to strengthen the notion that the domestic round of child care and housekeeping was primarily women's work, and women's prior responsibility. Nineteenth-century politicians had resisted moves which could serve to detach a woman from her dependence on a family setting. Twentieth-century feminists worked to wean the family away from its patriarchal tendencies, but did not themselves deny the central place of the mother within the family.

Suggestions for Further Reading

Degler, Carl N. *At Odds: Women and the Family in America from the Revolution to the Present.* New York, 1980.

Evans, Richard J. *The Feminists: Women's Emancipation Movements in Europe, America and Australasia 1840–1920.* London, 1977.

Kraditor, Aileen. *The Ideas of the Woman Suffrage Movement, 1890–1920.* New York, 1967.

Strachey, Ray. *The Cause: A History of the Women's Movement in Great Britain.* London, 1978.

Summers, Anne. "A Home from Home—Women's Philanthropic Work in the Nineteenth Century." In *Fit Work for Women,* edited by Sandra Burman. Canberra, 1979.

CHAPTER 14

Socialism

The factory system required of the individual worker a radical discipline of time and place. It imposed an increasingly efficient division of labor leading to tedium and fatigue. It differed from the traditional work rhythm of medieval craft regulation which had also expected a twelve- or fourteen-hour day, but which was geared largely to the energy of human muscles and allowed people to chat with a coworker or visitor. Work had been leisurely. Pay was neither regular, nor always sufficient, but livelihoods were generally integrated within a family environment with some personal control. The only object of consumer expenditures, after subsistence goods, was wine or ale. Factories, in contrast, offered a possible escape from oppressing intimacy and sometimes a regular source of income. On the other hand, the factory organization of production involved worker alienation, not only from ownership of tools but also from control of the daily routine. Workers and intellectuals perceived this as a problem very early in the industrialization process.

Philanthropic factory legislation was one liberal response. Insofar as women were concerned, it had brought ambivalent results, in the limitations on female access to wage labor, for example. But the major attempt to understand the causes of worker alienation comprehensively came from the socialist writers of the middle and later nineteenth century. In its analysis of capitalism and in its vision of future social and economic development, socialism as a theory appealed to many groups in society, including women. Socialism was adopted as a platform by many new political parties, legal or otherwise, organized primarily around unfranchised workers, and it seemed to offer a blueprint for society with some chance of future implementation. During the twentieth century many policies which had originally been proposed by socialists became commonplace features of modern states. For a generation after World War I, one nation-state, Soviet Russia, became a paradigm of the socialist utopia.

Engels and Bebel: Equality for All

In 1891 the second socialist International required its constituent national socialist parties to advocate women's equality as part of their political platforms. This commitment, together with women's sizable membership in national socialist parties, demonstrated a clear determination by the socialist hierarchy to include women in their vision of a new society. This was a practical translation of the frequently undeveloped discussion of women in socialist theory, but even there, the woman question attracted considerable intelligent discussion. The two staples of late-nineteenth-century feminist socialism were Engels's *Origin of the Family* (1881) and August Bebel's *Woman under Socialism* (1879). Neither work was totally original: Engels drew on Marx's anthropological guides Bachofen and Morgan and also on earlier utopian socialist mentors like Saint-Simon and Fourier, and Bebel synthesized much historical and contemporary scholarly thought on the nature of woman. With an excited sense of showing the way to a better future, these books expressed an appeal to women who could see for themselves an attractive place within a reconstructed social and economic system.

Engels and Bebel both identified the establishment of private property as the "first great revolution" in the history of woman's oppression. At the time of Bachofen's *Mutterrecht*, they asserted, there was community of property and likely sexual promiscuity, with identity transmitted along the female line. With the changeover to private ownership of property came male control of women's sexuality in order to ensure legitimate inheritance and security for that property. As Bebel wrote, "The reign of the mother-right implied communism; equality for all; the rise of the father-right implied the reign of private property, and, with it, the oppression and enslavement of women." He added, "It is difficult to trace in detail the manner in which the change was achieved. A knowledge of the events is lacking." A modern anthropologist, Kathleen Gough, supports their view of original human relationships:

> Morgan and Engels were probably right in thinking that the human family was preceded by sexual indiscriminacy. They were also right in seeing an egalitarian group-quality about early economic and marriage arrangements.[1]

Regardless of the primordial causes for women's secondary status, however, Engels and Bebel could both offer a strategy for contemporary and future generations of women in pursuit of equality. Their discussion of early societies was relevant as groundwork for their assertion that only after the dissolution of private property could women's proper place in society be restored to its early prelapsarian heights.

In the meantime, women must enter, or remain in, the industrialized work force. A woman's wages, inadequate though they might be even for subsistence, nevertheless provided a concrete contribution to a family's income and reduced her total dependency within it. Lending her support to the proletarian political struggle, she would hasten the revolution, after which, in a structurally reorganized socialist economy, her needs as a worker and as a woman would be met. "Class rule will have reached its end for all time, and, along with it, the rule of man over woman."[2]

> The woman of future society is socially and economically independent; she is no longer subject to even a vestige of dominion and exploitation;

she is free, the peer of man, mistress of her lot. Her education is the same as that of man, with such exceptions as the difference of sex and sexual functions demand. Living under natural conditions, she is able to unfold and exercise her mental powers and faculties. She chooses her occupation in such a way as corresponds with her wishes, inclinations, and natural abilities, and she works under conditions identical with man's. Even if engaged as a practical working-woman on some field or other, at other times of the day she may be educator, teacher, or nurse, at yet others she may exercise herself in art, or cultivate some branch of science, and at yet others may be filling some administrative function. She joins in studies, enjoyments or social intercourse with either her sisters or with men, as she may please or occasion may serve.

In the choice of love, she is, like man, free and unhampered. She woos or is wooed, and closes the bond from no consideration other than her own inclinations. This bond is a private contract. . . . Socialism creates in this nothing new: it merely restores, at a higher level of civilization and under new social forms, that which prevailed at a more primitive social stage, and before private property began to rule society.[3]

This woman of the future would be liberated by socialized domesticity: communal nurseries and schools, kitchens and eating places, baths and laundries, and electrical household appliances would all render nugatory much domestic work residually assigned to women.[4]

Later generations of socialist writers developed some of Engels's and Bebel's ideas, and some additionally grappled with gaps in their analysis: would communal property holding necessarily liberate women? Would the family as a protected institution be necessary? Was a sexual division of labor inevitable or desirable? One who uniquely explored further the connection between women in the family and women in society, and then had the opportunity actually to implement her ideas on a vast scale, was Aleksandra Kollontai.

Aleksandra Kollontai: Socialist Feminism in Action

Kollontai was born in 1872. Her father was a Russian general and her mother was the daughter of a Finnish wood merchant. Kollontai's childhood was divided between St. Petersburg and a country estate in Finland. She traveled abroad, and discovered the *Communist Manifesto* and other socialist literature. In 1893 she married an army officer who was a distant relative, Vladimir Kollontai, and bore a son. As a wife, she participated in philanthropic social work. In an 1896 visit to a textile factory, she saw industrial working conditions firsthand, and this led her to seek out revolutionary groups of the St. Petersburg intelligentsia under the leadership of Lenin. Two years later she left her husband, studied in Zurich and returned to St. Petersburg to work as an activist.[5] She became a full-time revolutionary after the 1905 revolution and turned her attention to the organization of women workers—primarily, it seems, to forestall their recruitment into the bourgeois feminist cause which, she contended, offered only false gods to the female proletariat.[6] Kollontai's

Aleksandra Kollontai, 1912

theories were developed in books, pamphlets, and speeches published in the ten years or so before 1918. By the time of the Bolshevik revolution she was a political force with strong allies. She was a member of the Central Committee of the Communist Party, helped organize the first Congress of Worker and Peasant Women in 1919, and was the first director of the *Zhenotdel*, or Women's Section of the Central Committee, established in 1919 in order to draw women into political commitment to the revolution.[7] Kollontai's ideas were tested not only in *Zhenotdel* activity, but also in the sweeping legislation introduced in 1917 and 1918 as the new Family Code.

Kollontai's major quarrel with bourgeois feminists had been that they ignored the importance of economic independence as a necessary foundation for woman's autonomy and hence control over her own destiny. Kollontai developed in a concrete way the notion of woman as an individual rather than as a member of a family. She concluded that Bebel's proposals of communal domestic arrangements—kitchens, nurseries, laundries, and so on—were a necessary first step toward releasing women from domestic drudgery into wage-earning freedom. With her slogan, "the separation of the kitchen from marriage is as vital as the separation of the church from the state," she insisted that since motherhood was a social function, providing the state with the next generation's population, the rearing of children should be a social responsibility, funded by the state. Consequently there should be day nurseries, and centralized and collective living arrangements. These the *Zhenotdel* hastened to

159

create, both in towns and in the more conservative countryside, although shortages of funds limited their scale. Nevertheless, visitors to Russia in the 1920s, together with contemporary Russian fiction, testified to the changed possibilities for women emerging at that time.[8]

The provision of communal domestic facilities for child rearing and household care allowed mothers to participate fully in the work force. Post-revolutionary legislation concerning marriage, divorce, and abortion offered the possibility that an adult woman could be as independent of involuntary family burdens as a man. The December, 1917, laws deprived the church of an official role in marriage and required marriages to be registered by the state only. In October, 1918, the Family Code abolished all distinction between children born within marriage and out of wedlock; gave each parent equal authority over their children; gave the husband and wife each control over their own earnings; made divorce easily obtainable, with equal division of marital property between the spouses at the time of divorce; abolished alimony, except when a spouse was disabled, in which case either spouse was eligible; and explicitly assumed women's work force participation. Abortion was legalized in 1920. This legislation, sweeping though it was, owed much to other Western countries' example. A judge of the USSR Supreme Court stated in 1925, when reforms were being debated, "our existing legislation on family and marriage relations was created by the methods of bourgeois law," as distinct from communist theory.[9] Very soon, however, the intentions of lawmakers and of the *Zhenotdel* were undermined by economic conditions following on civil war and the New Economic Policy of 1921 (NEP).

The NEP ended labor conscription, and began a partial return to private enterprise which led to the unemployment of many unskilled workers, most of whom were women. Fewer state resources were available for socialization of domestic tasks. A woman might find herself at the same time without a job, without nursery facilities for dependent children, and, especially if her marriage had not been registered, deprived of economic support from a spouse or partner. Moreover, in order to evade the obligation for property splits and spousal support in the event of divorce, a very large number of couples, particularly in the countryside where property was owned jointly by several family members, had lived together without benefit of civil registration. Consequently a woman, abandoned by her partner, had no legal recourse for her own support or that of her children if her man refused to support them. Social problems produced by the large number of abandoned poor women and children became apparent and in 1926 a new marriage law was passed which in many respects reneged on the progressive promise of 1918.

A major tenet of the new law was increased individual responsibility, and the consequent reduction in the state's obligations, within marriage. The assumption was that the woman was in need of protection. Alimony benefits were extended to divorced people of de facto marriages despite their nonregistration. In addition, a woman who was unemployed was entitled to economic support from her husband. This contradicted the principle Kollontai and others had advocated earlier, of a woman's claim on the state, rather than on her family, for the requisite economic foundation for individual autonomy. Kollontai herself had gradually lost influence in the party and had been replaced in 1922 as director of the *Zhenotdel* by Sofia Smidovich, who cautiously emphasized the transitional problems of a society undergoing revolution and favored a more conservative attitude toward family life.[10] In the debates on the new marriage law Kollontai argued that there could be sufficient economic prosperity for more employment and at the same time for state expansion in socialized household and child-rearing suppport systems. Even before that time, women were worthy of state support by virtue of their reproductive activity: they were producing the next generation of workers. The notion of family-funded alimony should, she argued, be abandoned, in favor of a national General Insurance Fund to which all workers would contribute on a graduated scale. Since there were sixty million workers, a sizeable fund would be created for the benefit of those in need. After three years the fund would no longer be a burden since economic growth could shortly be expected to expand the economy.

Kollontai was opposed by conservatives who wished to bolster the traditional family structure and also by those who wished to invest not in social experiment but in more rapid industrialization.[11] At a time of hot debate on ideology and priorities—for example, over the harmonizing of relations between peasant and urban proletariat—Kollontai's own political position was not central nor powerful enough to ensure success. She also suffered from her opponents' charges that her own personal life, and her writings on sexual morality, advocated promiscuity. In the event, her concept of the new woman, as unencumbered by family tentacles as a man, lost ground. Subsequent soviet legislation promoting communal child care centers, communal homes, state support to mothers whether married or single, and enabling women to participate in the work force on a scale rarely paralleled elsewhere in Western society, proceeded not so much from the feminist philosophy of Kollontai and her supporters as from the requirements of a society undergoing rapid industrialization and in need of total adult employment. Kollontai's primary achievement was that she was one of the few to distinguish woman as an individual from woman as member of a family in a materialist sense. Her spectacular achievement was her admittedly brief victory in establishing this concept, of an economically independent, sexually autonomous, emotionally sovereign new woman in the largest state of Europe after World War I.

No other Western socialist party experienced quite the same opportunity or success as Kollontai's Bolsheviks, but there were nevertheless intellectuals and workers who considered the problems of women and were able to suggest socialist solutions within the context of a pluralist society with its many competing and divergent interests.

Austromarxism: The Quality of Life

Viktor Adler, doctor and psychiatrist, was the founder of the Austrian Social Democratic party. In 1887 he identified two facets to the socialist movement:

> In a purely mechanical fashion the economic revolution goes its inexorable way . . . but a revolution in the consciousness of mankind goes

forward at the same time. . . . The revolutionizing of the brain is the real assignment, the immediate goal, of the proletarian parties of Social Democracy.[12]

One of the leaders of the women's socialist movement, Adelheid Popp, factory worker, journalist, party activist, and politician, throughout her life emphasized the dual appeal of socialism. Although she frequently acquiesced in the party's downgrading of women's issues, when she had the chance, in 1926, to help draft the party's platform of long-term goals, these were clearly expanded beyond women's economic involvement in the work force. "Social Democracy . . . demands for women full opportunity for the development of their personality," and this required relief from what she saw as woman's triple burden of employment, household work, and child raising.[13] The Austromarxist solution, insofar as women were concerned, was Bebel's program of communal and socialized domesticity: they called in addition for reproductive control, demanding the free distribution of birth control devices and information, and free, legal, hospitalized abortions.[14] The Austrian women socialists were more practical with respect to women in the work force, and possibly therefore appealed more to their constituents. Like Bebel and Marx they believed that women should be independent and educated, but they were also concerned to ensure women's physical safety in the work place. This led them to advocate not universal principles of regulated working conditions, but protective legislation for women only, consistent with the early 1893 International Socialist Congress which had demanded such rules as a safeguard to the exploitation of female workers.[15]

Socialist women had little influence on either the Social Democratic movement or on Austrian society in the post–World War I years. Austrian women gained suffrage in 1918 yet used their vote more conservatively then men. In 1927, 60 percent of the women voters (compared with 55 percent of the men) voted nonsocialist; and in 1930, 61 percent of the women (and 57 percent of the men) voted against the socialists and communists. The slight edge accorded to the more conservative political parties can be explained not so much by women's possible clerical susceptibilities and passiveness, as by their skepticism concerning socialist talk of progress within an all too familiar patriarchal environment. The reforms advocated in the 1920s by the women socialists were not legislated until 1975 in Austria.[16]

There was a clear split between the socialist women and the bourgeois women in the Austrian case. The latter were bitterly characterized by socialist Kaethe Leichter as selfish women seduced by superficialities who "did not realize that the issue was not opportunity for a few privileged women but the improvement of the miserable conditions of working women."[17] But differences went deeper than that. Bourgeois women managed with some degree of success to gain access to higher education and professional work in the nineteenth century. Unlike the socialist women, they persisted in fighting for women's suffrage in the years before World War I when the Social Democratic party had persuaded its women members to work for universal manhood suffrage only. More than tactics separated them. The bourgeois women did not advocate protective legislation for women—their constituency was not factory workers but professional and office workers whose health and safety were not so much at risk.[18] This division among feminists, people who wished to see women broaden their options in modern society, was by no means unique to Austria. It was present in most Western countries. It was, on the one hand, basically a class division, with working-class women (and men) suspicious of reforms pushed by the wives of capitalists and entrepreneurs. On the other hand, there was also a division between those who considered that women had special gifts (usually of spirituality and superior moral sensibility) and those who wanted to reduce rather than reinforce the gap between men's and women's experience.

Socialism and Reproduction: Radicals and Conservatives

One strain of thought within the socialist movement wished to provide women with greater access to sexual experience than was provided within the traditional monogamous family framework. It did not go undisputed. Indeed, this issue was used with effect against Kollontai. The German Marxist Clara Zetkin interviewed Lenin in 1920, and the interview was published in 1925. "You must be aware of the famous theory," said Lenin, "that in communist society the satisfaction of sexual desires, of love, will be as simple and unimportant as drinking a glass of water." He disapproved of this belief. "Of course, thirst must be satisfied. But will the normal man in normal circumstances lie down in the gutter and drink out of a puddle, or out of a glass with a rim greasy from many lips?"[19] Lenin's comments were interpreted as adverse criticism of Kollontai's passionate advocacy, and to some extent her own personal example, of free love for women. Nineteenth-century socialism had anticipated the withering away of the family as a concomitant feature of the new, revolutionary, classless society. Kollontai joyfully looked forward to that, too, since the traditional family had hindered, rather than helped, women, in her view. After her fall, however, her views on sexuality were identified with social irresponsibility and her opponents hastened to emphasize that the institution of the family, suitably buttressed by social welfare and liberalized by more permissive divorce procedures, was desirable.[20]

In other countries, any discussion of women's reproductive control—of contraception, abortion, or even the separation of sexual pleasure from procreation—tended to arouse suspicion in socialist men. Given the popularity of Malthusian theories of population control, whereby birth control was seen as an alternative to more appropriate means of social reform, their attitude was understandable. Capitalism's claim for more factory workers and militarist programs for more cannon fodder were counterbalanced by a socialist interest in breeding more workers for the revolution. Marie Stopes expressed contemporary beliefs when she argued on behalf of birth control since overcrowding in towns meant "we have been breeding revolutionaries."[21] Socialist feminists supported birth control not as dupes of the eugenicists but as theorists vitally alerted to the connection between economic and personal autonomy. Stella Browne, a progressive London librarian, emphasized the integration of birth control into orthodox socialist views of women: "No economic changes would give equality or self-determination to any woman unable to choose or refuse motherhood of her own free will." She was not averse to using the basic eugenics argument for her own purposes: selective procreation would "produce and build up a race fitted to carry out Communist and Feminist ideals."[22] Browne saw reproductive control as an essential prerequisite of a woman's self-determination, but was also prepared to support the birth control movement as a means of planning families in a planned society, an objective less threatening to political radicals who were also socially conservative.[23]

Aleksandra Kollontai was one of the few socialists to explore thoroughly woman's condition as a worker and as a mother, and to arrive at some viable means whereby in a socialist society, a woman could experience the same variety of options as a man. Few others approached her in energy or imagination. Even Stella Browne assumed that child rearing would remain women's work, and primarily a mother's concern and responsibility.[24] Other socialist writers, from the utopian socialist Flora Tristan in France through Engels and Bebel, seemed to consider that once women were participants in the industrial work force, their parity with men was assured.[25] The twentieth-century experience has shown otherwise. Kollontai understood that without social, collective involvement in child rearing and household care, women as workers would bear a double burden, for they would retain their traditional association with domestic work in addition to responsibilities attached to service or productive labor. Certainly the dual burden of job and home became a problem for Western women as more of them entered the work force. There are other unresolved problems, in particular the sexual division of labor within the work force itself, with managerial jobs largely male-dominated, and women confined predominantly to lower-level work. Even in the jobs where men and women both work, the socialist slogan of "equal pay for equal work" nominally accepted by governments and international organizations, has not prevented a wide, and increasing, differential between the rates of pay for women and men. Despite continuing sexual inequality, it is clear that socialism, with its emphasis on economic independence for women, and its advocacy of autonomy in terms of reproduction and sexuality as well, has provided feminists with both a theory and an image of an egalitarian society. Liberalism was unable to offer as much.

Suggestions for Further Reading

Bebel, August. *Woman under Socialism.* New York, 1904.

Boxer, Marilyn J., and Quataert, Jean H., eds. *Socialist Women: European Feminism in the Nineteenth and Early Twentieth Centuries.* New York, 1978.

Clements, Barbara Evans. *Bolshevik Feminist: The Life of Aleksandra Kollontai.* Bloomington, Ind., 1979.

Stites, Richard. *The Women's Liberation Movement in Russia: Feminism, Nihilism, and Bolshevism, 1860–1930.* Princeton, 1978.

CHAPTER 15

Fascism and War

During World Wars I and II women became more visible participants in public life than ever before. Reasons of state mobilized hitherto unrecognized national resources. War however was by no means the only agent hastening social change. The Great Depression affected women as well as men. Between the wars, in several Western countries, fascist governments attempted a radical reordering of society in accordance with racist chauvinist objectives. In the first years of the thousand-year Reich, for instance, women were quite explicitly involved. Beneath some of the more obvious changes introduced by fascism and war were significant long-term trends originating over a century before in the industrial revolution. The interaction of underlying and immediate factors is complex and often difficult to unravel. Both war and fascism led governments to regard their demographic resources in a different light. Some women benefited and others suffered as a result.

Jobs in World War I: Domestic Service Forsaken

During World War I, women's experiences in the countries involved in military action were comparable. Women became streetcar conductors, elevator operators, park attendants, bank workers, chimney sweeps, truck drivers—all as new visible substitutes for recently recruited or conscripted soldiers. They also entered factories in large numbers. Thousands worked in munitions plants, as riveters in shipbuilding, and in car production.[1] Governmental bureaucracies expanded to administer the war effort, and women were recruited into office work on a large scale. The nursing profession expanded and thousands enrolled in military nursing services. In Britain a Scottish woman doctor used the backing of the prewar suffragist society to support her organization of fourteen hospital units staffed by woman doctors which were dispatched to work for Allied armies (Belgian, French, Russian, and Serbian), having been told at the outbreak of hostilities by the War Office "to go home and keep quiet," since the British army did not want to be troubled by "hysterical women." By 1917 the War Office changed its view. Women's corps were introduced in the military with their own officers and uniform and employed over one hundred fifty thousand women. Housewives contributed to the war effort, through housing and feeding refugees and conserving food and energy. Many women were recruited into the British "land-army" part-time to work in agricultural food production.[2] In the United States the government for the first time hired women lawyers and doctors. Women substituted for men in practically every occupation and were praised for their patriotic contribution. For some prewar feminists, public approbation was a heady experience which justified a suspension of suffrage activity for the duration of the war. In Britain, for example, the militant Pankhurst wing declared a "Women's Armistice," and the constitutionalist wing shed its pacifist members and changed its name from the London Society for Women's Suffrage to the London Society for Women's Service.[3] Yet, with significant exceptions, the general picture of revolutionary change with respect to women in Western society as a result of the Great War is an illusion.

In the United States, the vast majority of women engaged in productive labor during the war had joined the labor force before the war: only 5 percent started to work for the first time.[4] The war years promoted changed activities, not new women workers. After the war, trade unions joined employers and governments to entreat the women either to return to their prewar jobs, or to leave the labor force altogether. In 1919 the Central Federated Union of New York said "the same patriotism which induced women to enter industry during the war should induce them to vacate their positions after the war." Compared with 1910, women's participation in the total United States labor force was the same (20.4 percent) in 1920 as in 1910 (20.9 percent).[5] In Europe, participation rates were higher than in the United States but prewar and postwar comparisons showed no dramatic change: in France in 1911, 36.9 percent of the economically active population were women, and in 1921 the figure was 39.6 percent; in Britain, the prewar and postwar percentages were identical (1911 and 1921, 29.5 percent); and in Germany the 1925 percentage of economically active women in the labor force was only slightly higher (35.9 percent) than in 1907 (30.7 percent).[6] In Britain after 1919, three-quarters of a million women left paid employment and "in practice, most women remained dependants."[7] The historian of the French Third Republic, Theodore Zeldin, wrote that "the war of 1914 did not produce any radical change in feminine attitudes, largely because it did not make all that much difference to the women."[8] However, the kind of women who were working, and the kind of jobs they did, did change.

More young middle-class French women had to contemplate working in the absence of a bourgeois private income.[9] One indisputable change caused by the war was the great reduction in the number of domestic servants; yet another was the expansion in clerical service work. Another trend which was doubtless accelerated by the war was the increase in the number of married women joining the labor force accompanied by a rise in the median age of the woman worker. By 1940 the median age of the woman worker in the United States had risen to over thirty, whereas in the 1890s it had been under twenty-five. In all Western countries the expansion of the service sector, in nursing, teaching, and social work as well as in white-collar office work, provided jobs for middle-class women when their families could no longer support adult single women. Before the Great War, most women had worked as servants, farm laborers, or unskilled factory workers, and the only "professional" job available to large numbers of women was teaching. Despite the efforts of nineteenth-century feminists to open up professional training and employment to women, little advance was made over the first initial steps. In the United States the proportion of women workers engaged in professional work increased only from 11.9 percent to 14.2 percent between 1920 and 1940.[10] Still, the pre–World War II picture was not identical with pre–1914. More women worked in offices, as distinct from farm or factory jobs; working women were predominantly but not exclusively single and young. A significant proportion of older, married women were in the work force. These novelties owed more to the development of the modern industrialized state, and to the relative impoverishment of the bourgeoisie, than to either women's experiences in World War I or the activities of the women's movement.

Women and Fascism: Rousseau Revisited

Changes brought to women by the Great War were largely limited to the duration of the war: they followed from governmental responses to a national crisis. Fascism also was directed from above, and manipulated women, often willingly, in the interest of a new society based on national purity and national purpose.[11] Fascist ideology was able to accommodate several roles for women, and the Third Reich was never efficient enough nor sufficiently monolithic to require total uniformity. The ideal Nazi woman was the mother of the nation's *Volk*, and as such fulfilled a highly esteemed reproductive role. "Woman's proper sphere is the family. There she is a sovereign queen. If we eliminated women from every realm of public life, we do not do it in order to dishonor her, but in order that her honor may be restored to her," said Goebbels to a

Ideal Nazi woman

group of women's leaders in 1934; but the Nazis never succeeded in the systematic elimination of non-Jewish women from public life. Within the family, a woman should receive the respect of her children, and the Nazi society wished to restore the high status enjoyed by women in their prehistoric past as described by Bachofen and the Nordic sagas.

The family, although of great importance, could not be considered in isolation from the community, and it was the communal good of society as a whole whose interests should always be paramount: "Gemeinnutz vor Eigennutz." Hence the Nazi woman was not circumscribed by her loyalty to her family. She, like all other citizens of the Reich, owed commitment to the state first and foremost. Such allegiance for many women could most appropriately be fulfilled by fecundity and patriotic parenthood; for other women—older unmarried women, widows, or wives whose husbands were sick or earning low wages—it could be consistent with employment in areas regarded as women's work, for example as teachers of girls, or as doctors for women patients.[12] Primacy of the general good meant that women could be called on to sacrifice time and comfort in the service of the Reich. Temporary sacrifice justified adjustments to the normally paramount role of race-mother, and explained the need for even mothers to work in factories if the state's security or well-being was at issue. Nazi ideology therefore encompassed a range of appropriate feminine behavior whose contradictions were only superficial. In her youth the Nazi woman was a healthy athlete and worked in the labor force. When she married, government policy encouraged her to quit work with an interest-free marriage loan (of approximately five months' wages) provided she withdrew from the labor force. The principal to be repaid was reduced by one quarter for each child born to the couple. Marriages increased significantly after the Nazis came to power in 1933, as did the birthrate after the introduction of the marriage loan policy. In 1933 there were 58.9 births per 1,000 women of childbearing age, in 1936 there were 77.4, and in 1939 there were 84.8. Deliberate government policy would not be the only determinant of an increased birthrate: improved economic circumstances after the severe depression years undoubtedly had an impact. Mothers were additionally fortified by legislation extending family allowances, allowances for children's vocational training, and some employers' support to families with numerous children.[13] Mothers of four or more children were publicly rewarded by medals which all party youth were required to salute after 1939.[14] A 1935 commentator pointed out that the Nazi governmental policy toward these women meant "little change, and certainly no sacrifice, but rather the glorification of the role to which they have always been committed."[15] Even the single adult woman who became pregnant was not disapproved by the government, despite her association with ideas of promiscuity and loose living. Himmler stressed that such a person was "not a married or an unmarried woman but a *mother*," and used this emphasis to support a policy of government support, after 1939, for certain illegitimate children.[16] Mothers whose husbands had sufficient pay were economically, as well as ideologically, preferred to single adult women or married women in the labor force who had neither equal pay nor welfare support.[17]

The situation changed in Germany after 1936, when the government became concerned about an insufficient labor supply. By that time, economic factors had combined with the deliberate government propaganda glorifying the race-mother to serve as a powerful disincentive for women, especially married women, to enter the labor force at all. A combination of increased wages for the head of the household and improved welfare provisions for the mother meant that "the material well-being of working-class households began to improve quite markedly." Reasons of state again reversed by 1939, when major armaments firms had to turn down contracts from the armed forces because they were suffering from such labor shortage that delivery dates could not be met. Yet, after men were conscripted for war, the separation allowances payable to wives were set at the highest rate for any European country: 85 percent of the husband's previous earnings. This suggests that the morale of soldiers at the front, comforted by the notion that their wives were well provided for, was considered a higher priority than the demands for an increased labor supply utilizing soldiers' wives at home.[18] Propaganda urging women to enter the labor force was halfhearted exhortation, appealing to patriotism and to the idea that women would be directly aiding their own husbands and sons. No conscription was introduced for women until 1943, when Goebbels declared Germany was in a state of "total war," and required women aged seventeen to forty-five to register.[19] Exemptions were permitted only for those already working forty-eight hours or more per week, those employed in agriculture or health, students, pregnant women, women with one child under six or two under fourteen. This law affected different sections of the community differently. Middle- and upper-class women evaded registration, thus inspiring the resentment of those other women whose economic resources or genuine patriotism led them to work. Bitterness over the injustice of uneven sacrifice was "not necessarily ideological hostility to fascism," but it existed, and was articulated.[20] Nazi policy also reflected the strength of the ideology of glorified motherhood with male leaders even when reasons of state would suggest such an outlook was outmoded.

The United States: World War II and Women's Work

Elsewhere in Western society the second World War, like the first, had a possibly more powerful effect on women's lives than in Germany, where ambivalent government policy tried to maintain many women in a protected domestic sphere. The experiences of the United States, Canada, and Britain with respect to women in the war effort illustrate in a different way the same general outlook toward women expressed in the Third Reich. At a time of national crisis, the good of the community took precedence; although woman's reproductive functions were to be protected, for the duration of the war she must sacrifice domestic comfort to the war effort. In all three countries women were involved in the armed forces, and in the labor force to an unprecedented degree. The governments designed support programs specifically for women, particularly mothers. Many developments were temporary and superficial, but others were structural and much more long lasting. Women's experiences during World War II were more significant in the long run than during World War I.

By 1945 in the United States, the female work force had increased by 50 percent over the prewar figure. Wages were higher, twice as many wives were at work than before, the number of women in unions had increased fourfold, and public opinion as reflected in the media and government appeared to support women working. The greatest single transformation had occurred, unsurprisingly, in those industries central to the war effort: the number of women in war industries grew 460 percent during the war.[21] One of the major centers of the shipbuilding industry, for example, was Portland, Oregon, where the American shipbuilding Kaiser Corporation dominated the area with three large shipyards. The experience of women working for Kaiser during the war offers an illustration of a widespread trend in industrial America.

A quarter of Kaiser's wartime work force of one hundred twenty-five thousand was women. Their wages were the same as men's for the same work. Child care centers catering to seven hundred children were created at the work place for working mothers who were explicitly recruited. Workers could buy precooked meals at the centers and reheat them at home for dinner. The major incentive to work, however, was provided less by available services than by high wages, which in 1943 averaged sixty-three dollars per week, compared with regular factory work wages of twenty-five dollars per week. In the shipyards, women did work which they had never formerly performed, yet a study by Karen Skold indicates that a sexual division of labor remained. Women were clustered mainly in the helper, laborer, and unskilled categories, although nearly all job categories had some, if only a few, women. In view of what happened after the war, it is interesting to note women's postwar intentions as of January 1944. Fifty-three percent of the women interviewed wished to continue in industrial work; 8 percent were undecided; the remainder wished to seek other jobs or return home. The shipyard newsletter, however, interpreted these figures according to Kaiser's interests. It emphasized that women really wanted to "put aside the welder's torch" and give it back to the men, and stay in "The Kitchen—Woman's Big Post-War Goal." Work in the shipyards was dramatically curtailed with the end of hostilities and by October, 1945, the Kaiser workforce was reduced to twenty-five thousand. A year later it was forty-five hundred with practically all jobs reserved for men.[22] In this instance, women's wartime employment was temporary and concentrated in the less skilled, helper-type jobs, regardless of the personal preferences of the women. Matters of state determined women's entry and participation in, and exit from, the masculine work force.

Canada: World War II and Government Support Services

The same principle determined women's wartime involvement in the Canadian work force, although there was a more intensive commitment to the requirement to mobilize a greater number of nontraditional workers. Unlike the United States, Canada after 1942 required the registration of all young women aged twenty to twenty-four. It passed a tax law in 1942 encouraging married women to work, by preserving the full married status exemption to a husband, regardless of the size of the wife's earnings. From 1943 onward, there was a campaign to attract women part-time into the labor force. By 1942, when the reserve of unemployed from the depression had been absorbed into either the armed forces or the work force, the prime minister declared that "recruitment of women for employment was 'the most important single feature of the program' " of National Selective Service. By October, 1944, there were an estimated 1,077,000 women in the work force compared with a 1939 figure of 638,000. The government propaganda appealed to patriotism, to sacrifice for the nation at war, and to "keep faith with the boys at the front" by work at home in Canada. Yet, according to a questionnaire conducted by the Women's Division of the Toronto Employment and Selective Service Office, 59 percent of the married applicants aged thirty-five or over who sought work identified as their prime motivation the "desire to supplement family income," as indeed was true also in the United States.[23] The importance of a financial incentive was recognized by the Canadian government in its tax legislation. The government also acted in providing a modicum of child support systems for working mothers: child care facilities were established in the two most industrialized provinces, Ontario and Quebec, with most of the cost borne by the federal and provincial governments.[24]

In Canada, as in the United States, such service, limited as it was, became unavailable after the war. Federal participation ceased in early 1946, and the centers were closed down, to the accompaniment of government explanations that "the Dominion share in financing this project was undertaken as a *war measure* for the reason that women whose children were in day care centers were engaged in *work of national importance.*" With the passing of the national emergency, the emergency welfare measures ceased. The tax concession also was rescinded: as of 1 January 1947, the tax law reverted, since the concession had been a wartime provision "justified only by the extreme state of emergency which then existed." The same agency which had been responsible for mobilizing women for the war effort after the war sought to "return married women to the home and to channel young unmarried women into traditionally female occupations."[25]

Great Britain: World War II and Conscription

In Britain, beleaguered and isolated in its opposition to Nazi Germany, there was an understandable siege mentality. Qualms about mobilizing women, although felt by some of the more influential war leaders, were set aside in the effort to free men for service in the armed forces. The minister of labor, Ernest Bevin, was a trade union leader who introduced the compulsory registration of women in March, 1941. From this register, women were selectively conscripted into industry, administration, or the armed forces after December 1941. Bevin also encouraged voluntary enlistment of women with few family responsibilities.[26] By September, 1943, however, all women up to the age of fifty-one were required to register. As in the United States, women worked in engineering and munitions factories where previously the work force had been male. Again the postwar period saw the return to prewar status. After the war, there were even fewer domestic servants, but the overall participation rate for women in the labor force in 1951 was identical to what it had been twenty years earlier: 34 percent.[27] More extensive participation in the work force was once again a temporary phenomenon. The war experience of most women in Britain, as in other Western countries, was symbolized not so much in access to work formerly denied, but in housekeeping problems of coping with food rationing and shortages, and in living under the strain of military attack without a husband. Some women were in military or intelligence service, many were involved as volunteers in hospital work, but most experienced the "discomfort and deprivation . . . not just sleeping in cellars and shelters, but always 'going without.' "[28]

Impact of World War II: Economic Advances for Women?

Two divergent scholarly views have emerged about the impact of World War II upon American women. William Chafe and Leila Rupp have both minimized the dramatic effect of the war. Chafe, however, argues that some of the changes wrought by war were indeed structural and long-lasting, while Rupp denies that such changes were directly related to the war at all. Chafe identified two changes of prime importance to women: the age and the marital status of new recruits to the labor force, during the war, in the United States. By war's end, half the women workers were married, and aged over forty, as compared with a prewar female work force of predominantly young single women. Eighty percent of the female wartime work force responding to a questionnaire stated that they wanted to remain in the work force after the war was over. Both the age and marital profile of women workers continued to be features of the postwar female work force, and Chafe concludes that the mobilization of women who formerly did not work in large numbers was a permanent result of their war experience. The new labor force participation was accompanied by corresponding changes in public opinion, particularly concerning the propriety of middle-class women working. In the 1950s, a time in America when, according to Betty Friedan, women were accepting the "feminine mystique" of domesticity, many other women were quietly consolidating economic gains made during the war.[29] Rupp in contrast argues "the impact of the war on public attitudes toward women was negligible" and moreover, the war "had no permanent impact on the female labor force."[30] The increased participation of married and older women in the labor force was merely an intensification of long-term economic trends consonant with the expansion of the service sector of the economy. The least that can now be said about the war's effect is that it cloaked with patriotism and public approval the initial steps of more women's more intense involvement in economic life. For many women, such support was necessary if they were to deviate from the standard approval of mother's place being in the home, still prevalent for many years after the war.[31]

What can be exclusively attributed to women's experience under both fascism and war is still debated. There is no question that some women suffered severely. Jewish women underwent humiliation and death in Hitler's final solution for the victory of Aryans. Also, in wartime, many women civilians and women in the military suffered directly from bombing and fighting. Some women were pacifists, and bravely maintained organizations for peace in both world wars.[32] Some women were active in resistance movements. But most maintained their prewar existence as far as they could, and the single most disruptive element in their lives would have been the novelty, for millions, of working for the first time, or of continuing to work at a time in their lives when they would normally expect to retire from the labor force and confine themselves to the home. For other millions, there was the novelty of working in areas previously monopolized by men. It is hard to discount these experiences entirely when assessing the milestones measuring women's gradual retirement from exclusively domestic concerns.

Suggestions for Further Reading

Bridenthal, Renate. "Something Old, Something New: Women Between Two World Wars." In *Becoming Visible: Women in European History*, edited by Renate Bridenthal and Claudia Koonz. Boston, 1977.

Chafe, William H. *The American Woman: Her Changing Social, Economic and Political Roles, 1920–1970*. Oxford, 1975.

Koonz, Claudia. "Mothers in the Fatherland: Women in Nazi Germany." In *Becoming Visible: Women in European History*, edited by Renate Bridenthal and Claudia Koonz. Boston, 1977.

Rupp, Leila J. *Mobilizing Women for War: German and American Propaganda, 1939–1945*. Princeton, 1978.

Stephenson, Jill. *Women in Nazi Society*. London, 1975.

Twentieth-Century Trends

Throughout the twentieth century women in all Western countries became more and more absorbed into the public sphere, the arena of politics, employment, and activities outside the home which had been theoretically formerly monopolized by men. In fact, of course, women had never been entirely absent. A few had been rulers. Upper-class hostesses through various stratagems had had some influence on matters of state. Poor women had always worked, as domestic servants, on the farm, or in factories. But by the 1970s in most Western countries practically all single women and at least half the married women belonged to the work force. Women's impact on politics was more difficult to gauge. All women possessed the vote, that symbol of public life which represented so much to the nineteenth-century suffrage workers, although women politicians were few in number. Participation in public life did not automatically bring prosperity or parity. As before, there were more poor women than poor men. As before, women continued to earn lower wages than men. Women's increased public work load did not involve a corresponding decrease in their domestic work load. This chapter examines women's involvement in the public sphere, and outlines some contemporary trends concerning women in the 1980s.

Votes for Women: Inert Victory

In their one objective, the vote, the women's movements in Western countries were successful. By the end of World War I about half of the European countries and the United States had enacted women's suffrage, often as part of a general measure of universal suffrage. (Women were enfranchised after World War I in Austria, Canada, Czechoslovakia, Denmark, Germany, Great Britain, Iceland, Luxembourg, the Netherlands, Poland, Sweden, the United States, the USSR. They were enfranchised after World War II in Albania, Belgium, Bulgaria, France, Greece, Hungary, Israel, Italy, Portugal, Rumania, Spain, Yugoslavia. Switzerland introduced woman suffrage in 1971.) Generally speaking, the vote was granted to women not from gratitude for their patriotic contribution to the war, nor as a belated recognition of the righteousness or power of the woman suffrage cause. According to Richard Evans's interpretation, newly empowered liberal or social democratic governments needed to consolidate their authority. The enfranchisement of women would help accomplish this aim, for women were seen as an essentially conservative group in the population.[1] Certainly women got the vote under particular circumstances where those politicians in power saw more advantage to be won than risked or lost. In the first two countries to give women the vote, New Zealand (1893) and Australia (1902), political sympathizers had emphasized not the justice but the expediency of a suffragist policy. "The effect of the admission of women to the suffrage will be distinctly Conservative," pronounced an editorial of the conservative New Zealand newspaper the *Evening Post*, "and the only possible corrective to the evils attendant on universal manhood suffrage." Prodded by a well-organized Women's Christian Temperance Union, the New Zealand government passed the measure in the hope that middle-class stability derived from the rurally based older settler families would be strengthened as against the rootless, the drunkards, and the profligates.[2] In Australia the Women's Christian Temperance Union campaigned for the vote as a means to effect prohibition. The temperance advocates found allies among the old governing parties dominated by established landowners and the middle classes, who wished to use women's votes to counterbalance the influence of male immigrant miners.[3]

A nationalist variation on the same theme, whereby the politicians in power sought the votes of women to reduce the political influence of their opposition, appeared in the two European countries to accord women the vote before World War I. In Finland, women's groups identified their interest with the nationalist liberals and social democrats who joined together at the time of the 1905 Russian Revolution to insist on a new Finnish constitution bringing more independence from Russia. This constitution granted universal suffrage for men and women. In the same year, the Norwegian government deposed their ruler, the Swedish king, and conducted a plebiscite about the new national monarchy. Four hundred thousand male votes were cast, but simultaneously the woman suffrage societies organized their own plebiscite and were able to register three hundred thousand votes, demonstrating both their nationalist and organizational credentials. During the 1906 election, the women suffragists worked for the Radical party which then became the government, and in 1907 the parliamentary vote was accorded to all women who already possessed the municipal vote based on a property franchise.[4] In 1913 women's suffrage, like men's, became universal. The alliance of suffrage activity with nationalist separatist movements can also be seen in another Scandinavian country, Iceland, and, in an interesting variation, within Icelandic immigrants to North America. One remarkable Icelander who emigrated to Canada in 1893, Margret Benedictsson, edited and published *Freyja*, (Woman), a magazine "devoted to Woman's Political, Economical, and Social Rights." In one article she wrote in 1904, she described her reading the work of Icelandic patriot Jon Sigurdsson who campaigned for Iceland's self-government from Denmark. She was inspired by his yearning for liberty.

> Angry and distressed I read the laments of oppressed persons, unhap-
> pily married women, and the misfortunes of young girls. And it is this
> evil that aroused in men and in all honorable persons, a yearning to
> break down all the fetters that tie people to evil and distress, all fetters by
> whatever name we call them.

She identified her own fight for women's rights with that of Sigurdsson fighting for Icelandic independence: it was "the same yearning, the same love of
liberty and plea for justice" that drove people to seek their rights.[5]

In every country where female enfranchisement was passed, male politicians calculated that women's votes would tend to benefit the party in power.
Moreover, in most countries much of the radical sting had already left the
women's suffrage movements. It is possible that extremist agitation, like that
organized by the Women's Social and Political Union in Britain before the war,
and by the Women's Party in the United States, would have recurred, had
politicians not been ready to grant women's suffrage shortly after the war.
Doubtless they did so partly to avoid resurrecting prewar militancy and the
bitterness engendered by a conflict between women's movements and intractable governments. But on the whole, women were enfranchised in order to
produce a generalized benefit, not necessarily benefits for women themselves.
In some countries women's votes at election time tended to maintain the social
supremacy of particular ethnic or class groups over others. It was no coincidence that prohibition was adopted in Canada and the United States at the
same time as female suffrage. The abolition of liquor was seen as a necessary
first step to the purification of public life and was considered to be a means of
controlling blacks and immigrants with their imagined tendency toward
revolution.[6] While postwar European governments did not share the Anglo-
American predilection for liquor as a universal scapegoat, they too thought that
a new political establishment could be well served by associating with that half
of the adult population regarded as socially conservative. Women were to be
the ballast of parliamentary democracy, a system which was often a legacy of
World War I.

The newly enfranchised women turned out to be sleeping partners in the
political sense. Nor should this be considered surprising. The vote had been
the only unifying goal of the nineteenth-century women's movement. Leaders
had tended to exaggerate the power which possession of the vote would bring.
Of necessity they had focused more on the campaign to acquire the vote than
on the purposes to which the vote should eventually be put. When woman
suffrage was obtained, many suffrage workers celebrated and reduced their
political role. Their departure from political activism was paralleled by a lack of
analysis on women's appropriate political activity as enfranchised citizens.[7]
Women's political abdication was not universal: as we have seen, Austromarxist women developed interesting and relevant policies, and during the twenties
feminists were able to influence government legislation on matters concerning
women in several Western countries. Still, women's organizations between the
wars tended to be apolitical.[8] Few women entered politics, and many erstwhile
suffragists expressed disappointment that a younger generation of women

were not continuing to struggle to achieve, for example, the inchoate ideals put forward by an advocate of equal suffrage in 1910: "Woman represents an idea of God, evidenced by her being created with feelings and powers different from man's. The development and influence of the woman ideal is essential to the true progress of humanity."[9] Many suffragists, particularly in North America where the Women's Christian Temperance Union was prominent in suffrage activity, had been so buoyed up by the notion of the superior moral purity of women that it came as a bitter shock that few women were prepared to walk through the political doors unbolted by the suffragists. On the other hand, in the relaxed postwar social atmosphere, women were only too ready to walk through other doors and avail themselves of pleasures formerly confined to men.[10] Young girls bobbed their hair, smoked cigarettes, danced to jazz, drank the demon rum and were unashamedly self-centered. Prewar suffragists could not provide political or ideological leadership for a postsuffrage situation. The political power of women lay dormant until the women's liberation movement of the 1960s rekindled the possibility of more women articulating issues particularly affecting women and promoting them in the political arena.

Women's Liberation: The Present and the Future

Chafe sees three ways in which the structure of the women's liberation movement differs from previous women's movements.

> It is grounded in and moving in the same direction as underlying social trends at work in the society; it has developed an organizational base that is diverse and decentralized; and it is pursuing a wide range of social objectives that strike at many of the root causes of sex inequality.[11]

Previous women's movements had used the rhetoric of universality but their goals stood to benefit only limited constituencies: unmarried middle-class women, for example, were the prime beneficiaries of the move to open up professional education and employment in the nineteenth century. Even the vote appeared irrelevant to many concerned women. "The call for 'Votes for Women' is a poor, cracked, treble call," wrote the English socialist Lily Gair Wilkinson at the turn of the century, unable to discern how improved economic conditions could ensue from women's distant involvement in an imperfect political system.[12] Seventy years later, however, "ideological protest and underlying social and economic changes appeared to be moving in a similar direction."[13] Women in the labor force were receptive to the feminist demand for parity in wages and promotion opportunity. Parents had to find day care and preschool supervision for young children, and could agree with the need for more and better child support services. Family units found the two-adult income a prerequisite for their way of life, and this reinforced the trend toward fewer births: the women's liberation call for individual self-fulfillment independent of the traditional maternal, nurturant role was heard by women who regarded that role as economically anachronistic or emotionally insufficient.[14] By the 1970s, also, birth control technology, although imperfect, had become relatively efficient in a preventive sense. A woman had the technical means to separate sexual enjoyment from possible pregnancy and the feminist insistence that personal autonomy must include sexual autonomy helped dissipate some of the cultural complex of guilt and confusion surrounding sexual relationships. "No longer was feminism irrelevant to most people's daily lives. Instead the message spoke to many of the realities of the contemporary society."[15] Organizationally, women's liberation was decentralized, with grass-roots appeal, in contrast to the earlier more centralized, hierarchical, and elitist women's movements. Finally, the women's liberation movement attacked the many barriers in the way of equality between men and women, in the number and diversity of its objectives, which included reform of abortion laws, reform of sex stereotyping in school books and the media, and, in some countries, affirmative action in hiring on the part of government-funded employers.[16] The single political issue of the vote was replaced by the hydra-headed monster of sexism: a more appalling prospect, but also a more realistic appraisal of the task facing feminists.

The main reason that the women's liberation movement's "egalitarian ethic" in tandem with a "liberation ethic" was so effective, according to Chafe's cheerful prognosis, was that it provided an ideology concordant with underlying economic realities. The realities concerning women's economic position were documented in a report published by the Organization for Economic Co-operation and Development (OECD) in 1979. (Members of the OECD are: Australia, Austria, Belgium, Canada, Denmark, Finland, France, the Federal Republic of Germany, Greece, Iceland, Ireland, Italy, Japan, Luxembourg, the Netherlands, New Zealand, Norway, Portugal, Spain, Sweden, Switzerland, Turkey, the United Kingdom, and the United States.) The OECD report examined the consequences of the growing participation and changing roles of women in the labor market and evaluated the various ways in which member countries coped with problems raised. The report was intended as information for governments to use for planning programs to bring about effective equality for all citizens. Its findings suggest that reports of successful "liberation" are premature.

Segregation in Society: Sexual Apartheid

The participation rates for women in the work force varied considerably. The highest participation rate (that is, the number of persons in the labor force expressed as a percentage of the population aged fifteen to sixty-four in 1975) was in the Scandinavian countries (see table 1). Sweden, for instance, had a participation rate for women of 67.6 percent, and for men 89.2 percent. The lowest participation rates—in Greece, Ireland, Italy, Portugal, and Spain—averaged 30 percent, as compared to the participation rate for men in those countries of 87 percent. When women were measured as a proportion of the civilian labor force, in 1975 they were 36 percent of the total, an increase of 3 percent over the previous decade. Thus more women than before participated in paid employment, and they formed a higher percentage of the total labor force (table 2). Since the participation rate for single women presently is almost as

TABLE 1.   Labor Force Participation Rates of Women and Men, 1975, in percentage of the Respective Female or Male Population Aged 15–64

Country	% Women	% Men
Australia	48.5%	88.8%
Austria	48.0	84.4
Belgium	43.9	83.8
Canada	50.0	86.2
Denmark	63.5	89.8
Finland	65.6	79.7
France	56.5	84.4
Germany	48.5	85.7
Greece	30.8	82.7
Iceland	45.1	93.9
Ireland	33.5	92.1
Italy	30.7	81.2
Japan	51.7	89.6
Luxembourg	31.1	85.5
Netherlands	26.9[a]	83.9[a]
New Zealand	39.0	88.0
Norway	53.3	85.9
Portugal	32.0	94.4
Spain	32.5	87.6
Sweden	67.6	89.2
Switzerland	54.6	94.6
Turkey	53.2	92.8
United Kingdom	55.3	91.5
United States	53.1	85.3
Yugoslavia	46.4	85.4
Average	46.2	87.7

Source: OECD, Equal Opportunities for Women (Paris, 1979), p. 17.

a. Labor force figures expressed in man-years.

high as that for single men, any increase will be among married women (table 3), with the highest rate of increase likely in married women of childbearing age. In the twenty to twenty-four age group, the participation rate has already increased from 44.8 percent in the United States in 1960 to 63 percent in 1974 (table 4). The participation is lowest for married women with preschool age children (32 percent in the United States in 1970.)[17]

The distribution of women among various occupations showed that they held over 40 percent of the jobs in the service sector, about 25 percent of the jobs in agriculture, and about 20 percent of the jobs in industry (table 5). In the industries where women were employed, however, they were concentrated in a narrower range of jobs than men, which carried lower pay, involved fewer skills, and required less education and training. Among women wage or salary earners, 87 percent (compared with 70 percent of the men) worked in only three categories: in community, social, and personal services (41 percent of all gainfully employed women); in wholesale and retail trade including hotels and restaurants (21 percent); and in manufacturing (25 percent). This pattern of

TABLE 2.   Women as a Percentage of Civilian Employment in Seventeen Countries

Country	Year	% Women	Year	% Women	Difference
Australia	1964	28.2%	1975	34.2%	6.0%
Austria	1968	38.4	1975	38.4	—
Belgium	1963	31.1	1975	34.4	3.3
Canada[a]	1963	28.4	1976	36.9	8.5
			1977	37.0	8.6
Denmark	1965	34.8	1975	41.6	6.8
Finland	1964	44.0	1975	46.8	2.8
France	1968	35.2	1975	37.2	2.0
Germany	1963	36.9	1975	37.7	0.8
Greece	1961	32.3	1971	27.5	−5.1
Italy	1964	28.2	1975	28.1	−0.1
Ireland	1966	26.6	1975	27.4	0.8
Japan	1964	39.8	1975	37.4	−2.4
New Zealand	1964	26.1	1975	30.4	4.3
Norway	1963	29.6	1975	37.4	7.8
Sweden	1964	36.7	1975	42.3	5.6
United Kingdom	1964	34.3	1975	38.8	5.5
United States	1963	34.1	1975	39.6	5.5

Source: OECD, Equal Opportunities for Women (Paris, 1979), p. 19.

a. Canadian figures from Statistics Canada, Labour Force Survey.

TABLE 3.   Labor Force Participation Rate of Married Women, in percentage

Year	United States	Germany	United Kingdom	Japan	Sweden[a]
1960	30.48%				
1961	32.74				
1962	32.72	33.5%			
1963	33.72	33.3	34.38%	50.12%	47.0%
1964	34.39	33.1	35.16	49.79	46.8
1965	34.72	33.7	36.14	49.77	47.2
1966	35.46	34.6	37.68	50.04	49.3
1967	36.80	33.3	37.71	50.26	49.8
1968	38.28	34.1	38.41	49.60	51.8
1969	39.59	34.5	39.36	48.71	53.4
1970	40.79	35.6	39.82	48.37	56.1
1971	40.78	36.2	39.18	46.98	58.2
1972	41.48	37.7	40.73	46.28	59.8
1973	42.23	38.90		47.05	61.2
1974		39.0			63.6
1975		39.1			66.2

Source: OECD, Equal Opportunities for Women (Paris, 1979), p. 27.

a. Although Sweden is not one of the countries included in this study, when data were available, they have been indicated.

TABLE 4. Female Labor Force Participation Rate by Age Group and Year

Country	Year	15–19	20–24	25–59	60–64	65+
Australia	1966	62.2	58.9	32.5	16.5	4.9
	1973	56.0	62.3	44.5	16.3	3.4
Austria	1961	75.4	75.2	49.9	19.8	7.1
	1971	60.0	68.0	50.0	13.2	3.2
Belgium	1961	40.6	52.2	27.9	9.4	3.7
	1970	34.5	60.9	33.9	7.6	2.2
Finland	1960	41.7	60.7	55.6	36.0	11.6
	1974	32.7	65.9	75.1	33.3	2.0
France	1968	31.3	62.3	45.3	32.4	8.2
	1974	21.8	65.8	53.9	31.3	5.4
Denmark	1965	60.8	61.9	44.0	28.0	7.8
	1973	44.4	71.2	66.9	32.6	5.3
Sweden	1965	40.8	56.2	41.0	27.0	5.1
	1974	53.1	71.0	69.7	36.3	3.8
United States	1960	27.6	44.8	41.0	29.4	10.1
	1974	49.0	63.0	52.7	33.1	7.8

Source: OECD, *Equal Opportunities for Women* (Paris, 1979), p. 28.

industrial segregation appeared static, at least during the decade ending in 1975.

Moreover, within occupational categories, even more pronounced segregation existed in all countries. Two illustrations indicate the prevalent situation of women concentrated in the occupations of clerks, typists, stenographers, nurses, teachers, child care workers, social workers, cleaning and household workers, sales clerks, and garment and textile workers. The breakdown in figures for Germany in 1976 was the following. Women comprised 99 percent of health workers, 97 percent of the secretaries, 58 percent of the clerks, 60 percent of the wholesale and retail trade workers and 75 percent of the textile workers. By way of contrast, women comprised 2 percent of carpenters, 6 percent of electricians and 5 percent of chemists, physicists, and mathematicians. Similarly in the United States: in 1977 women were 98 percent of the

TABLE 5. Female Share of the Labor Force and Sectoral Employment, 1976, in percentage

	Average for All OECD Countries	Highest Female Share	Lowest Female Share
Female share of the total labor force	34.6%	45.6% (Finland 1976)	26.0% (Netherlands 1971)
Female share of agricultural employment	27.9	52.5 (Germany 1976)	9.0 (Ireland 1971)
Female share of industrial employment	21.2	29.2 (Finland 1976)	7.5 (Luxembourg 1970)
Female share of service employment	42.3	60.3 (Finland 1976)	10.1 (Turkey 1975)

Source: OECD, *Equal Opportunities for Women* (Paris, 1979), p. 28.

stenotypists, 74 percent of the clerical workers, 74 percent of the noncollege teachers and 58 percent of the service workers. At the same time, women were 1 percent of the carpenters and 5 percent of the construction workers. As workers, women enjoyed lateral mobility, but not upward mobility: they could move more easily than men from one employer to another, doing similar work, but had less facility than men in advancing within their occupations.[18]

Women experience the economic reality of a large and increasing work force which is highly segregated. Women's wages are lower, overall, than men's (70–75 percent) for the same or similar work. The objective of equal pay for work of equal value has met with limited success among employers, governments, and trade unions.[19] The continued female concentration in segregated occupations suggests that any increase of female representation in professional, management, and executive levels is of only small significance in the overall context of female employment.

The reasons for continuing disparity within the labor force derive from ancient assumptions concerning male authority and female subordination and continue to be reinforced by environmental facts which have been only slowly changing during the twentieth century. There is a vicious cycle whereby the narrow range of jobs performed by women perpetuates the stereotype, but both expectations and opportunities for women broaden as a result of nonsegregated education and training. Just as significant is the continuing expectation of women, and society, that women will bear prime responsibility for reproductive tasks: homemaking, and child rearing, as well as childbearing. Consequently women perceive their interest to be best served by choosing training for occupations which will allow maximum flexibility for combining work and family responsibilities. The low pay attached to work regarded as predominantly female deters men from entering such occupations and consequently helps to maintain the segregated work force. The OECD report emphasized nevertheless that women can be expected to participate more fully in the labor force, both in the service sector, which is expected to expand, and in other, less traditional occupations as ideological barriers weaken. It documented several ways in which governments have already weakened obstacles to a less segregated work force.

Imbalance and Equilibrium: Future Goals

For the future, the overall OECD objective is "a better equilibrium in the distribution of roles and tasks (occupational and family obligations) between the sexes."[20] To achieve this aim, governments should encourage employers and their own agencies, by human rights legislation, by antidiscrimination provisions, and by tax incentives, to provide nonsegregated educational and training opportunities for both sexes, to work toward more flexible working arrangements for men and women, and to acknowledge in a material way the responsibility of the state in the welfare of all citizens.

Superficially, it may appear that immense advances had been made in education by 1975. This is certainly true, in comparison with the limited literacy and minimal opportunities for advanced and professional training of a hundred years earlier. The school-leaving age in most countries was raised during the depression in order to reduce the number of young people in the labor market: this had the dual effect of helping form a largely literate population and at the same time reducing the competition for jobs among adults who had graduated from school. The trend to longer periods of education continued after World War II. Graduation from secondary schools, however, was still more common for boys than girls, and participation in higher education (universities and technical colleges) also showed a higher rate for men than women.[21] But the aims of nineteenth-century reformers have been achieved. Formal barriers to women's entry into such institutions have been largely banished, but informal obstacles remain. Educational agencies and students themselves resist a balanced sex ratio in technical and vocational training: business and commercial education, typing and bookkeeping, electronics, mechanical trades, and so on. Such resistance comes from the entrenched role prejudice which sees occupations as more appropriate for one sex or the other. The notion of androgynous occupations still taxes the imagination, and in schools peer pressure can exert a powerful influence to maintain existing proprieties: typing is for girls, mechanics is for boys. To a limited extent, some OECD countries offer adult education courses which enable older people to acquire technical training related to more mature considerations. Even at a later stage in their life span, however, women are barely represented in adult vocational training courses most likely to lead to job possibilities and advancement.[22] Their motivation is low: they still prefer to work with other women, and most of the better jobs do not provide female company. However, the tighter a family budget becomes in inflationary terms, the more incentive there is for an older woman to maximize her economic potential to the full, and the more motivation she may have to take advantage of second-chance training opportunity.

It remains to be seen which of the two major forces competing for the attention of women—and men—will dominate: economic necessity, or role ideology and socialization emanating from thousands of years of largely unquestioned experience. While public institutions can reduce discrimination by dismantling formal prohibitions on women's participation in educational preparation, they cannot alone overcome deep-rooted feelings held within an entire culture. Nevertheless, they are not entirely powerless. In the immediate future schools and other educational institutions can examine their own curricula, admissions policies, counseling services, and their own examples as employers to ensure they neither wittingly nor unwittingly perpetuate the prejudices which education can do so much to understand and change.

If women and men are to share responsibility for productive work in a society, equity suggests they share responsibility for reproductive work also. While much of this is likely based on a family, it is not confined to it. The rearing of children to maturity is a complex and wide-ranging task, as is the maintenance of a home. The physical and psychological demands made on parents by their children vary over the life cycle.[23] So do the demands of productive work. Time flexibility is one way that individual workers can be helped to find "solutions to the problems arising from the accumulation of employment and family responsibilities." Rigid systems, whereby daily, weekly, monthly, and yearly time schedules are always the same, create problems for parents who work. Businesses in several countries have tried experiments in coping with the problem. The introduction of flexible hours, for example, can allow parents to synchronize their working day with their children's illnesses or school hours. Other measures are ambiguous. Part-time work does not necessarily benefit parents, since traditionally it has carried inferior pay and benefits. A lifelong alternation of gainful and nongainful activity could be attractive to parents who wish to devote energy full time to either family or work, depending on the demands of the situation: a newborn infant, for example, needs full-time supervision from someone. If this is to be a real option, the disadvantages of discontinuous employment—in the loss of seniority and benefits—will have to be counterbalanced. If the leave is brief, such disadvantages can easily be overcome, and many countries have legislation protecting the fringe benefits of mothers who take maternity leave, for example. Longer absences, possibly related to professional and educational development as well as to family life, may require more thoroughgoing adjustment.[24] Within the family also there is much room for a redistribution of time commitments. Women still ordinarily spend more time than men do on household work. Work of a reproductive nature is still seen as mainly women's, even for those working in the labor force.[25]

Although participation rates vary, mothers of young children continue to enter the labor force in increasing numbers. In Sweden, for example, 37 percent of the mothers of preschool children were employed in 1965, but the number had risen to 66 percent by 1977.[26] While most parents will probably continue to assert their own responsibility in ensuring their children receive proper care, clearly an increasing number require that care be provided by persons other than themselves. The demand for child care, both preschool and after school, is already large and is likely to increase. It is, however, a demand with limits, for there are fewer children per family than formerly. Nevertheless, the OECD report found a universal shortage of adequate facilities for all age groups. The vast majority of children were cared for in unregulated, unlicensed premises, and received custodial care without reference to the educational or intellectual development of the child.

Since early education can have such a beneficial effect on children, many governments already acknowledge their responsibility in the provision of good facilities, but well-funded nursery schools are still comparatively rare. Low priority has been assigned to their provision, largely because of a lack of consensus within Western society generally about who should look after babies and infants. An Australian governmental committee of 1976 expressed the prevalent view: "Young children are dependent for emotional security on a limited number of adults, of whom the mother (or an acceptable substitute) is usually the most important."[27] Advice books to young parents continue to stress the role of the mother in parenting, urging also that the early preschool development of the infant is of such critical significance that any knots tied then cannot later be undone. At least some psychologists demur. "The whole of development is important, not merely the early years. There is as yet no indication that a given stage is clearly more formative than others; in the long term all may be important."[28] In the meantime, young parents will doubtless continue to work, and care for children must be seen as a responsibility shared not only within the family unit, but among society at large.

Government Services: Women's Welfare Benefits

The principle that the state accepts welfare responsibilities for its nationals is no longer in question. The actual extent of welfare benefits continue to generate discussion about priorities for government spending. Social security programs, whereby the state provides either money or services to cope with old age, industrial accident, death, unemployment, sickness, or poverty, exist in all OECD countries. They are financed by contributions made by workers, by employers, and by governments. They vary in the amount of assistance provided and in the standards of eligibility imposed for recipients. Employed single women with a continuous career until retirement generally enjoy equality of treatment with men in the same situation. Other women who experience an interruption of employment, or a change in marital status, or lower wages, are disadvantaged in the benefits for which they are eligible. Each particular program often reflects more than one goal, and this too may contribute to disparity in the way women are treated. For example, a pension plan is designed first to provide a minimum income for all old persons and simultaneously to relate pension benefits to past earnings. The more contributions a person makes, the higher the pension on retirement. Since most women's wage-related contributions are low, and often interrupted, a working woman's pension will also be low. A wife who did not herself contribute to a pension scheme may benefit only as a dependent of her contributing husband. The OECD report describes several ways in which member countries have addressed the problem whereby those persons in the population most in need of assistance do not always receive it.[29] The issue may possibly become less difficult as more women participate more continuously in the labor force and can receive benefits in their own right. Government programs in the areas of education and employment, and improved, more flexible working conditions in the work place together will inevitably influence social security programs. Clearly, a multifaceted approach to government programs and policies is the only sensible one.

In the meantime, grave problems and inequities exist which require more immediate action in that they can be literally a question of life and death. In Canada, for example, in 1975, out of 7.5 million adult women, 1.2 million were considered "poor" according to an official government definition: "families spending 62 percent or more of their income to provide themselves with the minimum necessities of food, shelter and clothing." One adult woman out of six, but only one man in nine, was classified as poor. An investigation found that the "great financial vulnerability of women" was based on the incorrect assumption that "most of them will always have a father or husband on whom they can count": Harriet Martineau's "false supposition" of 1859. The Canadian study echoed the conclusions of the OECD analysis in its statement of what needed to be done to ameliorate women's position.

Unless governments vigorously intervene to stop the damaging effects of sexual stereotyping in our schools and media, to reform family law to make the spouses more equal, to pursue employment policies aimed at advancing women's position in the labor market, to give more support to daycare and other measures of assistance to parents, and to improve income security programs for disadvantaged women there is no reason to believe that future generations of Canadian women will be any less vulnerable to poverty.[30]

Assumptions about women's roles must be detached from the Western cultural context and examined for their usefulness. The major achievement of both the nineteenth- and twentieth-century women's movements was that they inspired this ongoing process, but it is by no means complete. The concepts of equality and justice continue to inform Western thought. In the last century they inspired the first women's rights reformers to formulate their goals and strategies. The work they initiated continues. The nineteenth-century goal was to remove the man-made barriers to women's involvement in public life, and many of these have been dismantled. Feminists a hundred and fifty years later wish to restructure life, domestic as well as public, altogether.

Suggestions for Further Reading

Chafe, William H. *The American Woman: Her Changing Social, Economic and Political Roles, 1920–1970.* Oxford, 1975.

———. *Women and Equality: Changing Patterns in American Culture.* New York, 1977.

Evans, Richard J. *The Feminists: Women's Emancipation Movements in Europe, America and Australasia 1840–1920.* London, 1977.

Freeman, Jo, ed. *Women: A Feminist Perspective.* Palo Alto, Ca., 1975.

Lerner, Gerda. *The Majority Finds Its Past: Placing Women in History.* New York, 1981.

Organization for Economic Co-operation and Development. *Equal Opportunities for Women.* Paris, 1979.

Postscript

As we survey the centuries in our search for women's experience in the Western tradition, some familiar landmarks recur. Paramount among these persistent features is the historical placing of women within their families. It is true of the Gortyn heiress on Crete in the fifth century B.C., of fourteenth-century peasants in Montaillou in the French Pyrenees, and of English middle-class women in the nineteenth century. Behind this confinement of women within the family was the perceived need to protect and control their sexuality. The family must know the paternity of its daughters' children, a matter of considerable importance for a family of property. Concern for the transmission of private property helps explain society's physical circumscription of women and women's exclusion from privileges which might make them less mindful of their family's importance. The institutions, customs, and laws mutually reinforcing this central fact transcend cultural and economic variables down the centuries of the Western tradition. Yet there are tantalizing glimpses of a previous unchained woman.

Anthropologists and archaeologists have unearthed evidence of a time when women were active, revered, self-confident, visible. The women of Catal Huyuk and Minoan Crete seem to have more in common with the hypothesized women of Bachofen's *Mutterrecht* than with their suppressed descendants in civilized society. Socialists argued that the development of the concept of property held privately, rather than in common, ended a freedom of action women had once enjoyed—Engels's famous "world historical defeat of the female sex." In default of a more convincing explanation, we still invoke it today. We are nevertheless aware that the distinction between public and private property was never so precise as Engels asserted. At least Bebel sounded a laconic note of caution. "It is difficult to trace in detail the manner in which the change was achieved. A knowledge of the events is lacking." So we allude to the Neolithic goddesses and the ecstatic princesses and infer that women before the first millennium B.C. knew more freedom than Aristotle's women in the Golden Age of Greece. We are ever mindful that future scholars may find themselves painting a more bleak, as well as a more precise, picture.

Within the family the women have been able to exercise domestic authority, and in societies with competing clans and tribes, women have been able to exercise political authority too. Even the segregated Athenian woman had power over her young children. Feudal heiresses could exact tribute and respect due to the lord of a fief. When state interests replaced dynastic interests the political power of the women in great families was commensurately reduced. So long as the family was the microcosm and the state was the macrocosm, the hierarchical relations of the one were rehearsed in the other, and each reinforced the other. The monarch exacted unquestioning obedience from the subject, and within the family, the lady lived through the same formula of deference and submission to her lord. We know from scraps of surviving literature that prescriptions of womanly obedience were not universally followed, but church and state together exercised a powerful influence enjoining submission to authority.

The French Revolution heralded the end of that ancient regime. Anticipated by the Renaissance and Reformation, the Enlightenment philosophers of the eighteenth century subjected received wisdom to critical analysis, and the same methodology was accessible for women to question their official inferiority to men. At the same time, industrialization drove a wedge into time-honored relations between the vast majority of men and women subsisting in an agrarian economy. Before the industrial revolution, the household economy represented a collaboration in production between a peasant woman and her husband. The ablebodied adults of a family unit contributed their productive, as well as their reproductive, work to the family, and this understanding was maintained even after the inception of the factory system dislocated the dual demands of work and family care. But by the end of the nineteenth century wages were increasing; fewer families required more than one adult wage earner; women were expected to invest more time in their reproductive activity; and it seemed as though industrialization was confining more women than ever before to the household and banishing them from the public sphere.

Not all women, however, lived with men whose income sufficed to support a family. The nineteenth century saw a new concern for single adult women who outnumbered adult men, those "redundant" women who could not count on perpetual protection from a father or husband. While few reformers at the time foresaw the detachment of most women totally from the confines of family, middle-class reformers worked to provide suitable employment for middle-class spinsters so that they could avoid burdening their relatives. Originally promoted in the interests of a minority, middle-class employment for women swiftly became the experience of practically all women for some period of their lives. Populations expanded, the number of jobs increased, aspirations rose and so did prices. By the 1980s, consumption in Western countries had drawn the majority of women back into productive occupations. Marriage was again reverting to a preindustrial pattern of economic collaboration between the spouses.

One difference between women of the twentieth century and preindustrial peasant women is the physical separation of productive and reproductive activity. But just as the nature of women's productive work has changed, from primarily agrarian and domestic service work to manufacturing and administrative service sector work, so also have the demands of reproductive investment.

Until World War II women found it expedient to exploit their reproductive potential. A child represented a future wage earner for the family economy, and as an adult, a child could care for parents in their dotage. By the first quarter of the twentieth century child mortality was waning, and Western states had welfare programs to provide minimum social security for old, sick, and unemployed people. It was no longer as important for a woman to maximize her reproductive capacity. A woman was released from a predominantly reproductive imperative at the same time that there was more opportunity to be involved once again in productive life. The nineteenth-century women's movement had opened professional and office employment to single women, so some formal impediments were already dismantled. Within a modern industrialized economy the historically long integration for women between reproduction and production was again, tentatively, resumed, only this time with the addition of a political ideology of equality to inspire a more egalitarian balance between the sexes.

Twentieth-century women no longer suffer the same constraints as their ancestors for the same reasons. Reproduction can be managed less imperfectly: fewer pregnancies need be taken to term for survival, and the simple economic value of children in Western society is much reduced. Also, the physical disposition of private property is less important when the assets producing a family's livelihood lie not in its inherited land but in the educated skills and intelligence of its youth. Education has become a substitute for land and plow. As always, a young woman must be trained with her future in mind. In the schools and colleges of the late twentieth century we recognize one of the old features of women's historical landscape. Women still perceive themselves with the foremost responsibility for reproductive work and they consequently choose their occupation with an eye to mobile auxiliary work, secondary in importance to a husband's. Increasingly more women depart from this pattern, but the pattern is still there, clearly defined and reinforced by every young woman who enters nursing, teaching, and secretarial work. These life choices are no longer predetermined by ancient law and religious regulation. Modern sanctions substitute with similar effect. Old habits die hard: when so many factors mutually reinforce one another, monumental effort is required to arrive at egalitarian principles of institutional and personal practice.

That is still in the future. What I have attempted to do in this book is to show what the past has meant for Western women. For we cannot deny our history. There is so much we can learn from it, and as more historians unravel more of women's experience in the past, we shall discover in greater measure what our cultural resources are.

Notes

CHAPTER 1

1. Susan Moller Okin, *Women in Western Political Thought* (London, 1980), pp. 5–11.

2. Lorenne M. G. Clark and Lynda Lange, eds., *The Sexism of Social and Political Theory: Women and Reproduction from Plato to Nietzsche* (Toronto, 1979), p. viii.

3. Germaine Greer, *The Obstacle Race: The Fortunes of Women Painters and Their Work* (London, 1979).

4. Mary Beard, *Woman As Force in History* (New York, 1946).

5. Carl N. Degler, *Is There a History of Women?* (Oxford, 1975), pp. 6 and passim.

6. G. M. Trevelyan, *English Social History* (London, 1944), p. vii.

7. E. LeRoy Ladurie, *The Territory of the Historian* (Brighton, 1979), pp. 17–31; Carroll Smith-Rosenberg, "The New Woman and the New History," *Feminist Studies* 2 (1975):185–98; Lawrence Stone, "The Revival of Narrative: Reflections on a New Old History," *Past and Present* 85 (1979):15.

8. Gerda Lerner, "Placing Women in History: A 1975 Perspective," in *Liberating Women's History: Theoretical and Critical Essays* ed. Berenice A. Carroll (Urbana, Ill., 1976), pp. 357–67.

9. Mary Beth Norton, "American History," *Signs* 5 (1979):328.

10. Mary Lyndon Shanley, "The History of the Family in Modern England," *Signs* 4 (1979):740–50; Carl N. Degler, *At Odds: Women and the Family in America from the Revolution to the Present* (Oxford, 1980), pp. vi, vii, 3–6.

11. Lawrence Stone, *The Family, Sex and Marriage in England 1500–1800* (London, 1977); Natalie Zemon Davis, "Women's History in Transition: The European Case," *Feminist Studies* 3 (1976):83–103.

12. Virginia Woolf, *A Room of One's Own* (London, 1975), p. 45.

CHAPTER 2

1. Geoffrey Barraclough, ed., *The Times Atlas of World History* (Maplewood, N.J., 1979), pp. 32–37; Nancy Tanner and Adrienne Zihlman, "Women

in Evolution Part I: Innovation and Selection in Human Origins," *Signs* 1(1976):585–608; Adrienne Zihlman, "Women in Evolution Part II: Subsistence and Social Organization Among Early Hominids," *Signs* 4(1978):4–20; Louise Lamphere, "Anthropology," *Signs* 2 (1977):612–27; Rayna Rapp, "Anthropology," *Signs* 4 (1979):497–513.

2. E. Evans-Pritchard, "The Position of Women in Primitive Societies," in *The Position of Women in Primitive Societies and Other Essays in Social Anthropology*, ed. E. Evans-Pritchard (London, 1965), pp. 38–39; Elizabeth Fee, "The Sexual Politics of Victorian Social Anthropology," in *Clio's Consciousness Raised: New Perspectives on the History of Women*, ed. Mary S. Hartman and Lois Banner (New York, 1974), p. 101.

3. Sally Slocum, "Woman the Gatherer: Male Bias in Anthropology," in *Toward an Anthropology of Women*, ed. Rayna R. Reiter (New York, 1975), pp. 39, 42, 43, 45; Zihlman, "Women in Evolution Part II," p. 18.

4. Kathleen Gough, "The Origin of the Family," in *Toward an Anthropology of Women*, ed. Reiter, pp. 51–76.

5. Martin King Whyte, *The Status of Women in Preindustrial Societies* (Princeton, 1978), pp. 108–12.

6. James Mellaart, "Catal Huyuk, A Neolithic City in Anatolia," *Proceedings of the British Academy* 51 (1965):201–13; Kathleen Kenyon, *Royal Cities of the Old Testament* (New York, 1971), p. 6.

7. James Mellaart, *Catal Huyuk: A Neolithic Town in Anatolia* (New York, 1967), pp. 202–5, 224–26.

8. Jacquetta Hawkes, *Dawn of the Gods* (New York, 1968), p. 24.

9. Ibid., p. 70.

10. Ibid., pp. 52, 69, 153.

11. Joan Bamberger, "The Myth of Matriarchy: Why Men Rule in Primitive Society," in *Woman, Culture and Society*, ed. Michelle Zimbalist Rosaldo and Louise Lamphere (Stanford, 1974). pp. 263–65.

12. Paula Webster, "Matriarchy: A Vision of Power," in *Toward an Anthropology of Women*, ed. Reiter, p. 144.

13. Fee, "Sexual Politics," p. 88.

14. Webster, "Matriarchy: A Vision of Power," p. 145; Bamberger, "The Myth of Matriarchy," p. 266.

15. Eleanor Leacock, "Women in Egalitarian Societies," in *Becoming Visible: Women in European History*, ed. Renate Bridenthal and Claudia Koonz (Boston, 1977), p. 25.

16. Judith K. Brown, "Iroquois Women: An Ethnohistorical Note," in *Toward an Anthropology of Women*, ed. Reiter, pp. 237, 241.

17. Ibid., pp. 237, 251.

18. Whyte, *Status of Women*, pp. 167–68.

19. Ibid., p. 116.

20. Ibid., p. 172.

21. Ibid., pp. 153–57, 160–61.

22. Ibid., p. 165.

23. Ibid., p. 182.

CHAPTER 3

1. Aristotle, *The Politics*, trans. B. Jowett (Oxford, 1957) p. 52; Verena Zinserling, *Women in Greece and Rome* (New York, 1973), p. 22.

2. Homer, *The Iliad*, trans. E. V. Rieu (London, 1978), pp. 69, 122; Mary R. Lefkowitz and Maureen Fant, *Women in Greece and Rome* (Toronto, 1977), p. 50.

3. Sarah B. Pomeroy, *Goddesses, Whores, Wives, and Slaves: Women in Classical Antiquity* (New York, 1975), pp. 17–18, 97–101.

4. Marylin Arthur, " 'Liberated' Women: The Classical Era," in *Becoming Visible: Women in European History*, ed. Renate Bridenthal and Claudia Koonz, (Boston, 1977), p. 71; Euripides, *Medea*, trans. Philip Vellacott (London, 1971), p. 24.

5. Sarah B. Pomeroy, "A Classical Scholar's Perspective on Matriarchy," in *Liberating Women's History: Theoretical and Critical Essays*, ed. Berenice Carroll (Urbana, Ill., 1976), p. 223; C. G. Thomas, "Matriarchy in Early Greece: The Bronze and Dark Ages," *Arethusa* 6 (1973):190.

6. W. K. Lacey, *The Family in Classical Greece* (Ithaca, N.Y., 1968), pp. 198, 200–201, 206; Pomeroy, *Goddesses, Whores, Wives, and Slaves*, pp. 36, 38.

7. Lacey, *The Family in Classical Greece*, pp. 208–216; Pomeroy, *Goddesses, Whores, Wives, and Slaves*, pp. 39–42.

8. Pomeroy, *Goddesses, Whores, Wives, and Slaves*, pp. 45–46.

9. Judith P. Hallett, "Sappho and Her Social Context: Sense and Sensuality," *Signs* 4 (1979):450, 457–58; Lefkowitz and Fant, *Women in Greece and Rome*, pp. 3–6; Pomeroy, *Goddesses, Whores, Wives, and Slaves*, pp. 53–55.

10. Marylin Arthur, "Classics," *Signs* 2 (1976):387–91; David M. Schaps, *The Economic Rights of Women in Ancient Greece* (Edinburgh, 1979), pp. 3, 97–98.

11. Pomeroy, *Goddesses, Whores, Wives, and Slaves*, p. 168.

12. Lacey, *The Family in Classical Greece*, pp. 157–58; K. J. Dover, "Classical Greek Attitudes to Sexual Behavior," *Arethusa* 6 (1973):163.

13. Lacey, *The Family in Classical Greece*, pp. 100, 103.

14. Pomeroy, *Goddesses, Whores, Wives, and Slaves*, p. 69.

15. Aristotle, *Politics*, p. 7.

16. Ibid., p. 295.

17. Pomeroy, *Goddesses, Whores, Wives, and Slaves*, p. 79.

18. Lefkowitz and Fant, *Women in Greece and Rome*, pp. 22–24.

19. Lacey, *The Family in Classical Greece*, pp. 163, 171.

20. Philip E. Slater, *The Glory of Hera: Greek Mythology and the Greek Family* (Boston, 1968), pp. 8–14, 28–30, 33–38.

21. Aristotle, *Politics*, p. 51.

22. Pomeroy, *Goddesses, Whores, Wives, and Slaves*, pp. 75–78.

23. Ibid., pp. 126–28.

24. Ibid., pp. 134–36.

25. Ibid., pp. 76, 121–25, 127, 130, 142–43.

26. Sheila McNally, "The Maenad in Early Greek Art," *Arethusa* 11 (1978):102.

CHAPTER 4

1. Judith P. Hallett, "The Role of Women in Roman Elegy: Counter-Cultural Feminism," *Arethusa* 6 (1973):105.

2. J. P. Dacre Balsdon, *Roman Women* (London, 1962), pp. 76–77, 202, 236.

3. Sarah B. Pomeroy, *Goddesses, Whores, Wives, and Slaves: Women in Classical Antiquity* (New York, 1975), pp. 150–57.

4. Vern L. Bullough and Bonnie Bullough, *The Subordinate Sex: A History of Attitudes Toward Women* (Baltimore, Md., 1974), p. 88.

5. Balsdon, *Roman Women*, p. 47; Hallett, "Role of Women in Roman Elegy," p. 107.

6. Balsdon, *Roman Women*, pp. 47–48.

7. Pomeroy, *Goddesses, Whores, Wives, and Slaves*, pp. 150, 157, 160; Balsdon, *Roman Women*, pp. 214, 245.

8. Balsdon, *Roman Women*, p. 194; Jerome Carcopino, *Daily Life in Ancient Rome: The People and the City at the Height of the Empire* (London, 1978), p. 104.

9. Pomeroy, *Goddesses, Whores, Wives, and Slaves*, pp. 165, 167.

10. Balsdon, *Roman Women*, p. 196.

11. Mary R. Lefkowitz and Maureen Fant, *Women in Greece and Rome* (Toronto, 1977), p. 111.

12. Balsdon, *Roman Women*, pp. 270–71; Marylin Arthur, " 'Liberated' Women: The Classical Era," in *Becoming Visible: Women in European History*, ed. Renate Bridenthal and Claudia Koonz (Boston, 1977), p. 84.

13. Balsdon, *Roman Women*, p. 62.

14. Verena Zinserling, *Women in Greece and Rome* (New York, 1973), pl. 94, 95.

15. Balsdon, *Roman Women*, p. 261.

16. Ibid., p. 265.

17. Pomeroy, *Goddesses, Whores, Wives, and Slaves*, pp. 190–93.

18. Susan Treggiari, "Libertine Ladies," *Classical World* 64 (1971):198; Pomeroy, *Goddesses, Whores, Wives, and Slaves*, pp. 193–97.

19. Pomeroy, *Goddesses, Whores, Wives, and Slaves*, pp. 200–201.

20. Hallett, "Role of Women in Roman Elegy," pp. 103, 112–15, 120.

CHAPTER 5

1. Mary R. Lefkowitz and Maureen Fant, *Women in Greece and Rome* (Toronto, 1977), p. 92.

2. Sarah B. Pomeroy, *Goddesses, Whores, Wives, and Slaves: Women in Classical Antiquity* (New York, 1975), pp. 76–77.

3. J. P. Dacre Balsdon, *Roman Women* (London, 1962), p. 200.

4. Pomeroy, *Goddesses, Whores, Wives, and Slaves*, pp. 208–9, 218, 213–14, 223.

5. Ibid., p. 171.

6. Henry Chadwick, *The Early Church* (London, 1977), pp. 55–56.

7. Hans Jonas, *The Gnostic Religion* (Boston, 1958), pp. 31–34, 42–47.

8. Elaine H. Pagels, "What Became of God the Mother? Conflicting Images of God in Early Christianity," *Signs* 2 (1976):294–95.

9. Elaine H. Pagels, *The Gnostic Gospels* (New York, 1979), pp. xiii–xxxvi.

10. Phyllis Bird, "Images of Women in the Old Testament," in *Religion and Sexism*, ed. Rosemary Reuther (New York, 1974), pp. 51–54.

11. Ibid., pp. 57–70.

12. Luke 15:3–7, 8–10; Luke 13:18–21.

13. Luke 10:42; John 8:3–11; Matthew 19:1–9; Constance F. Parvey, "The Theology and Leadership of Women in the New Testament," in *Religion and Sexism*, ed. Reuther, pp. 139–41.

14. Pagels, *Gnostic Gospels*, p. 64.

15. Acts 17:11–12; Parvey, "Women in the New Testament," p. 144.

16. Joan Morris, *Against Nature and God* (London, 1973), p. 1.

17. Acts 9:36–43; Parvey, "Women in the New Testament," p. 145.

18. Derrick Sherwin Bailey, *The Man-Woman Relation in Christian Thought* (London, 1959), pp. 15–16; Joel 2:28.

19. Parvey, "Women in the New Testament," pp. 123–26.

20. I Corinthians 6:9–20; 6:1–4; 5:1–2; Parvey, "Women in the New Testament," pp. 124–25.

21. I Corinthians 14:40; Parvey, "Women in the New Testament," p. 130; Morris, *Against Nature and God*, pp. 118–23.

22. Chadwick, *Early Church*, p. 60.

23. Balsdon, *Roman Women*, p. 283.

24. Morris, *Against Nature and God*, pp. 4–8.

25. Pagels, "What Became of God the Mother?" p. 300.

26. Ibid.

27. Ibid., p. 294.

28. Morris, *Against Nature and God*, p. 12.

29. Bailey, *The Man-Woman Relation in Christian Thought*, p. 44.

30. Rosemary Reuther, "Misogynism and Virginal Feminism in the Fathers of the Church," in *Religion and Sexism*, ed. Reuther, pp. 157, 159; Bailey, *The Man-Woman Relation in Christian Thought*, p. 24.

31. Bailey, *The Man-Woman Relation in Christian Thought*, pp. 49–51.

32. Ibid., pp. 26, 30, 62.

33. Ibid., pp. 74, 83–84, 88, 93.

34. Ibid., p. 44.

CHAPTER 6

1. Robert W. Hanning, "From 'Eva' and 'Ave' to Eglentyne and Alisoun: Chaucer's Insight into the Roles Women Play," *Signs* 2 (1977):580–99.

2. Georges Duby, *The Early Growth of the European Economy: Warriors and Peasants from the Seventh to the Twelfth Centuries* (New York, 1974), pp. 8, 24.

3. Ibid., pp. 15, 18, 22.

4. Meg Bogin, *The Women Troubadours* (New York, 1980), p. 36.

5. Ibid., pp. 49, 55, 72.

6. R. W. Southern, *Western Society and the Church in the Middle Ages* (London, 1978), p. 80.

7. Eleanor Commo McLaughlin, "Equality of Souls, Inequality of Sexes: Women in Medieval Theology," in *Religion and Sexism*, ed. Rosemary Reuther (New York, 1974), pp. 213–32.

8. Julia O'Faolain and Lauro Martines, eds., *Not In God's Image: A History of Women in Europe from the Greeks to the Nineteenth Century* (New York, 1973), p. 102.

9. Doris Stenton, *The English Woman in History* (New York, 1977), pp. 11, 23.

10. Jo-Ann McNamara and Suzanne F. Wemple, "Marriage and Divorce in the Frankish Kingdom," in *Women in Medieval Society*, ed. Susan Mosher Stuard (Philadelphia, 1976), p. 108.

11. Ibid., p. 102; Georges Duby, *Le Chevalier, la Femme et le Pretre* (Paris, 1981).

12. Stenton, *The English Woman in History*, pp. 15–16; Emily James Putnam, *The Lady: Studies of Certain Significant Phases of Her History* (Chicago, 1970), pp. 69–105.

13. Stenton, *The English Woman in History*, pp. 40, 41.

14. Eileen Power and M. Postan, *Medieval Women* (Cambridge, 1975), p. 99.

15. Joan Morris, *Against Nature and God* (London, 1973), pp. 55, 69, 85.

16. Southern, *Western Society and the Church*, pp. 242, 280–81.

17. Ibid., p. 263.

18. Brenda M. Bolton, "Mulieres Sanctae," in *Women in Medieval Society*, ed. Stuard, p. 149; Sally Thompson, "The Problem of the Cistercian Nuns in the Twelfth and the Early Thirteenth Centuries," in *Medieval Women: Essays Presented to Rosalind Hill*, ed. Derek Baker (Oxford, 1978), p. 242.

19. Bolton, "Mulieres Sanctae," p. 145.

20. McLaughlin, "Equality of Souls, Inequality of Sexes," pp. 242–43.

21. LeRoy Ladurie, *Montaillou: The Promised Land of Error* (New York, 1978), pp. viii–ix.

22. Marina Warner, *Alone of All Her Sex: The Myth and the Cult of the Virgin Mary* (New York, 1976), pp. 131, 121–32.

23. Bogin, *The Women Troubadours*, pp. 57–61.

24. Warner, *Alone of All Her Sex*, pp. 147–48.

25. David Hugh Farmer, ed., *The Oxford Dictionary of Saints* (Oxford, 1978), p. 404; S. Baring-Gould, *The Lives of the Saints* (London, 1898), 8:488–89.

26. Stenton, *The English Woman in History*, pp. 6, 32–33.

27. David Herlihy, "Land, Family and Women in Continental Europe, 701–1200," in *Women in Medieval Society*, ed. Stuard, pp. 30, 31.

28. O'Faolain and Martines, *Not In God's Image*, pp. 98, 100.

29. Stenton, *The English Woman in History*, pp. 80–84.

30. Eileen Power, *Medieval People* (London, 1950), pp. 99, 103.

31. Emily Coleman, "Infanticide in the Early Middle Ages," in *Women in Medieval Society*, ed. Stuard, pp. 62–64; Evelyne Patlagean, "Birth Control in the Early Byzantine Empire," in *Biology of Man in History, Vol. 1: Selections from*

the Annales: Economies, Societies, Civilizations, ed. Robert Forster and Orest Ranum (Baltimore, 1975), p. 9.

32. Power and Postan, *Medieval Women,* p. 55.

33. Duby, *Early Growth of the European Economy,* pp. 186–210; M. M. Postan, *The Medieval Economy and Society: An Economic History of Britain, 1100–1500* (London, 1975), pp. 30–80.

34. David Herlihy, "Life Expectancies for Women in Medieval Society," in *The Social History of Italy and Western Europe 700–1500,* ed. David Herlihy (London, 1978), 13:5–13; Herlihy, "The Medieval Marriage Market," in *ibid.,* 14:16–19; Herlihy, "Women in Medieval Society," in *ibid.,* 9:5.

35. Ladurie, *Montaillou,* pp. 25, 153, 169, 178, 179.

36. Ibid., pp. 186–89, 192–93, 194, 197–200, 224, 248, 253–55.

37. Power, *Medieval People,* pp. 18–26; Power and Postan, *Medieval Women,* pp. 55–57, 59.

38. O'Faolain and Martines, *Not In God's Image,* pp. 154, 155.

39. Ibid., p. 162; Power and Postan, *Medieval Women,* p. 60; R. Lis and H. Soly, *Poverty and Capitalism in Pre-Industrial Europe: 1350–1850* (Brighton, 1979), pp. 18–20; Kathleen Casey, "The Cheshire Cat: Reconstructing the Experience of Medieval Women," in *Liberating Women's History: Theoretical and Critical Essays,* ed. Berenice Carroll (Urbana, Ill., 1976), pp. 224–49.

40. Barbara A. Hanawalt, "The Female Felon in Fourteenth Century England," in *Women in Medieval Society,* ed. Stuard, pp. 135, 138.

41. James A. Brundage, "Prostitution in the Medieval Canon Law," *Signs* 1 (1976):830, 835–38.

42. Marina Warner, *Joan of Arc: The Image of Female Heroism* (New York, 1981).

43. Geoffrey Chaucer, *The Canterbury Tales,* trans. Neville Coghill (London, 1977), p. 310.

CHAPTER 7

1. J. H. Plumb, *The Penguin Book of the Renaissance* (London, 1969), p. 25.

2. Judy Chicago, *The Dinner Party* (New York, 1979), p. 79–82.

3. Ann Sutherland Harris and Linda Nochlin, *Women Artists 1550–1950* (Los Angeles, 1976), pp. 20–21, 25–27; Germaine Greer, *The Obstacle Race: The Fortunes of Women Painters and Their Work* (London, 1979), p. 207.

4. Julia O'Faolain and Lauro Martines, eds., *Not In God's Image: A History of Women in Europe from the Greeks to the Nineteenth Century* (New York, 1973), pp. 190–93.

5. Christine de Pisan, "The Boke of the Cyte of Ladyes," in *Distaves and Dames: Renaissance Treatises for and About Women,* ed. Diane Bornstein (New York, 1978).

6. O'Faolain and Martines, *Not In God's Image,* p. 181; Susan Groag Bell, "Comment on Sheila Delany's 'Review of The Order of the Rose: The Life and Times of Christine de Pisan,' " *Signs* 4 (1979):592–93.

7. Joan Kelly-Gadol, "Did Women Have a Renaissance?" in *Becoming Visible: Women in European History,* ed. Renate Bridenthal and Claudia Koonz (Boston, 1977), pp. 139, 161.

8. O'Faolain and Martines, *Not In God's Image*, p. 183.

9. Ibid., pp.184, 188.

10. Doris Stenton, *The English Woman in History* (New York, 1977), p. 142.

11. Galatians 4:28; Joel 2:28.

12. Stenton, *The English Woman in History*, p. 175.

13. Roland H. Bainton, *Women of the Reformation in Germany and Italy* (Boston, 1974), pp. 98, 105–6.

14. Ibid., pp. 62–63, 66.

15. Owen Chadwick, *The Reformation* (London, 1977), p. 74.

16. Bainton, *Women of the Reformation*, p. 26.

17. Ibid., pp. 145–58; Chadwick, *The Reformation*, pp. 188–210; Roger Thompson, *Women in Stuart England and America: A Comparative Study* (London, 1974), p. 88.

18. Claire Cross, " 'He-Goats Before the Flocks': A Note on the Part Played by Women in the Founding of some Civil War Churches," in *Popular Belief and Practice*, ed. G. J. Cuming and Derek Baker (Cambridge, 1972), pp. 195–202.

19. Keith Thomas, "Women and the Civil War Sects," *Past and Present* 13 (1958):52.

20. Christopher Hill, *The World Turned Upside Down* (London, 1975), p. 311.

21. Ibid., pp. 42–43, 210.

22. Ibid., p. 315.

23. Thomas, "Women and the Civil War Sects," p. 47.

24. Stenton, *The English Woman in History*, p. 179; Thomas, "Women and the Civil War Sects," pp. 47–48; Mary Maples Dunn, "Women of Light," in *Women of America*, ed. Carol Ruth Berkin and Mary Beth Norton (Boston, 1979), p. 120.

25. Natalie Zemon Davis, "City Women and Religious Change," in *Society and Culture in Early Modern France*, ed. Natalie Zemon Davis (Stanford, 1975), pp. 79, 82.

26. Stenton, *The English Woman in History*, p. 105.

27. Lawrence Stone, *The Family, Sex and Marriage in England 1500–1800* (London, 1977), p. 140.

28. Stenton, *The English Woman in History*, p. 109.

29. Bainton, *Women of the Reformation*, p. 67.

30. Davis, *Society and Culture in Early Modern France*, pp. 83, 85.

31. Hill, *The World Turned Upside Down*, pp. 137, 319.

32. G. R. Quaife, *Wanton Wenches and Wayward Wives: Peasants and Illicit Sex in Early Seventeenth Century England* (London, 1979), pp. 186–201.

33. E. William Monter, "Women in Calvinist Geneva, 1550–1800," *Signs* 6 (1980):208.

34. Ibid., pp. 191–93; Quaife, *Wanton Wenches and Wayward Wives*, pp. 192–93.

35. O'Faolain and Martines, *Not In God's Image*, pp. 267–68.

36. Davis, *Society and Culture in Early Modern France*, p. 89.

37. E. William Monter, "Pedestal and Stake," in *Becoming Visible*, ed.

Bridenthal and Koonz, p. 133; Keith Thomas, *Religion and the Decline of Magic* (London, 1971), pp. 436, 438.

38. O'Faolain and Martines, *Not In God's Image*, p. 210.

39. Monter, "Pedestal and Stake," p. 130; Thomas, *Religion and the Decline of Magic*, pp. 450–52.

40. E. William Monter, *Witchcraft in France and Switzerland: The Borderlands During the Reformation* (Ithaca, N.Y., 1976), pp. 197–200.

41. Thomas, *Religion and the Decline of Magic*, p. 49.

CHAPTER 8

1. Olwen Hufton, *The Poor of Eighteenth-Century France 1750–1789* (Oxford, 1974), pp. 11–24, 115.

2. G. R. Elton, *England under the Tudors* (London, 1962); Allison Heisch, "Queen Elizabeth I: Parliamentary Rhetoric and the Exercise of Power," *Signs* 1 (1975):31–55; J. E. Neale, *Elizabeth I and Her Parliaments* (London, 1966).

3. C. A. Macartney, *Maria Theresa and the House of Austria* (London, 1969), pp. 47, 144.

4. Ibid., passim; Edward Crankshaw, *Maria Theresa* (London, 1969).

5. Vincent Cronin, *Catherine, Empress of All the Russians* (London, 1978).

6. Isabel De Madariaga, *Russia in the Age of Catherine the Great* (New Haven, Conn., 1981).

7. Arthur M. Wilson, " 'Treated Like Imbecile Children' (Diderot): The Enlightenment and the Status of Women," in *Woman in the Eighteenth Century and Other Essays*, ed. Paul Fritz and Richard Morton (Toronto, 1976), p. 95.

8. Carolyn Lougee, *Le Paradis Des Femmes: Women, Salons, and Social Stratification in Seventeenth-Century France* (Princeton, 1976), pp. 4–7.

9. Ibid., pp. 136, 214.

10. Hugo P. Thieme, *Woman: Women of Modern France* (Philadelphia, 1907), pp. 231, 236, 265.

11. Doris Stenton, *The English Woman in History* (New York, 1977), pp. 270–72; Alison Adburgham, *Women in Print* (London, 1972), p. 135.

12. Jean Jacques Rousseau, *Emile*, trans. Barbara Foxley (London, 1963), 5:321–444; *Julie ou la Nouvelle Heloise* (Paris, 1930); Condorcet, "Esquisse d'un tableau historique des progres de l'esprit humain," in *Oeuvres Complètes* (Paris, 1804), p. 8.

13. Montesquieu, *Persian and Chinese Letters*, trans. J. Davison (Washington, 1901), pp. 288–89; *The Spirit of the Laws*, trans. T. Nugent (New York, 1949), pp. 94–108.

14. Rousseau, *Emile*, pp. 325–442; *Confessions*, trans. J. M. Cohen (London, 1960), pp. 374–453.

15. James Leith, *The Idea of Art as Propaganda in France, 1750–1799: A Study in the History of Ideas* (Toronto, 1965), pp. 106–7.

16. Ruth Graham, "Rousseau's Sexism Revolutionized," in *Woman in the Eighteenth Century*, ed. Fritz and Morton, pp. 130–31.

17. Condorcet, *Sketch for a Historical Picture of the Progress of the Human Mind*, trans. J. Barraclough (London, 1955), p. 193.

18. Wilson, " 'Treated Like Imbecile Children,' " p. 94.

19. Molière, "Les Femmes Savantes," in *The Comedies* (London, 1961), 2:309–61.

20. Eleanor Flexner, *Mary Wollstonecraft* (Baltimore, Md., 1973), p. 71.

21. Adburgham, *Women in Print*, p. 110.

22. Mary Wollstonecraft, *A Vindication of the Rights of Woman*, ed. Carol H. Poston (New York, 1975), pp. 77–115.

23. Flexner, *Mary Wollstonecraft*, p. 162.

24. Wollstonecraft, *A Vindication of the Rights of Woman*, pp. 168, 178.

25. Ibid., p. 150.

26. Ibid., pp. 28–29, 63, 148, 191.

27. Ibid., p. 143.

28. Ibid., p. 3.

29. Flexner, *Mary Wollstonecraft*, p. 70.

30. Jane Austen, *The Watsons* (London, 1975), p. 109.

31. Margaret Drabble, "Introduction," in Jane Austen, *Lady Susan, The Watsons, Sanditon* (London, 1975), p. 20.

32. Rousseau, *Emile*, p. 328.

33. Pierre de Beaumarchais, *The Barber of Seville and The Marriage of Figaro*, trans. John Wood (London, 1976), p. 199.

34. L. H. Butterfield, M. Friedlaender, and M. J. Kline, eds., *The Book of Abigail and John* (Cambridge, 1975), pp. 121, 123.

CHAPTER 9

1. Eleanor Flexner, *Mary Wollstonecraft* (Baltimore, Md., 1973), p. 195.

2. Jane Abray, "Feminism in the French Revolution," *American Historical Review* 80 (1975):46–47.

3. Ruth Graham, "Rousseau's Sexism Revolutionized," in *Woman in the Eighteenth Century and Other Essays*, ed. Paul Fritz and Richard Morton (Toronto, 1976), p. 130.

4. Ibid., p. 133.

5. Darline Gay Levy, Harriet Branson Applewhite, and Mary Durham Johnson, eds., *Women in Revolutionary Paris, 1789–1795* (Urbana, Ill., 1979), p. 40.

6. Ruth Graham, "Women in the French Revolution," in *Becoming Visible: Women in European History*, ed. Renate Bridenthal and Claudia Koonz (Boston, 1977), p. 241.

7. Abray, "Feminism in the French Revolution," p. 48.

8. Ibid., p. 50; Graham, "Rousseau's Sexism Revolutionized," p. 138.

9. Levy, Applewhite, and Johnson, eds., *Women in Revolutionary Paris*, pp. 62–64.

10. Ibid., pp. 5, 105–6.

11. Elizabeth Racz, "The Women's Rights Movement in the French Revolution," *Science and Society* 16 (1952):169.

12. Levy, Applewhite, and Johnson, eds., *Women in Revolutionary Paris*, p. 205.

13. Abray, "Feminism in the French Revolution," p. 52.

14. Ibid., p. 56.

15. Olwen Hufton, "Women in Revolution 1789–1796," *Past and Present* 53 (1971):102.

16. Abray, "Feminism in the French Revolution," p. 58; Graham, "Women in the French Revolution," p. 251; Levy, Applewhite, and Johnson, eds., *Women in Revolutionary Paris*, p. 272.

17. Racz, "Women's Rights Movement in the French Revolution," p. 161; Hufton, "Women in Revolution 1789–1796," pp. 100–101.

18. Abray, "Feminism in the French Revolution," p. 59.

19. Ibid., p. 55.

20. James Leith, *The Idea of Art as Propaganda in France, 1750–1799: A Study in the History of Ideas* (Toronto, 1965), pp. 107–9.

21. Hufton, "Women in Revolution 1789–1796," p. 101.

22. Ibid., p. 98.

23. Ibid., pp. 96–97.

24. Ibid., pp. 103–5.

24. Olwen Hufton, *The Poor of Eighteenth-Century France 1750–1789* (Oxford, 1974), p. 24.

26. Hufton, "Women in Revolution 1789–1796," p. 108.

27. Racz, "Women's Rights Movement in the French Revolution," pp. 162–65.

28. Sheila Rowbotham, *Women, Resistance and Revolution: A History of Women and Revolution in the Modern World* (London, 1972), p. 38.

CHAPTER 10

1. Eleanor Flexner, *Mary Wollstonecraft* (Baltimore, Md., 1973), p. 60.

2. Gregory King, "Natural and Political Observations and Conclusions upon the State and Condition of England," in *Two Tracts* (Baltimore, Md., 1936), p. 31; Emmanuel LeRoy Ladurie, "Peasants," in *Companion Volume to the New Cambridge Modern History*, ed. Peter Burke (Cambridge, 1979), 13:115.

3. Ivy Pinchbeck, *Women Workers and the Industrial Revolution, 1750–1850* (London, 1969), pp. 33, 312–13.

4. Ibid., p. 37.

5. Ibid., pp. 7–16.

6. Ibid., pp. 16–26.

7. J. D. Chambers and G. E. Mingay, *The Agricultural Revolution 1750–1880* (London, 1966), pp. 206–9.

8. B. Seebohm Rowntree, *Poverty: A Study of Town Life* (London, 1903), p. 14.

9. Julia O'Faolain and Lauro Martines, eds., *Not In God's Image: A History of Women in Europe from the Greeks to the Nineteenth Century* (New York, 1973), pp. 154, 203.

10. M. Phillips and W. S. Tomkinson, *English Women in Life and Letters* (New York, 1971), pp. 7, 366.

11. Alice Clark, *The Working Life of Women in the Seventeenth Century* (New York, 1968), pp. 151, 197–235, and passim.

12. Jean Donnison, *Midwives and Medical Men: A History of Inter-Professional Rivalries and Women's Rights* (London, 1977), pp. 1–61.

13. O'Faolain and Martines, *Not In God's Image*, pp. 291–303.

14. Louise A. Tilly and Joan A. Scott, *Women, Work, and Family* (New York, 1978), pp. 124, 196.

15. Ibid., pp. 91, 95, 99.

16. Michael Anderson, "Household Structure and the Industrial Revolution: Mid-nineteenth Century Preston in Comparative Perspective," in *Household and Family in Past Time*, ed. Peter Laslett and Richard Wall (Cambridge, 1977), p. 230.

17. Rowntree, *Poverty: A Study of Town Life*, p. 39.

18. Ibid., pp. 298–99; Tilly and Scott, *Women, Work, and Family*, p. 132.

19. Tilly and Scott, *Women, Work, and Family*, pp. 143–44.

20. Pinchbeck, *Women Workers and the Industrial Revolution*, pp. 19–22.

21. Tilly and Scott, *Women, Work, and Family*, pp. 198, 204–5; Phyllis Deane, *The First Industrial Revolution* (Cambridge, 1969), p. 253.

22. Tamara K. Hareven, "Family Time and Historical Time," in *The Family*, ed. Alice S. Rossi, Jerome Kagan, and Tamara K. Hareven (New York, 1978), pp. 68–69.

CHAPTER 11

1. Lee Holcombe, *Victorian Ladies at Work: Middle-Class Working Women in England and Wales, 1850–1914* (Hamden, Conn., 1973), pp. 216–17.

2. Peter N. Stearns, "Working Class Women in Britain, 1890–1914," in *Suffer and Be Still: Women in the Victorian Age*, ed. Martha Vicinus (Bloomington, Ind., 1973), pp. 110–12.

3. Nancy F. Cott, *The Bonds of Womanhood: "Woman's Sphere" in New England, 1780–1835* (New Haven, 1977), pp. 55, 74.

4. Theresa M. McBride, *The Domestic Revolution: The Modernization of Household Service in England and France 1820–1920* (London, 1976), pp. 14, 36, 45.

5. Peter Laslett, *The World We Have Lost: England Before the Industrial Age* (London, 1968), p. 64; Gregory King, "Natural and Political Observations and Conclusions upon the State and Condition of England," in *Two Tracts* (Baltimore, Md., 1936), p. 22.

6. Jonathan Swift, *Directions to Servants* (New York, 1964), p. 51.

7. Dorothy Marshall, *The English Domestic Servant in History* (London, 1969), pp. 8–9.

8. Ibid., pp. 26–27.

9. Geoffrey Best, *Mid-Victorian Britain 1851–1875* (New York, 1971), pp. 82–83.

10. McBride, *Domestic Revolution*, p. 20; Patricia Branca, *Silent Sisterhood: Middle-Class Women in the Victorian Home* (London, 1975), p. 55.

11. McBride, *Domestic Revolution*, p. 42.

12. Ibid., pp. 62, 85.

13. Guy Routh, *Occupation and Pay in Great Britain 1906–1960* (Cambridge, 1965), p. 95.

14. Ivy Pinchbeck, *Women Workers and the Industrial Revolution, 1750–1850* (London, 1969), pp. 316–21.

15. Standish Meacham, *A Life Apart: The English Working Class, 1890–1914* (London, 1977), p. 100; Jill Liddington and Jill Norris, *One Hand Tied Behind Us* (London, 1978), pp. 85, 87.

16. Meacham, *A Life Apart*, pp. 70, 235; Maud Pember Reeves, *Round About A Pound A Week* (London, 1979), p. 213.

17. Liddington and Norris, *One Hand Tied Behind Us*, pp. 85, 94.

18. Ibid., pp. 105–7.

19. Meacham, *A Life Apart*, pp. 99–100.

20. Stearns, "Working Class Women in Britain," p. 115.

21. Margaret Hewitt, *Wives and Mothers in Victorian Industry* (London, 1958), pp. 192–93; Meacham, *A Life Apart*, pp. 100, 241–42.

22. Philip S. Foner, ed., *The Factory Girls: A Collection of Writings on Life and Struggles in the New England Factories of the 1840s* (Chicago, 1977), p. xxi; Benita Eisler, ed., *The Lowell Offering: Writings by New England Mill Women* (New York, 1977), p. 22.

23. Eisler, *The Lowell Offering*, pp. 53, 64, 208–10.

24. Foner, *The Factory Girls*, p. xxiv.

25. Carl N. Degler, *At Odds: Women and the Family in America from the Revolution to the Present* (Oxford, 1980), p. 371.

26. Ibid., pp. 372, 374; Joan W. Scott and Louise A. Tilly, "Women's Work and the Family in Nineteenth Century Europe," in *The Economics of Women and Work*, ed. Alice H. Amsden (London, 1980), p. 94.

27. Degler, *At Odds*, pp. 395–401; Carole Turbin, "And We Are Nothing But Women: Irish Working Women in Troy," in *Women of America: A History*, ed. Carol Ruth Berkin and Mary Beth Norton (Boston, 1979), p. 204; Eleanor Flexner, *Century of Struggle: The Woman's Rights Movement in the United States* (Cambridge, 1975), p. 141; see also James J. Kenneally, *Women and American Trade Unions* (St. Alban's, Vt., 1978).

28. Meacham, *A Life Apart*, pp. 100–101, 106–7; Liddington and Norris, *One Hand Tied Behind Us*, pp. 93, 106.

29. Sheila Lewenhak, *Women and Trade Unions* (London, 1977), p. 69.

30. Ibid., p. 97; Meacham, *A Life Apart*, p. 104; Kenneally, *Women and American Trade Unions*, p. 218.

31. Meacham, *A Life Apart*, p. 106.

32. Scott and Tilly, "Women's Work and the Family," pp. 95–96.

33. Josephine Kamm, *Indicative Past: A Hundred Years of the Girls' Public Day School Trust* (London, 1971), p. 38.

34. Alison Adburgham, *Women in Print* (London, 1972), p. 38.

35. Eleanor Flexner, *Mary Wollstonecraft* (Baltimore, Md., 1973), pp. 47–49.

36. J. Steven Watson, *The Reign of George III, 1760–1815,* (Oxford, 1960), p. 39.

37. Adburgham, *Women in Print*, p. 191.

38. Wanda F. Neff, *Victorian Working Women* (New York, 1929), p. 153; Holcombe, *Victorian Ladies at Work*, p. 14; M. Jeanne Person, "The Victorian

Governess: Status Incongruence in Family and Society," in *Suffer and Be Still,* ed. Vicinus, p. 8.

39. Holcombe, *Victorian Ladies at Work,* p. 12.

40. Ibid., pp. 7, 8, 18.

41. Angeline Goreau, *Reconstructing Aphra: A Social Biography of Aphra Behn* (New York, 1980), pp. 6–13, 164–65.

42. Adburgham, *Women in Print,* pp. 26, 28.

43. Ibid., p. 45.

44. Jane Austen, *Northanger Abbey* (Oxford, 1948), p. 106.

45. Holcombe, *Victorian Ladies At Work,* Appendix pp. 203–17, and pp. 34, 40, 43, 62, 79, 103, 139, 175, 188.

46. Christopher Kent, "Image and Reality: The Actress and Society," in *A Widening Sphere: Changing Roles of Victorian Women,* ed. Martha Vicinus (Bloomington, Ind., 1977), pp. 100, 106, 113.

47. Degler, *At Odds,* pp. 377, 379, 394; Richard Evans, *The Feminists: Women's Emancipation Movements in Europe, America and Australasia 1840–1920* (London, 1977), pp. 50–52; Flexner, *Century of Struggle,* pp. 117–21, 237.

CHAPTER 12

1. Barbara Welter, "The Cult of True Womanhood 1820–1860," *American Quarterly* 18 (1966):152.

2. Kate Millett, *Sexual Politics* (New York, 1970), pp. 128–51.

3. Constance Rover, *Love, Morals and the Feminists* (London, 1970), pp. 73–74.

4. Ray Strachey, *The Cause: A History of the Women's Movement in Great Britain* (London, 1978), p. 204.

5. Ibid., pp. 197–98; Constance Rover, *Women's Suffrage and Party Politics in Britain 1866–1914* (London, 1967), p. 2.

6. See A. Bebel, *Woman under Socialism,* trans. D. de Leon (New York, 1904); F. Engels, *Origin of the Family, Private Property and the State* (London, 1940); J. F. C. Harrison, *Robert Owen and the Owenites in Britain and America* (London, 1969); Charles Knowlton, *The Fruits of Philosophy,* ed. Drysdale (London, 1977); William Thompson, *Appeal of one half of the human race, women, against the pretensions of the other half, men, to retain them in political and thence in civil and domestic slavery* (London, 1825).

7. Raymond Lee Muncy, *Sex and Marriage in Utopian Communities* (Baltimore, Md., 1974), pp. 54–57.

8. Angus McLaren, *Birth Control in Nineteenth Century England: A Social and Intellectual History* (London, 1978), pp. 152, 195.

9. Sheila Rowbotham, *Hidden from History: Rediscovering Women in History from the 17th Century to the Present* (London, 1973), p. 67; Sheila Rowbotham and Jeffrey Weeks, *Socialism and the New Life: The Personal and Sexual Politics of Edward Carpenter and Havelock Ellis* (London, 1977), p. 21.

10. Sheila Rowbotham, *Women, Resistance and Revolution: A History of Women and Revolution in the Modern World* (London, 1972), pp. 81–84.

11. Muncy, *Sex and Marriage in Utopian Communities,* pp. 8, 56–59.

12. Ibid., pp. 60–62.

13. Ibid., pp. 165, 171–72, 180–96.

14. Olive Schreiner, *Woman and Labor,* ed. Jane Graves (London, 1978), p. 3.

15. Hannah Mitchell, *The Hard Way Up* (London, 1968), p. 88.

16. Rowbotham, *Hidden from History,* p. 95.

17. Jill Liddington and Jill Norris, *One Hand Tied Behind Us* (London, 1978), p. 14.

18. Rowbotham and Weeks, *Socialism and the New Life,* pp. 165–66, 169; Ruth Hall, *Marie Stopes* (London, 1978), p. 129.

19. Hall, *Marie Stopes,* p. 128.

20. Marie Stopes, *Radiant Motherhood* (London, 1920), pp. 214–15, 218–36.

21. Havelock Ellis, *The Task of Social Hygiene* (London, 1927), pp. 31–44.

22. Linda Gordon, *Woman's Body, Woman's Right: A Social History of Birth Control in America* (New York, 1976), p. 122.

23. Muncy, *Sex and Marriage in Utopian Communities,* pp. 190–91.

24. Stopes, *Radiant Motherhood,* pp. 27, 30.

25. McLaren, *Birth Control in Nineteenth Century England,* p. 161.

26. Ibid., p. 164.

27. Rowbotham and Weeks, *Socialism and the New Life,* p. 14.

28. Rover, *Love, Morals and the Feminists,* pp. 97–98; McLaren, *Birth Control in Nineteenth Century England,* p. 201.

29. Louise A. Tilly and Joan A. Scott, *Women, Work, and Family* (New York, 1978), p. 101.

30. Hall, *Marie Stopes,* p. 213.

31. Gordon, *Woman's Body, Woman's Right,* pp. 341–59.

32. Carl N. Degler, "What Ought To Be and What Was," *American Historical Review* 79 (1974):1467.

33. Hall, *Marie Stopes,* p. 230.

34. Degler, "What Ought To Be and What Was," pp. 1470, 1483–84, 1486.

35. Ellis, *Social Hygiene,* pp. 126, 130.

CHAPTER 13

1. Ivy Pinchbeck, *Women Workers and the Industrial Revolution 1750–1850* (London, 1969), p. 188.

2. Ibid., p. 200.

3. Ibid., p. 249.

4. Ibid., pp. 246, 267.

5. E. L. Woodward, *The Age of Reform 1815–1870* (Oxford, 1954), p. 144.

6. Nancy F. Cott, *The Bonds of Womanhood: "Woman's Sphere" in New England, 1780–1835* (New Haven, 1978), pp. 134–35; Keith E. Melder, *Beginnings of Sisterhood: The American Woman's Right Movement 1800–1850* (New York, 1977), pp. 38–43.

7. F. K. Prochaska, "Women in English Philanthropy, 1790–1830," *International Review of Social History* 19 (1974):428, 430.

8.Ibid., pp. 429–30, 432, 434.

9. Anne Summers, "A Home from Home—Women's Philanthropic Work in the Nineteenth Century," in *Fit Work for Women*, ed. Sandra Burman (Canberra, 1979), p. 38.

10. David Owen, *English Philanthropy 1660–1960* (Cambridge, 1964), pp. 148, 167, 413–20.

11. Brian Harrison, *Separate Spheres: The Opposition to Woman Suffrage in Britain* (London, 1978), p. 55.

12. Elaine Showalter, "Florence Nightingale's Feminist Complaint: Women, Religion and 'Suggestions for Thought,' " *Signs* 6 (1981):407.

13. Ray Strachey, *The Cause: A History of the Women's Movement in Great Britain* (London, 1978), p. 404.

14. Summers, "A Home from Home," p. 55.

15. Owen, *English Philanthropy*, pp. 389–90.

16. Doris Stenton, *The English Woman in History* (New York, 1977), p. 343.

17. Harrison, *Separate Spheres*, p. 112.

18. Aileen S. Kraditor, *The Ideas of the Woman Suffrage Movement, 1890–1920* (New York, 1967), p. 142.

19. Eleanor Flexner, *Century of Struggle: The Woman's Rights Movement in the United States* (Cambridge, 1975), p. 215.

20. Josephine Kamm, *Indicative Past: A Hundred Years of the Girls' Public Day School Trust* (London, 1971), pp. 14–44.

21. Vera Brittain, *The Women at Oxford* (London, 1960), pp. 152–54.

22. Rita McWilliams-Tullberg, "Women and Degrees at Cambridge University, 1862–1897," in *A Widening Sphere: Changing Roles of Victorian Women*, ed Martha Vicinus (Bloomington, Ind., 1977), p. 145.

23. Kamm, *Indicative Past*, p. 27.

24. Ann D. Gordon, "The Young Ladies Academy of Philadelphia," in *Women of America: A History*, ed. Carol Ruth Berkin and Mary Beth Norton (Boston, 1979), p. 69.

25. Kathryn Kish Sklar, "The Founding of Mount Holyoke College," in *Women of America*, ed. Berkin and Norton, pp. 178, 183, 197.

26. Ibid., p. 179; Carl N. Degler, *At Odds: Women and the Family in America from the Revolution to the Present* (Oxford, 1980), p. 308.

27. Degler, *At Odds*, pp. 310–12.

28. Phyllis Stock, *Better Than Rubies: A History of Women's Education* (New York, 1978), pp. 126, 129–213.

29. Melder, *Beginnings of Sisterhood*, p. 143.

30. Marylynn Salmon, "Equality or Subversion? Feme Covert Status in Early Pennsylvania," in *Women of America*, ed. Berkin and Norton, pp. 93–98; Flexner, *Century of Struggle*, pp. 86–89.

31. Lee Holcombe, "Victorian Wives and Property: Reform of the Married Women's Property Law, 1857–1882," in *A Widening Sphere*, ed. Vicinus, pp. 16, and passim.

32. Ibid., pp. 20, 25.

33. Roger Fulford, *Votes for Women* (London, 1958), p. 65.

34. See Catherine Cleverdon, *The Woman Suffrage Movement in Canada:*

The Start of Liberation (Toronto, 1974); S. Encel, N. McKenzie, and M. Tebbutt, eds., *Women and Society: An Australian Study* (Melbourne, 1975); Richard T. Evans, *The Feminist Movement in Germany 1894–1933* (London, 1976); Richard J. Evans, *The Feminists: Women's Emancipation Movements in Europe, America and Australasia 1840–1920* (London, 1977); Flexner, *Century of Struggle*; Fulford, *Votes for Women*; Patricia Grimshaw, *Woman's Suffrage in New Zealand* (Wellington, 1972); Harrison, *Separate Spheres*; Kraditor, *The Ideas of the Woman Suffrage Movement*; Jill Liddington and Jill Norris, *One Hand Tied Behind Us* (London, 1978); Andrew Rosen, *Rise up, Women! The Militant Campaign of the Women's Social and Political Union, 1903–1914* (London, 1974); Constance Rover, *Women's Suffrage and Party Politics in Britain 1866–1914* (London, 1967); Richard Stites, *The Women's Liberation Movement in Russia: Feminism, Nihilism, and Bolshevism, 1860–1930* (Princeton, 1978); Strachey, *The Cause*; Theodore Zeldin, *France, 1848–1945, vol. 1* (London, 1974).

35. Rover, *Women's Suffrage and Party Politics in Britain*, pp. 211–33.

36. Ibid., pp. 120, 124.

37. Harrison, *Separate Spheres*, p. 204.

38. Fulford, *Votes for Women*, pp. 73–74.

39. Liddington and Norris, *One Hand Tied Behind Us*, pp. 211–30.

40. Ibid., pp. 182, 227–28; Rover, *Women's Suffrage and Party Politics in Britain*, pp. 29–30, 34.

41. See chapter 16, Twentieth-Century Trends.

42. Millicent Fawcett, *What I Remember* (Westport, Conn., 1976), p. 118.

CHAPTER 14

1. August Bebel, *Woman Under Socialism*, trans. D. De Leon (New York, 1904), p. 30; Kathleen Gough, "The Origin of the Family," in *Toward an Anthropology of Women*, ed. Rayna Reiter (New York, 1975), p. 74; Michelle Z. Rosaldo, "The Use and Abuse of Anthropology: Reflections on Feminism and Cross-Cultural Understanding," *Signs* 5 (1980):389–91; Bernice Glatzer Rosenthal, "Love on the Tractor: Women in the Russian Revolution," in *Becoming Visible: Women in European History*, ed. Renate Bridenthal and Claudia Koonz (Boston, 1977), pp. 370–99.

2. Bebel, *Woman Under Socialism*, p. 349.

3. Ibid., p. 343.

4. Ibid., pp. 323–42.

5. Barbara Evans Clements, *Bolshevik Feminist: The Life of Aleksandra Kollontai* (Bloomington, Ind., 1979), pp. x–xi; Alexandra Kollontai, *Love of Worker Bees*, trans. Cathy Porter (London, 1977), pp. 7–9.

6. Richard Stites, *The Women's Liberation Movement in Russia: Feminism, Nihilism, and Bolshevism, 1860–1930* (Princeton, 1978), p. 250.

7. Beatrice Brodsky Farnsworth, "Communist Feminism: Its Synthesis and Demise," in *Women, War and Revolution*, ed. Carol R. Berkin and Clara M. Lovett (New York, 1980), p. 148.

8. Ibid., pp. 147–48.

9. Beatrice Brodsky Farnsworth, "Bolshevik Alternatives and the Soviet

Family: The 1926 Marriage Law Debate," in *Women in Russia*, ed. Dorothy Atkinson, Alexander Dallin, and Gail Warshovsky Lapidus (Brighton, 1978), p. 140.

10. Farnsworth, "Communist Feminism," p. 150.

11. Beatrice Brodsky Farnsworth, "Bolshevism, The Woman Question, and Aleksandra Kollontai," in *Socialist Women: European Feminism in the Nineteenth and Early Twentieth Centuries*, ed. Marilyn J. Boxer and Jean H. Quataert (New York, 1978), pp. 194–95.

12. Ingrun Lafleur, "Five Socialist Women: Traditionalist Conflicts and Socialist Visions in Austria, 1893–1934," in *Socialist Women*, ed. Boxer and Quataert, p. 218.

13. Ibid., p. 239.

14. Ibid., p. 241.

15. Ibid., p. 237; see also Charles A. Gulick, *Austria from Habsburg to Hitler* (Berkeley, 1948), 1:505–43.

16. Lafleur, "Five Socialist Women," pp. 235, 244; see also Jane S. Jacquette, *Women in Politics* (New York, 1974), p. xxi.

17. Lafleur, "Five Socialist Women," p. 230.

18. Ibid., p. 237.

19. Stites, *Women's Liberation Movement in Russia*, p. 377.

20. Clements, *Bolshevik Feminist*, pp. 240–41.

21. Sheila Rowbotham, *A New World for Women: Stella Browne, Socialist Feminist* (London, 1977), p. 24.

22. Ibid., p. 28.

23. Ibid., pp. 37, 42.

24. Ibid., pp. 73–74.

25. S. Joan Moon, "Feminism and Socialism: The Utopian Synthesis of Flora Tristan," in *Socialist Women*, ed. Boxer and Quataert, pp. 41, 45; Charles Sowerwine, "The Organization of French Socialist Women 1880–1914: A European Perspective for Women's Movements," *Historical Reflections* 3 (1976):3–23.

CHAPTER 15

1. William H. Chafe, *The American Woman: Her Changing Social, Economic and Political Roles, 1920–1970* (Oxford, 1975), p. 51; Norbert C. Soldon, *Women in British Trade Unions 1874–1976* (London, 1978), p. 80.

2. Ray Strachey, *The Cause: A History of the Women's Movement in Great Britain* (London, 1978), pp. 338, 345–47.

3. David Mitchell, *Queen Christabel* (London, 1977), p. 248; Millicent Fawcett, *What I Remember* (Westport, Conn., 1976), p. 221.

4. Chafe, *The American Woman*, p. 52.

5. Ibid., p. 53.

6. B. R. Mitchell, *European Historical Statistics 1750–1970* (London, 1975), pp. 155–56, 163; Renate Bridenthal, "Something Old, Something New: Women Between Two World Wars," in *Becoming Visible: Women in European History*, ed. Renate Bridenthal and Claudia Koonz (Boston, 1977), p. 426.

7. Eric Richards, "Women in the British Economy since about 1700: An

Interpretation," *History* 59 (1974):353; Gail Braybon, *Women Workers in the First World War: The British Experience* (London, 1981), pp. 216–28.

8. Theodore Zeldin, *France 1848–1945*, (Oxford, 1973), 1:350; Chafe, *The American Woman*, p. 54.

9. Zeldin, *France 1848–1945*, 1:351.

10. Chafe, *The American Woman*, pp. 55, 56, 58; Bridenthal, "Something Old, Something New," pp. 434–38.

11. See Jill Stephenson, *The Nazi Organisation of Women* (London, 1981).

12. Leila J. Rupp, "Mother of the *Volk:* The Image of Women in Nazi Ideology," *Signs* 3 (1977):365, 368, 374.

13. Tim Mason, "Women in Nazi Germany, Part I," *History Workshop* 1 (1976):95, 98.

14. Claudia Koonz, "Mothers in the Fatherland: Women in Nazi Germany," in *Becoming Visible*, ed. Bridenthal and Koonz, p. 462.

15. Rupp, "Mother of the *Volk*," p. 375.

16. Jill Stephenson, *Women in Nazi Society* (London, 1975), pp. 64, 68–70.

17. Tim Mason, "Women in Nazi Germany, Part II," *History Workshop* 2 (1976):7–9.

18. Ibid., pp. 10, 13, 19.

19. Leila J. Rupp, *Mobilizing Women for War: German and American Propaganda, 1939–1945* (Princeton, 1978), p. 170.

20. Leila J. Rupp, " 'I don't all that *Volksgemeinschaft*': Women, Class and War in Nazi Germany," in *Women, War and Revolution*, ed. Carol R. Berkin and Clara M. Lovett (New York, 1980), pp. 38, 47–48; Leila J. Rupp, "Woman's Place is in the War: Propaganda and Public Opinion in the United States and Germany, 1939–1945," in *Women of America: A History*, ed. Carol R. Berkin and Mary Beth Norton (Boston, 1979), p. 355.

21. Chafe, *The American Woman*, pp. 139–40.

22. Karen Skold, "The Job He Left Behind: American Women in the Shipyards during World War II," in *Women, War and Revolution*, ed. Berkin and Lovett, pp. 55, 58, 61, 67, 68; Chafe, *The American Woman*, p. 144.

23. Ruth Pierson, "Women's Emancipation and the Recruitment of Women into the Labor Force in World War II," in *The Neglected Majority: Essays in Canadian Women's History*, ed. Susan Mann Trofimenkoff and Alison Prentice (Toronto, 1977), pp. 126, 133, 135, 145; Rupp, *Mobilizing Women for War*, p. 170.

24. Pierson, "Recruitment of Women," p. 138.

25. Ibid., pp. 136, 142, 145.

26. Mason, "Women in Nazi Germany, Part II," p. 22.

27. Richards, "Women in the British Economy," p. 354.

28. Mary Stott, *Organization Woman: The Story of the National Union of Townswomen's Guilds* (London, 1978), pp. 58–59, 67.

29. Chafe, *The American Woman*, pp. 145, 146, 182–84.

30. Rupp, "Woman's Place is in the War," p. 357; Rupp, *Mobilizing Women for War*, p. 177.

31. Rupp, *Mobilizing Women for War*, p. 180; Rosalynn Baxandall, Linda Gordon, and Susan Reverby, eds., *America's Working Women: A Documentary History, 1600 to the Present* (New York, 1976), pp. 299–308.

32. Richard J. Evans, *The Feminists: Women's Emancipation Movements in Europe, America and Australasia 1840–1920* (London, 1977), pp. 196, 206, 226; Barbara J. Steinson, "The Mother Half of Humanity: American Women in the Peace and Preparedness Movements in World War I," in *Women, War and Revolution*, ed. Berkin and Lovett, pp. 259–81; Vera Brittain, *Testament of Experience* (London, 1957), pp. 220–21.

CHAPTER 16

1. Richard J. Evans, *The Feminists: Women's Emancipation Movements in Europe, America and Australasia 1840–1920* (London, 1977), p. 219.

2. Patricia Grimshaw, *Women's Suffrage in New Zealand* (Wellington, 1972), pp. 64, 65.

3. Evans, *The Feminists*, pp. 215–16.

4. Ibid., pp. 217–18; Margaret Bernhard, ed., *The Present Position of Woman Suffrage* (London, 1929), p. 5.

5. Mary Kinnear, "Margret Benedictsson and *Freyja*," *Logberg-Heimskringla* 42 (1979):15, 16.

6. Evans, *The Feminists*, p. 227.

7. Melville Currell, *Political Woman* (London, 1974), pp. 122–29; Jane Lewis, *The Politics of Motherhood: Child and Maternal Welfare in England, 1900–1939* (London, 1981), p. 222; Carl N. Degler, *At Odds: Women and the Family in America from the Revolution to the Present* (Oxford, 1980), p. 359.

8. William H. Chafe, *The American Woman: Her Changing Social, Economic and Political Roles, 1920–1970* (Oxford, 1975), pp. 25–47; Mary Stott, *Organization Woman: The Story of the National Union of Townswomen's Guilds* (London, 1978), pp. 23–24.

9. Ramsay Cook and Wendy Mitchinson, eds., *The Proper Sphere: Woman's Place in Canadian Society* (Toronto, 1976), p. 284.

10. Nellie L. McLung, *The Stream Runs Fast* (Toronto, 1965), p. 181.

11. William H. Chafe, *Women and Equality: Changing Patterns in American Culture* (New York, 1977), p. 117.

12. Lily Gair Wilkinson, "Women's Freedom," in *Women in Rebellion 1900*, ed. Suzie Fleming (London, 1973), p. 22.

13. Chafe, *Women and Equality*, p. 119.

14. There were many people still receptive to romantic images of woman as angel of the hearth. Marabel Morgan's *The Total Woman* was the top-selling book of 1975 in the United States. Ellen Ross, " 'The Love Crisis': Couples Advice Books of the late 1970s," *Signs* 6 (1980):119.

15. Chafe, *Women and Equality*, p. 123; Robert V. Wells, "Women's Lives Transformed: Demographic and Family Patterns in America, 1600–1970," in *Women of America: A History*, ed. Carol R. Berkin and Mary Beth Norton (Boston, 1979), pp. 26–33; Sara Evans, *Personal Politics* (New York, 1980), p. 222.

16. Jo Freeman, "The Women's Liberation Movement: Its Origins, Structures, Impact and Ideas," in *Women: A Feminist Perspective*, ed. Jo Freeman (Palo Alto, Ca., 1975), pp. 457–59.

17. See Tables I, II, III, and IV in Organization for Economic Co-

operation and Development, *Equal Opportunities for Women* (Paris, 1979), pp. 17, 19, 25–27.

18. See Table V in Ibid., pp. 27–29, 31.

19. Ibid., pp. 75–77, 94–105.

20. Ibid., p. 37.

21. Ibid., pp. 47, 49.

22. Ibid., p. 51.

23. Alice S. Rossi, "Life-Span Theories and Women's Lives," *Signs* 6 (1980):25–26.

24. *Equal Opportunities for Women,* pp. 112, 114–26.

25. Susan Clark and Andrew S. Harvey, "The Sexual Division of Labor: The Use of Time," *Atlantis* 2 (1976):44–66; Gerda Lerner, *The Majority Finds Its Past: Placing Women in History* (New York, 1981), p. 136.

26. *Equal Opportunities for Women,* p. 128.

27. Ibid., p. 149.

28. Ann M. Clarke and A. D. B. Clarke, eds., *Early Experience: Myth and Evidence* (London, 1976), p. 372.

29. *Equal Opportunities for Women,* pp. 164–204.

30. National Council of Welfare, *Women and Poverty* (Ottawa, 1979), pp. 7, 51–52.

Selected Bibliography

Abray, Jane. "Feminism in the French Revolution." *American Historical Review* 80 (1975):43–62.

Adburgham, Alison. *Women in Print*. London, 1972.

Amsden, Alice H., ed. *The Economics of Women and Work*. London, 1980.

Aristotle. *The Politics*. Translated by B. Jowett. Oxford, 1957.

Arthur, Marylin. "Classics." *Signs* 2 (1976):387–403.

Arthur, Marylin; Bridenthal, Renate; Kelly-Gadol, Joan; and Lerner, Gerda. *Conceptual Frameworks for Studying Women's History*. New York, 1975.

Atkinson, Dorothy; Dallin, Alexander; and Warshovsky Lapidus, Gail, eds. *Women in Russia*. Brighton, 1978.

Austen, Jane. *Lady Susan, The Watsons, Sanditon*. Introduction by Margaret Drabble. London, 1975.

———. *Northanger Abbey*. Oxford, 1948.

Bailey, Derrick Sherwin. *The Man-Woman Relation in Christian Thought*. London, 1959.

Bainton, Roland H. *Women of the Reformation in Germany and Italy*. Boston, 1974.

Baker, Derek, ed. *Medieval Women: Essays presented to Rosalind Hill*. Oxford, 1978.

Balsdon, J. P. Dacre. *Roman Women*. London, 1962.

Baring-Gould, S. *The Lives of the Saints*. London, 1898.

Barraclough, Geoffrey, ed. *The Times Atlas of World History*. Maplewood, N.J., 1979.

Baxandall, Rosalynn; Gordon, Linda; and Reverby, Susan, eds. *America's Working Women: A Documentary History, 1600 to the Present*. New York, 1976.

Beard, Mary. *Woman As Force in History*. New York, 1946.

Bebel, August. *Woman Under Socialism*. Translated by Daniel De Leon. New York, 1904.

Bell, Susan Groag. "Comment on Sheila Delany's 'Review of The Order of the Rose: The Life and Times of Christine de Pisan.' " *Signs* 4 (1979):592–93.

Berkin, Carol Ruth, and Lovett, Clara M., eds. *Women, War and Revolution*. New York, 1980.

Berkin, Carol Ruth, and Norton, Mary Beth, eds. *Women of America: A History*. Boston, 1979.

Bernhard, Margaret, ed. *The Present Position of Woman Suffrage*. London, 1929.

Best, Geoffrey. *Mid-Victorian Britain 1851–1875*. New York, 1971.

Bogin, Meg. *The Women Troubadours*. New York, 1980.

Bornstein, Diane, ed. *Distaves and Dames: Renaissance Treatises for and About Women*. New York, 1978.

Boxer, Marilyn J., and Quataert, Jean H., eds. *Socialist Women: European Feminism in the Nineteenth and Early Twentieth Centuries*. New York, 1978.

Branca, Patricia. *Silent Sisterhood: Middle-Class Women in the Victorian Home*. London, 1975.

———. *Women in Modern Europe since 1750*. London, 1978.

Braybon, Gail. *Women Workers in the First World War: The British Experience*. London, 1981.

Bridenthal, Renate, and Koonz, Claudia, eds. *Becoming Visible: Women in European History*. Boston, 1977.

Brittain, Vera. *Testament of Experience*. London, 1957.

———. *The Women at Oxford*. London, 1960.

Brundage, James A. "Prostitution in the Medieval Canon Law." *Signs* 1 (1976):825–45.

Bullough, Vern L., and Bullough, Bonnie. *The Subordinate Sex: A History of Attitudes Toward Women*. Baltimore, Md., 1974.

Burke, Peter, ed. *Companion Volume to the New Cambridge Modern History*. Vol. 13. Cambridge, 1979.

———. *Popular Culture in Early Modern Europe*. London, 1978.

Burman, Sandra, ed. *Fit Work for Women*. Canberra, 1979.

Butterfield, L. H.; Friedlaender, M.; and Kline, M. J., eds. *The Book of Abigail and John*. Cambridge, 1975.

Canadian National Council of Welfare. *Women and Poverty*. Ottawa, 1979.

Carcopino, Jerome. *Daily Life in Ancient Rome: The People and the City at the Height of the Empire*. London, 1978.

Carroll, Berenice, ed. *Liberating Women's History: Theoretical and Critical Essays*. Urbana, Ill., 1976.

Chadwick, Henry. *The Early Church*. London, 1977.

Chadwick, Owen. *The Reformation*. London, 1977.

Chafe, William H. *The American Woman: Her Changing Social, Economic and Political Roles, 1920–1970*. Oxford, 1975.

———. *Women and Equality: Changing Patterns in American Culture*. New York, 1977.

Chambers, J. D., and Mingay, G. E. *The Agricultural Revolution 1750–1880*. London, 1966.

Chaucer, Geoffrey. *The Canterbury Tales*. Translated by Neville Coghill. London, 1977.

Chicago, Judy. *The Dinner Party*. New York, 1979.

Clark, Alice. *The Working Life of Women in the Seventeenth Century*. New York, 1968.

Clark, Lorenne M. G., and Lange, Lynda, eds. *The Sexism of Social and Political Theory: Women and Reproduction from Plato to Nietzsche*. Toronto, 1979.

Clark, Susan, and Harvey, Andrew S. "The Sexual Division of Labor: The Use of Time." *Atlantis* 2 (1976):44–66.

Clarke, Ann M., and Clarke, A. D. B., eds. *Early Experience: Myth and Evidence.* London, 1976.

Clements, Barbara Evans. *Bolshevik Feminist: The Life of Aleksandra Kollontai.* Bloomington, Ind., 1979.

Cleverdon, Catherine. *The Woman Suffrage Movement in Canada: The Start of Liberation.* Toronto, 1974.

Condorcet, *Oeuvres Complets.* Paris, 1804.

————. *Sketch for a Historical Picture of the Progress of the Human Mind.* Translated by J. Barraclough. London, 1955.

Cook, Ramsay, and Mitchinson, Wendy, eds. *The Proper Sphere: Woman's Place in Canadian Society.* Toronto, 1976.

Cott, Nancy F. *The Bonds of Womanhood: "Woman's Sphere" in New England, 1780–1835.* New Haven, 1977.

Crankshaw, Edward. *Maria Theresa.* London, 1969.

Cronin, Vincent. *Catherine, Empress of All the Russians.* London, 1978.

Cuming, G. J., and Baker, Derek, eds. *Popular Belief and Practice.* Cambridge, 1972.

Currell, Melville. *Political Woman.* London, 1974.

Davis, Natalie Zemon, ed. *Society and Culture in Early Modern France.* Stanford, 1975.

Davis, Natalie Zemon. "Women's History in Transition: The European Case." *Feminist Studies* 3 (1976):83–103.

Deane, Phyllis. *The First Industrial Revolution.* Cambridge, 1969.

de Beaumarchais, Pierre. *The Barber of Seville and The Marriage of Figaro.* Translated by John Wood. London, 1976.

de Beauvoir, Simone. *The Second Sex.* New York, 1952.

Degler, Carl N. *At Odds: Women and the Family in America from the Revolution to the Present.* New York, 1980.

————. *Is There A History of Women?* Oxford, 1975.

————. "What Ought To Be and What Was." *American Historical Review* 79 (1974):1467–90.

De Madariaga, Isabel. *Russia in the Age of Catherine the Great.* New Haven, 1981.

Donnison, Jean. *Midwives and Medical Men: A History of Inter-Professional Rivalries and Women's Rights.* London, 1977.

Dover, K. J. "Classical Greek Attitudes to Sexual Behavior." *Arethusa* 6 (1973):59–73.

Duby, Georges. *Le Chevalier, la Femme et le Pretre.* Paris, 1981.

————. *The Early Growth of the European Economy: Warriors and Peasants from the Seventh to the Twelfth Centuries.* New York, 1974.

Eisler, Benita, ed. *The Lowell Offering: Writings by New England Mill Women.* New York, 1977.

Ellis, Havelock. *The Task of Social Hygiene.* London, 1927.

Elton, G. R. *England Under the Tudors.* London, 1962.

Encel, S.; McKenzie, N.; and Tebbutt, M., eds. *Women and Society: An Australian Study.* Melbourne, 1975.

Engels, Friedrich. *Origin of the Family, Private Property and the State.* London, 1940.

Epstein, Cynthia F., and Coser, Rose L., eds. *Access to Power: Cross-National Studies of Women and Elites.* London, 1981.

Euripides. *Medea.* Translated by Philip Vellacott. London, 1971.

Evans, Richard J. *The Feminists: Women's Emancipation Movements in Europe, America and Australasia 1840–1920.* London, 1977.

Evans, Richard T. *The Feminist Movement in Germany 1894–1933.* London, 1976.

Evans-Pritchard, E. E., ed. *The Position of Women in Primitive Societies and Other Essays in Social Anthropology.* London, 1965.

Farmer, David Hugh, ed. *The Oxford Dictionary of Saints.* Oxford, 1978.

Fawcett, Millicent. *What I Remember.* Westport, Conn., 1976.

Flandrin, Jean Louis. *Le Sexe et l'Occident.* Paris, 1981.

Fleming, Suzie, ed. *Women in Rebellion 1900.* London, 1973.

Flexner, Eleanor. *Century of Struggle: The Woman's Rights Movement in the United States.* Cambridge, 1975.

———. *Mary Wollstonecraft.* Baltimore, Md., 1973.

Foner, Philip S., ed. *The Factory Girls: A Collection of Writings on Life and Struggles in the New England Factories of the 1840s.* Chicago, 1977.

Forster, Robert, and Ranum, Orest, eds. *Biology of Man in History, Vol. 1: Selections from the Annales: Economies, Societies, Civilisations.* Baltimore, Md., 1975.

Freeman, Jo. *The Politics of Women's Liberation: A Case Study of an Emerging Social Movement and Its Relation to the Policy Process.* New York, 1975.

Fritz, Paul, and Morton, Richard, eds. *Woman in the Eighteenth Century and Other Essays.* Toronto, 1976.

Fulford, Roger. *Votes for Women.* London, 1958.

Gordon, Linda. *Woman's Body, Woman's Right: A Social History of Birth Control in America.* New York, 1976.

Goreau, Angeline. *Reconstructing Aphra: A Social Biography of Aphra Behn.* New York, 1980.

Goulianos, Joan, ed. *By a Woman Writt: Literature from Six Centuries by and About Women.* Baltimore, Md., 1974.

Greer, Germaine. *The Obstacle Race: The Fortunes of Women Painters and Their Work.* London, 1979.

Grimshaw, Patricia. *Woman's Suffrage in New Zealand.* Wellington, 1972.

Gulick, Charles A. *Austria from Habsburg to Hitler.* Berkeley, 1948.

Hall, Ruth. *Marie Stopes.* London, 1978.

Hallett, Judith P. "Sappho and Her Social Context: Sense and Sensuality." *Signs* 4 (1979):447–64.

———. "The Role of Women in Roman Elegy: Counter-Cultural Feminism." *Arethusa* 6 (1973):103–24.

Hanning, Robert W. "From 'Eva' and 'Ave' to Eglentyne and Alisoun: Chaucer's Insight into the Roles Women Play." *Signs* 2 (1977):580–99.

Harris, Ann Sutherland, and Nochlin, Linda. *Women Artists 1550–1950.* Los Angeles, 1976.

Harrison, Brian. *Separate Spheres: The Opposition to Woman Suffrage in Britain.* London, 1978.

Harrison, J. F. C. *Robert Owen and the Owenites in Britain and America*. London, 1969.

Hartman, Mary S., and Banner, Lois, eds. *Consciousness Raised: New Perspectives on the History of Women*. New York, 1974.

Hawkes, Jacquetta. *Dawn of the Gods*. New York, 1968.

Heisch, Allison. "Queen Elizabeth I: Parliamentary Rhetoric and the Exercise of Power." *Signs* 1 (1975):31–55.

Herlihy, David, ed. *The Social History of Italy and Western Europe 700–1500*. Variorum Reprints, vol. 14. London, 1978.

Hewitt, Margaret. *Wives and Mothers in Victorian Industry*. London, 1958.

Hill, Christopher. *The World Turned Upside Down*. London, 1975.

Holcombe, Lee. *Victorian Ladies at Work: Middle-Class Working Women in England and Wales, 1850–1914*. Hamden, Conn., 1973.

Homer. *The Iliad*. Translated by E. V. Rieu. London, 1978.

Hufton, Olwen. *The Poor of Eighteenth-Century France 1750–1789*. Oxford, 1974.

———. "Women in Revolution 1789–1796." *Past and Present* 53 (1971):90–108.

Jacquette, Jane S. *Women in Politics*. New York, 1974.

Jonas, Hans. *The Gnostic Religion*. Boston, 1958.

Kamm, Josephine. *Indicative Past: A Hundred Years of the Girls' Public Day School Trust*. London, 1971.

Kenneally, James J. *Women and American Trade Unions*. St. Albans, Vt., 1978.

King, Gregory. *Two Tracts*. Baltimore, Md., 1936.

Kinnear, Mary. "Margret Benedictsson and *Freyja*." *Logberg-Heimskringla* 42 (1979):15–16.

Knowlton, Charles. *The Fruits of Philosophy*. London, 1977.

Kollontai, Alexandra. *Love of Worker Bees*. Translated by Cathy Porter. London, 1977.

Kraditor, Aileen S. *The Ideas of the Woman Suffrage Movement, 1890–1920*. New York, 1967.

Lacey, W. K. *The Family in Classical Greece*. Ithaca, N.Y., 1968.

Ladurie, Emmanuel LeRoy. *Montaillou: The Promised Land of Error*. New York, 1978.

———. *The Territory of the Historian*. Brighton, 1979.

Lamphere, Louise. "Anthropology." *Signs* 2 (1977):612–27.

Laslett, Peter. *The World We Have Lost: England Before the Industrial Age*. London, 1968.

Laslett, Peter, and Wall, Richard, eds. *Household and Family in Past Time*. Cambridge, 1977.

Lefkowitz, Mary R., and Fant, Maureen. *Women in Greece and Rome*. Toronto, 1977.

Leith, James. *The Idea of Art as Propaganda in France, 1750–1799: A Study in the History of Ideas*. Toronto, 1965.

Lerner, Gerda. *The Majority Finds Its Past: Placing Women in History*. New York, 1981.

Levy, Darline Gay; Applewhite, Harriet Branson; and Johnson, Mary Durham, eds. *Women in Revolutionary Paris, 1789–1795*. Urbana, Ill., 1979.

Lewenhak, Sheila. *Women and Trade Unions*. London, 1977.

Lewis, Jane. *The Politics of Motherhood: Child and Maternal Welfare in England, 1900–1939*. London, 1981.

Liddington, Jill, and Norris, Jill. *One Hand Tied Behind Us*. London, 1978.

Lis, R., and Soly, H. *Poverty and Capitalism in Pre-industrial Europe: 1350–1850*. Brighton, 1979.

Lougee, Carolyn. *Le Paradis Des Femmes: Women, Salons, and Social Stratification in Seventeenth-Century France*. Princeton, 1976.

Macartney, C. A. *Maria Theresa and the House of Austria*. London, 1969.

Marshall, Dorothy. *The English Domestic Servant in History*. London, 1969.

Mason, Tim. "Women in Nazi Germany, Part I." *History Workshop* 1 (1976):74–113.

———. "Women in Nazi Germany, Part II." *History Workshop* 2 (1976):5–32.

Marx, Karl. *Early Writings*. Edited by T. Bottomore. London, 1963.

McBride, Theresa M. *The Domestic Revolution: The Modernization of Household Service in England and France 1820–1920*. London, 1976.

McLaren, Angus. *Birth Control in Nineteenth Century England: A Social and Intellectual History*. London, 1978.

McLung, Nellie. *The Stream Runs Fast*. Toronto, 1965.

McNally, Sheila. "The Maenad in Early Greek Art." *Arethusa* 11 (1978):101–35.

Meacham, Standish. *A Life Apart: The English Working Class, 1890–1914*. London, 1977.

Melder, Keith E. *Beginnings of Sisterhood: The American Woman's Right Movement 1800–1850*. New York, 1977.

Mellaart, James. "Catal Huyuk, A Neolithic City in Anatolia." *Proceedings of the British Academy* 51 (1965):202–13.

———. *Catal Huyuk: A Neolithic Town in Anatolia*. New York, 1967.

Millett, Kate. *Sexual Politics*. New York, 1970.

Mitchell, B. R. *European Historical Statistics 1750–1970*. London, 1975.

Mitchell, David. *Queen Christabel*. London, 1977.

Mitchell, Hannah. *The Hard Way Up*. London, 1968.

Mitchell, Juliet. *Woman's Estate*. New York, 1973.

Molière. *The Comedies*. Introduction by F. C. Green. London, 1961.

Monter, E. William. *Witchcraft in France and Switzerland: The Borderlands During the Reformation*. Ithaca, N.Y., 1976.

———. "Women in Calvinist Geneva, 1550–1800." *Signs* 6 (1980):189–209.

Montesquieu. *Persian and Chinese Letters*. Translated by J. Davison. Washington, 1901.

———. *The Spirit of the Laws*. Translated by T. Nugent. New York, 1949.

Morris, Joan. *Against Nature and God*. London, 1973.

Muncy, Raymond Lee. *Sex and Marriage in Utopian Communities*. Baltimore, Md., 1974.

Neale, J. E. *Elizabeth I and Her Parliaments*. London, 1966.

Neff, Wanda F. *Victorian Working Women*. New York, 1929.

Norton, Mary Beth. "American History." *Signs* 5 (1979):324–37.

Oakley, Ann. *The Sociology of Housework*. London, 1974.

Organization for Economic Co-operation and Development (OECD). *Equal Opportunities for Women*. Paris, 1979.

O'Faolain, Julia, and Martines, Lauro, eds. *Not In God's Image: A History of Women in Europe from the Greeks to the Nineteenth Century.* New York, 1973.

Okin, Susan Moller. *Women in Western Political Thought.* London, 1980.

Owen, David. *English Philanthropy 1660–1960.* Cambridge, 1964.

Pagels, Elaine H. *The Gnostic Gospels.* New York, 1979.

———. "What Became of God the Mother? Conflicting Images of God in Early Christianity." *Signs* 2 (1976):293–303.

Phillips, M., and Tomkinson, W. S. *English Women in Life and Letters.* New York, 1971.

Pinchbeck, Ivy. *Women Workers and the Industrial Revolution, 1750–1850.* London, 1969.

Plumb, J. H. *The Penguin Book of the Renaissance.* London, 1969.

Pomeroy, Sarah B. *Goddesses, Whores, Wives, and Slaves: Women in Classical Antiquity.* New York, 1975.

Postan, M. M. *The Medieval Economy and Society: An Economic History of Britain, 1100–1500.* London, 1975.

Power, Eileen. *Medieval People.* London, 1950.

Power, Eileen, and Postan, M. *Medieval Women.* Cambridge, 1975.

Prochaska, F. K. "Women in English Philanthropy, 1790–1830." *International Review of Social History* 19 (1974):426–45.

Putnam, Emily James. *The Lady: Studies of Certain Significant Phases of Her History.* Chicago, 1970.

Quaife, G. R. *Wanton Wenches and Wayward Wives: Peasants and Illicit Sex in Early Seventeenth Century England.* London, 1979.

Racz, Elizabeth. "The Women's Rights Movement in the French Revolution." *Science and Society* 16 (1952):151–74.

Rapp, Rayna. "Anthropology." *Signs* 4 (1979):497–513.

Reeves, Maud Pember. *Round About A Pound A Week.* London, 1979.

Reiter, Rayna, ed. *Toward an Anthropology of Women.* New York, 1975.

Reuther, Rosemary, ed. *Religion and Sexism.* New York, 1974.

Richards, Eric. "Women in the British Economy since about 1700: An Interpretation." *History* 59 (1974):337–57.

Richards, Janet Radcliffe. *The Sceptical Feminist: A Philosophical Enquiry.* London, 1980.

Riemer, Eleanor S., and Fout, John C., eds. *European Women: A Documentary History, 1789–1945.* New York, 1980.

Rosaldo, Michelle Z., "The Use and Abuse of Anthropology: Reflections on Feminism and Cross-Cultural Understanding." *Signs* 5 (1980):389–417.

Rosaldo, Michelle Z., and Lamphere, Louise, eds. *Women, Culture and Society.* Stanford, 1974.

Rosen, Andrew, *Rise up, Women! The Militant Campaign of the Women's Social and Political Union, 1903–1914.* London, 1974.

Ross, Ellen. " 'The Love Crisis': Couples Advice Books of the late 1970s." *Signs* 6 (1980):109–22.

Rossi, Alice S. "Life-Span Theories and Women's Lives." *Signs* 6 (1980):4–32.

Rossi, Alice S., ed. *The Feminist Papers: From Adams to De Beauvoir.* New York, 1973.

Rossi, Alice S.; Kagan, Jerome; and Hareven, Tamara S., eds. *The Family*. New York, 1978.

Rousseau, Jean Jacques. *Confessions*. Translated by J. M. Cohen. London, 1960.

———. *Emile*. Translated by Barbara Foxley. London, 1963.

———. *Julie, ou la Nouvelle Héloise*. Paris, 1930.

Routh, Guy. *Occupation and Pay in Great Britain 1906–1960*. Cambridge, 1965.

Rover, Constance. *Love, Morals and the Feminists*. London, 1970.

———. *Women's Suffrage and Party Politics in Britain 1866–1914*. London, 1967.

Rowbotham, Sheila. *A New World for Women: Stella Browne, Socialist Feminist*. London, 1977.

———. *Hidden from History: Rediscovering Women in History from the 17th Century to the Present*. London, 1973.

———. *Women, Resistance and Revolution: A History of Women and Revolution in the Modern World*. London, 1972.

Rowbotham, Sheila, and Weeks, Jeffrey. *Socialism and the New Life: The Personal and Sexual Politics of Edward Carpenter and Havelock Ellis*. London, 1977.

Rowntree, B. Seebohm. *Poverty: A Study of Town Life*. London, 1903.

Rupp, Leila J. *Mobilizing Women for War: German and American Propaganda, 1939–1945*. Princeton, 1978.

———. "Mother of the *Volk*: The Image of Women in Nazi Ideology." *Signs* 3 (1977):362–79.

Schaps, David M. *The Economic Rights of Women in Ancient Greece*. Edinburgh, 1979.

Schreiner, Olive. *Woman and Labor*. Edited by Jane Graves. London, 1978.

Shanley, Mary Lyndon. "The History of the Family in Modern England." *Signs* 4 (1979):740–50.

Showalter, Elaine. "Florence Nightingale's Feminist Complaint: Women, Religion and 'Suggestions for Thought,' " *Signs* 6 (1981):395–412.

Slater, Philip E. *The Glory of Hera: Greek Mythology and the Greek Family*. Boston, 1968.

Smith-Rosenberg, Carroll. "The New Woman and the New History." *Feminist Studies* 2 (1975):185–98.

Soldon, Norbert C. *Women in British Trade Unions 1874–1976*. London, 1978.

Southern, R. W. *Western Society and the Church in the Middle Ages*. London, 1978.

Sowerwine, Charles. "The Organization of French Socialist Women 1880–1914: A European Perspective for Women's Movements." *Historical Reflections* 3 (1976):3–23.

Stenton, Doris. *The English Woman in History*. New York, 1977.

Stephenson, Jill. *The Nazi Organisation of Women*. London, 1981.

———. *Women in Nazi Society*. London, 1975.

Stites, Richard. *The Women's Liberation Movement in Russia: Feminism, Nihilism, and Bolshevism, 1860–1930*. Princeton, 1978.

Stock, Phyllis. *Better Than Rubies: A History of Women's Education*. New York, 1978.

Stone, Lawrence. *The Family, Sex and Marriage in England 1500–1800*. London, 1977.

———. "The Revival of Narrative: Reflections on a New Old History." *Past and Present* 85 (1979):3–24.

Stopes, Marie. *Radiant Motherhood.* London, 1920.

Stott, Mary. *Organization Woman: The Story of the National Union of Townswomen's Guilds.* London, 1978.

Strachey, Ray. *The Cause: A History of the Women's Movement in Great Britain.* London, 1978.

Stuard, Susan Mosher, ed. *Women in Medieval Society.* Philadelphia, 1976.

Swift, Jonathan. *Directions to Servants.* New York, 1964.

Tanner, Nancy, and Zihlman, Adrienne. "Women in Evolution Part I: Innovation and Selection in Human Origins." *Signs* 1 (1976):585–608.

Thieme, Hugo P. *Woman: Women of Modern France.* Philadelphia, 1907.

Thomas, C. G. "Matriarchy in Early Greece: The Bronze and Dark Ages." *Arethusa* 6 (1973):173–95.

Thomas, Keith. *Religion and the Decline of Magic.* London, 1971.

———. "Women and the Civil War Sects." *Past and Present* 13 (1958):42–62.

Thompson, Roger. *Women in Stuart England and America: A Comparative Study.* London, 1974.

Thompson, William. *Appeal of one half of the human race, women, against the pretensions of the other half, men, to retain them in political and thence in civil and domestic slavery.* London, 1825.

Tilly, Louise A., and Scott, Joan A. *Women, Work, and Family.* New York, 1978.

Treggiari, Susan. "Libertine Ladies." *Classical World* 64 (1971):196–98.

Trevelyan, G. M. *English Social History.* London, 1944.

Trofimenkoff, Susan Mann, and Prentice, Alison, eds. *The Neglected Majority: Essays in Canadian Women's History.* Toronto, 1977.

Vicinus, Martha, ed. *A Widening Sphere: Changing Roles of Victorian Women.* Bloomington, Ind., 1977.

———. *Suffer and Be Still: Women in the Victorian Age.* Bloomington, Ind., 1973.

Warner, Marina. *Alone of All Her Sex: The Myth and the Cult of the Virgin Mary.* New York, 1976.

———. *Joan of Arc: The Image of Female Heroism.* New York, 1981.

Watson, J. Steven. *The Reign of George III, 1760–1815.* Oxford, 1960.

Welter, Barbara. "The Cult of True Womanhood 1820–1860." *American Quarterly* 18 (1966):151–74.

Whyte, Martin King. *The Status of Women in Preindustrial Societies.* Princeton, 1978.

Wollstonecraft, Mary. *A Vindication of the Rights of Woman.* Edited by Carol H. Poston. New York, 1975.

Woodward, E. L. *The Age of Reform 1815–1970.* Oxford, 1954.

Woolf, Virginia. *A Room of One's Own.* London, 1975.

Zeldin, Theodore. *France 1848–1945.* Vol. 1. London, 1974.

Zihlman, Adrienne. "Women in Evolution Part II: Subsistence and Social Organization Among Early Hominids." *Signs* 4 (1978):4–20.

Zinserling, Verena. *Women in Greece and Rome.* New York, 1973.

Index